Microcomputers
in school administration

'Of course we won't be getting rid of you now that
we have a computer. They can do a lot of things but
they can't make tea.'

Microcomputers in school administration

Patrick Bird

Hutchinson

London   Melbourne   Sydney   Auckland   Johannesburg

Hutchinson & Co. (Publishers) Ltd

An imprint of the Hutchinson Publishing Group

17-21 Conway Street, London W1P 6JD

Hutchinson Group (Australia) Pty Ltd
30-32 Cremorne Street, Richmond South, Victoria 3121
PO Box 151, Broadway, New South Wales 2007

Hutchinson Group (NZ) Ltd
32-34 View Road, PO Box 40-086, Glenfield, Auckland 10

Hutchinson Group (SA) (Pty) Ltd
PO Box 337, Bergvlei 2012, South Africa

First published 1984
© Patrick Bird 1984
Illustrations © Hutchinson & Co 1984

Computerized phototypesetting by First Page Ltd.,
Watford, Herts.

Printed and bound in Great Britain by
Anchor Brendon Ltd,
Tiptree, Essex

British Library Cataloguing in Publication Data

Bird, Patrick
  Microcomputers in school administration.
  1. School management and administration
  ——Data processing——England
  2. Microprocessors
  I. Title
  371.2′028′5404   LB2846

ISBN 0 09 154510 2

Contents

Foreword   7
Preface   8
Acknowledgements   10
Reading this book   12

1   History and background   13

1.1   Microprocessors and microcomputers   14
1.2   Mainframes and microcomputers   14
1.3   Computers, administration and management   16
1.4   Microcomputer based administration   18
1.5   'Where are we?'   19
1.6   School timetabling   19
1.7   Option choices   24
1.8   Pupil record systems   26
1.9   Marks and reports   29
1.10 Attendance   30
1.11 Statistics   30
1.12 The school library   32
1.13 Accounting   33
1.14 Careers   33
1.15 Benefits and implications   33
1.16 General benefits   34
1.17 Social implications   36
1.18 Where are we now?   39

2   Tasks for the microcomputers   41

2.1   Pupil record systems – databases   42
2.2   A database for school microcomputers   44
2.3   Pupil record systems – tasks   47
2.4   School timetabling   55
2.5   Wordprocessing   63
2.6   Accounts   65
2.7   Stock control   66
2.8   The school library   67
2.9   Other tasks   67

3   Microcomputer hardware for school administration   69

3.1   'Will it be technical?'   70
3.2   The heart of the matter   71
3.3   Memory   73

3.4	RAM and ROM	74
3.5	The 'ins' and 'outs' of hardware	75
3.6	Choosing your hardware	87
3.7	Specific systems	90
3.8	Supplies	97

4 Microcomputer software for school administration — 99

4.1	What is software?	100
4.2	Developing software	101
4.3	Documentation	104
4.4	User friendliness	104
4.5	Buying software	107
4.6	Record systems	108
4.7	Option choices systems	113
4.8	Examination administration	117
4.9	Timetable planning	124
4.10	Timetable scheduling and printing	128
4.11	Cover for absent staff	135
4.12	Timetabling parents' evenings	136
4.13	Wordprocessing	138
4.14	Accounts	144
4.15	Library applications	145
4.16	Stock control	146

5 A practical guide for individual schools — 147

5.1	Reasons for beginning MCBA	148
5.2	The initiative to begin MCBA	150
5.3	Problems in beginning MCBA	151
5.4	Key factors for success	161
5.5	How to begin MCBA	163

6 Prospects for the future — 167

6.1	The Local Authority's role	168
6.2	The modular concept	171
6.3	The requirements of in-service training	174
6.4	Policies for the future	176
6.5	Hardware for the future	177

| Appendix 1 Software sources for microcomputers in school administration | 182 |
| Appendix 2 Useful addresses | 197 |

Bibliography	199
Glossary	203
Index	205

Foreword

Ray Bolam, Director of the National Development Centre for Training in School Management

This book is very timely. Recent initiatives by the Department of Education and Science to promote the training of heads and senior staff have highlighted the need for practical and relevant training materials. The relationship of microcomputers and school management is clearly a topic which is going to be of central and continuing interest and initiative.

This book provides cogent and coherent arguments as to why microcomputers should be taken seriously and utilized, especially in secondary schools. Of the three reasons given in Chapter 5 – that the sensible use of microcomputers will save time, improve efficiency and strengthen the quality of the information needed to make good management decisions – it is the latter which I regard as most important. All schools are complex whether they be large or small. Just as the classroom teacher is compelled by force of circumstance to make hundreds of decisions – some of them crucial, every lesson, every hour – so too the heads, deputies and other senior staff with management responsibilities are similarly faced by the need to decide and act quickly and frequently. The danger is that the pressure of day to day events forces school managers into a reactive stance, whereas ideally they ought to be in a pro-active forward-looking stance anticipating the many problems and decisions which they have to face. This book demonstrates that this process can be considerably helped by the appropriate use of the microcomputer.

Moreover, by exploring the practical factors associated with the successful use of microcomputers, including the essential support role of the local education authority, this book ensures that the reader will at least be aware of what has to be done.

Perhaps most important of all this book is very readable. Chapters 3 and 4 provide an extremely clear and easily understood account of the technicalities of microcomputers. So I commend Patrick Bird's book to the reader as being timely, relevant, practical and readable.

August 1983

Preface

The age of the microcomputer dawned for me on a rather pleasant spring day in 1978. Tony Hay, a sixth form pupil on one of my computer appreciation courses came to my office and suggested that we could have our own computer at school rather than use the large and distant machine at the Polytechnic. I was about to ridicule the suggestion and expound on the difficulties when he produced Volume 1, Number 1 of *Personal Computer World*. I needed little more convincing. Tony Hay was right. Within a few months our first RML 380Z was on the way.

When our disk machine arrived it didn't take me long to realize two things. Firstly, I had an awful lot of new experience to gain in the unknown world of the microcomputer. Secondly, I found the machine much more powerful than I had expected. Clearly it was just as much a tool as it was equipment for educational experience. I felt it should be used to help with as many chores of my school administration as possible.

Despite a long-standing amateur interest in computers, and several attempts to use them in my tasks both as a Deputy and as a Head, I found microcomputing a strange new world. Those with whom I must now, by need, consult often used strange and unfamiliar terms. One was much closer to the 'hardware' too, and this required a clear understanding of how the computer actually functioned. It was necessary that I should become much more 'computer literate' than ever before.

Early in 1979, through the good offices of the University of Bristol School of Education, I was able to meet HMI Brian Kay with whom I talked of the possibilities for microcomputers in school administration. With his support the DES funded a small research project to investigate this interesting development. The project was generously supported, too, by my Local Authority, Avon, who released me for one day each week over two years. My involvement with microcomputers in school administration had really begun.

One of my conclusions in the final report to the DES was that the application of microcomputers in school administration was vitally important for the future. I suggested that all management focused training courses for senior school staff should contain an element of this new development. Since then I've had countless opportunities to address such courses and it is clear that interest and the desire for information and knowledge is rapidly increasing. This has been particularly true following the Department of Industry's initiative to place a microcomputer in every school. Additionally, I have been able to keep in contact with many individual teachers and schools pressing forward with developments in the field. It has been a special privilege to use, appraise or see

8

in action many of the programs which have been developed for school administration, and I have tried to pioneer the exchange of information about this software. Schools beginning to experiment with their microcomputer for administrative tasks have been hungry for help, advice and information. All this suggested that I should try to share my accumulated knowledge on a wider basis.

Another factor has also come to my attention. While it's not strictly necessary to fully understand the workings of a microcomputer in order to use it, a little knowledge certainly helps. We've heard a great deal about the need to make our pupils 'computer literates'. It has to be a good idea for teachers, including Heads, to understand something of the new technology, too.

This, then, is the book's *raison d'être*. Its prime target audience comprises Heads, Deputy Heads and senior staff in secondary schools and those who would join these ranks. Additionally, I hope it will prove a useful resource and guide to Local Education Authority Officers, Advisers and Inspectors, and Further and Higher Education lecturers with interests or responsibilities in school computing or management training, and their students. The book aims to examine the microcomputer's role in tasks with which most of these people will be familiar, and to be a practical guide to the many facets of this role. Along the way it attempts to use the reader's familiarity with school administration and management to enlighten the world of computing and the microprocessor. I have tried to direct such efforts towards the reader who has little or no knowledge of computers. A basic exposition within the familiar context will provide the foundation to enhance their comprehension of the main theme. I hope that those readers who are already knowledgeable in these fields will bear with this necessity.

I hope that in this book there is something productive for everyone. If it helps the reader to progress in the application of new technology to old skills, it will have served its basic purpose. If, in addition, it helps the reader to share the excitement and enjoyment which I have derived from working with microcomputers then I shall, to quote Byron, 'let joy be unconfined'. To a barely literate mathematician the effort of writing will all have been worthwhile.

Patrick Bird, 1983

Acknowledgements

The foundations of this book were laid during a research project entitled 'The use of low cost microprocessor based computer systems in school administration and management'. This was funded by the Department of Education and Science, supported by the University of Bristol School of Education, and for which purpose my own Local Education Authority in the County of Avon generously seconded me for one day per week over two years. I acknowledge the support of the staff of Hengrove School over this period, and particularly the Deputy Heads Bill Fletcher, Basil Rogers and initially Olga Place, but latterly Ann Pert, who carried extra burdens over this period. I am grateful for the support of many heads, deputies and teachers who gave their time during the project both to welcome me to their schools and to respond to letters and questionnaires.

Many people have contributed to the production of this book, both directly and indirectly. I wish to record my thanks for assistance received from the following sources: all the program authors whose work is identified and who provided software, documentation, and comments on my description of their programs; Research Machines Limited and Commodore Business Machines (UK) Limited, who provided technical comment and photographic material; the Tandy Corporation (UK) for technical comment; the Assistant Masters and Mistresses Association for consent to reproduce their code of practice for computers in schools; Central Press Features Limited.

Some contributions have been exceptionally practical and have made considerable demands on that valuable commodity, time. I am deeply grateful to the following four colleagues who read the original manuscript and whose comments enabled significant improvements to be made: Dr Bernard Chapman of the University of Bristol School of Education; Simon Pratt, of the same School (whose enthusiasm initiated the original project); Philip Waterhouse, my predecessor at Hengrove, and former Director of the Avon Resources for Learning Development Unit, now with CET; and Dr Bob Campbell of the Department of Education, University of York, whose detailed comments proved particularly valuable. I also record my gratitude to: Dr Ray Bolam, Director of the National Centre for Training in School Management for contributing the Foreword; Lesley Williams, who so quickly mastered wordprocessing techniques to type the original manuscript onto disk; and Bob Osborne and his staff at Hutchinson Education for a great deal of advice, support and encouragement.

Finally, without my wife Mary this book could not have been written. She has encouraged and supported in so many practical ways, not only in making it practically possible for me to write, but also by reading the manuscript several times, being a stern critic of spelling, grammar and turn of phrase, and undertaking those many other mundane, but essential tasks without which completion would have been impossible. It is as much her book as it is mine, and for her I record my very special thanks.

P. B. 1983

Reading this book.

Those investigating the use of microcomputers in school administration for the first time, or students seriously studying the field can follow the text continuously. Others may like to abbreviate the reading as follows:

Not interested in the historical background and development?
Omit Sections 1.6 to 1.14 inclusive.

Already totally familiar with hardware?
Omit Chapter 3.

Happy with the way you have set up microcomputer based administration in the school so far?
Omit Chapter 5.

Interested only in software and future prospects?
Read Chapter 1 to Section 1.5
      Chapter 2
      Chapter 4
      Chapter 6
      and browse through Appendix 1.

1 History and background

or 'How it all began'

' . . . and with our latest program it will easily do your timetable . . ..'

History and background

There is nothing new about using computers for school administration. Computers have been around for more than thirty-five years, and have been used widely in business and commerce for the last twenty-five. In education we have been a bit slower off the mark but there's evidence of spasmodic activity in schools stretching back some twenty years. What is new is the explosion of interest generated by the introduction of the microcomputer into schools. As recently as 1977 few could have believed that every school would soon own even one, let alone several computers. The rapid introduction of this new technology has given fresh impetus to the idea that computers might be useful in the administration of large secondary schools, and has led to new efforts to examine the range of applications which are possible in this field.

1.1 Microprocessors and microcomputers

It is worthwhile at this very early stage to make a distinction between 'microcomputers' and 'microprocessors'. The two words are often used synonymously, even by those who should know better. To me there is a clear distinction. A 'microprocessor' is nothing more than a highly sophisticated silicon chip, or to give this its technical name, a 'large scale integrated circuit', smaller than a little finger nail, encapsulated in a plastic package from which emerge a number of 'legs' or contacts through which it communicates with the outside world. A first year pupil of mine very aptly described one which I passed around in class as 'a black plastic centipede with silver-metal pointed legs'! When provided with the proper source of power the microprocessor will exhibit the characteristics of a computer to the electronics engineer. To the layman the microprocessor on its own is almost certainly totally useless.

A microcomputer employs a great deal more circuitry, both 'large scale integrated' and otherwise, than the simple microprocessor which is at its heart. In addition it will need other paraphernalia such as a keyboard – for you to communicate with it – and a screen (or visual display unit) – for it to communicate with you – to name but two. In short, a microprocessor is a single device; a microcomputer is a collection of them.

1.2 Mainframes and microcomputers

A microcomputer is a rather different beast to its big brother 'mainframe' (that is a large computer such as has evolved from the first valve types of the 1940s). Although they have shrunk considerably in size during the last ten years, mainframe machines will still require a room, or even a suite, to themselves. This is largely on account of the wide range of often bulky peripheral machinery (such as fast line printers, large disk units and bulky tape drives) which they require to be fully efficient. Although large, some of this equipment is very delicate and the environment of such a computer suite needs to be carefully controlled for temperature and humidity. While the reliability of mainframe computers has increased rapidly with advances in electronic engineering, most companies using such machines will pay considerable sums for maintenance and may have to make frequent calls upon their contract. Some larger installations require a permanent service engineer on site to ensure continuous running. This is not to say that such machines are unreliable; but they are extremely complex and there is nothing so expensive as an idle computer. Compare this with the average microcomputer. Although dirty, dusty or damp environments are not recommended, especially with disk systems, and while you might not expect it to survive unscathed if knocked from a desk, I have known these machines work away faultlessly in the corner of a busy classroom, subjected to the probing fingers of a multitude of children, and also enduring frequent journeys in the boot of a teacher's car in extremes of temperature, without attention from the maintenance company for four or five years. It has been said that if the electronics survive the first six months there will be no problems for the first six years.

The method of working with mainframe computers tends to be somewhat different, too. Mainframes can usually execute tasks much faster than microcomputers. Despite this, the pressures for time in conducting tasks on a mainframe are greater, largely because there are many more tasks to be carried out, often simultaneously, by several users. On this account the processing of work has to be much more carefully organized on mainframes than on microcomputers and this task is, these days, usually carried out by the machine itself. Even so, the delays can still be so frustrating that in large companies the desktop microcomputer is being used in preference to the mainframe for some tasks.

It is unusual for the user to be anywhere near a mainframe computer when asking it to process tasks. There are two modes of use – 'batch' and 'on-line' processing. 'Batch' processing was by far the most common mode in the 1950s and 1960s. In this mode the user usually prepared programs or data on a special coding sheet. This was translated by keyboard operators into some other medium - perhaps punched cards or paper tape. The length of time it took to translate your data depended on the length of the queue or your priority in the system – a bit like getting letters typed in a school: the Head's will be typed today, Deputy's 'tomorrow', anyone else's 'by the end of the week'! Once the punched medium was prepared you still waited your turn for the operator to 'run' your work – again in some hierarchical system. Later you returned to collect your results – usually on paper output by the printer. It was often frustrating to receive a single sheet with a cryptic message such as 'Coding error in Line 10' dutifully printed upon it.

Working 'on-line' is much more usual these days. In this mode you are still 'remote' from the computer itself but have a direct connection with it either via a telephone line to a distant location or a direct wire to the computer suite within the building. The feeling is much more like working at a microcomputer. A keyboard accepts information for the computer, and a screen, or perhaps a teletype, conveys information back to you. Such a workstation is called a 'terminal'. However the 'on-line' mode still has its disadvantages. It's rather inefficient for conveying a large amount of data especially if your keyboard skills are not very good. Such users are discouraged from operating in this mode as they tend to tie up computer time unnecessarily whilst others wait. Depending on the type of computer you will not be aware of this if a small number of terminals is 'logged in'. If the number is large, however, the delays in getting a response to your input can be infuriatingly long. At worst you may even get repeated messages such as 'Busy – try later'!

Compare this with the personal microcomputer where the whole machine is yours for the session. Admittedly your session length may be limited by other users' needing the machine, but so it will be on a terminal. At least responses are immediate and, as long as programs work, the length of time which is taken to execute them is, within reason, not so vital. I remember once writing a program for a task on a mainframe machine in 'batch' mode. The total processing time was returned as thirty-five minutes with a note from the computer manager saying that he was concerned about this. A friend re-wrote the program in a more efficient language to reduce the processing time to seven minutes. The computer manager was still unhappy. Eventually we got the program to run on another machine in twenty seconds and everyone was happy. Such efficiency need not concern anyone save the most fastidious microcomputer user. If administrative programs are going to take time, then so be it. While the microcomputer carries out its data-processing routines perhaps we can be away doing other tasks.

1.3 Computers, administration and management

But what have these differences to do with school administration? I believe that the remoteness and slow turn-around times for batch-processed work in most mainframe installations have been largely responsible for the slow tempo of development in the use of computers in this field. It is also possible to cite reasons such as lack of proper programs to do the job, lack of people able to communicate with the machines, lack of in-service training and poor dissemination of the possibilities. Such factors, however, don't seem to have delayed developments following the delivery of microcomputers. The immediacy of the equipment and the speedy output of results have certainly had a stimulating influence. Interest amongst senior members of school staffs has grown enormously in the last two years.

Perhaps it is about time. Schools have generally been tardy in recognizing that management techniques have much to offer the organization of our large institutions. 'Management' training for the senior staff of secondary schools did not really begin until the late 1960s or early 1970s – some years after such techniques were applied in industry and commerce. Indeed, such needs for Heads and potential Heads were only fully recognized by Central Government in the 1980s. Perhaps this was due to the independent nature of the British school and its headteacher, perhaps due to the lack of compulsory in-service training, or the different pressures to which schools and commercial organizations are subjected. Whatever the reason, schools have always been at least ten years behind in terms of their approach to management techniques, and this has been as much true about computer use as any other. In 1966 Peter Drucker was exhorting managers to engage in self analysis: 'Which of the activities on my time log could be done by somebody else just as well, if not better?'

Geoffrey Lyons was still pointing out similar truths to schools in 1976 in his work on the major administrative tasks of senior secondary school staff, by saying 'many so-called major administrative tasks are clerical, or very little more than clerical', and 'Deputy Heads should not be high level clerks or administrative assistants'.

Yet Lyons' book has but one reference to the use of a computer in school administration, and that to a publication concerned with school timetabling. By contrast, a textbook on management written six years earlier (Coventry, 1970) contains almost a dozen references to the use of a computer as an aid to management techniques, including the advice that: ' . . .in view of the complex nature of model building, it is virtually essential to make extensive use of a computer'.

Apart from the purely clerical chores which have to be undertaken in schools, Lyons acknowledges that there are a number of major administrative tasks which have a strong managerial content, requiring decisions necessitating careful analysis and evaluation. Amongst these will be the design of a curriculum, the production of a timetable, budgeting and accounting in the management of school finance, and the allocation of pupils to teaching groups (for example, in options systems). Such tasks will depend on model building. Models exist, or can be designed, to present the problems and variables in a suitable mathematical form for analysis by a computer. An example of such a model, which may be familiar to the reader, is the style of curriculum analysis proposed by T. I. Davies in his well known book *School organization* published in 1969. Use of this model can highlight certain features of any designed curriculum very effectively. The deterrent of the somewhat tedious calculations is overcome very quickly using a computer, demonstrating the soundness of Coventry's advice.

Few schools which have given serious consideration to the use of a computer for clerical tasks need a great deal of convincing about its potential. Nevertheless, there remains a justifiable need for scepticism. Not every avenue of exploration will produce similar benefits in every school. There are bound to be some blind alleys and some disappointments. Because of the great variety in our schools, what is a blind alley for some may prove a motorway for others. One important avenue remains to be explored. Where computers have been introduced in commerce for administrative purposes their use in analysis and planning has rapidly followed. Such tasks are among the most important for management. In schools we have not yet fully considered the management potential of the computer model or computer report. It is here that I believe that the case to apply this new technology is strongest.

As will be evident, I believe that there is a difference between administration and management. Consider a school's external examination policy and its implementation. In the first instance decisions must be taken about which subjects candidates should study, which syllabuses will be studied, how many subjects candidates might enter, and how much time shall be allocated to each subject within the curriculum. Such decisions require value judgements to be made. I regard the processes leading to these decisions as 'management' functions. Once the decisions have been taken the candidates must be entered for the correct examinations with accurate birthdates and correctly spelled names. They must know their timetables, be seated properly in the examination room, have their papers marked, and receive their results. These tasks do not require high order value judgements, but they do require precision, an efficient organization, and control of a large amount of information. The conduct of such tasks I regard as 'administration'.

As far as the use of microcomputers in school administration and management is concerned, I shall take 'administration' to be the facilitation of the orderly progress of the organization – in educational terms, the conducting of those background tasks without which the day-to-day work of a school could not take place. 'Management' I shall take to relate to planning and decision-making tasks, particularly those where data needs to be processed, rearranged and considered and which may well affect the future success or failure of the organization. Much of the work a microcomputer will do must be purely administrative, but where it can process the data to provide information for enlightened decision making then its use will be managerial. In this sense its administrative function is a subset of its wider managerial role.

The distinction I make is not universally recognized and the reader is referred to Dunsire (1973) for a full discussion of the various meanings of the word 'administration'. Its use in the title of this book does not imply neglect of the managerial function of microcomputers. I shall stress those cases where I consider that such a function is being attempted.

1.4 Microcomputer based administration

What can we call this new management or administrative tool? It is certainly cumbersome continually referring to 'the use of microcomputers in school administration'. While researching the topic I noted that several of my contacts used terms such as 'computer assisted administration' or 'computer based administration'. The word 'assist' always seemed to ascribe a minor roll when perhaps we had high hopes of bigger things. The word 'based' was used in an important report for the Local Authorities Management Services and Computer Committee (LAMSAC) in 1974 entitled *Towards a computer based education management information system*. In this context it seemed to say a great deal more about our aspirations and so the term 'microcomputer based administration' was coined. Eventually, for quick reference in conversation this was abbreviated to MCBA. More recently I have noticed that SAM (school administration by microcomputer) is becoming popular. It is certainly easier to say, but for the remainder of this book I shall use my original acronym, MCBA.

1.5 'Where are we?'

There is a great maxim in Barry and Tye's book *Running a school*. It suggests planning by the following directions:

Where are you?
Where are you going?
How do you intend to get there?
How will you know when you have got there?

In the rest of this book I hope to follow these directions concerning the development of microcomputers in school management and administration. The remainder of this chapter is devoted to the first question – 'Where are we?'. Chapter 2 will examine the second question – 'Where are we going?'. The remainder of the book will consider questions three and four – 'How do you intend to get there?' and 'How will you know when you are there?'

It's a long way to journey from a scratch position to the frontiers of knowledge even in a comparatively new development like MCBA. We can learn a great deal by treading the paths that others have trodden and learning from their experience. Although microcomputers have been with us for a comparatively short time, experience has been gained with mainframes and, despite the difficulties already noted, some early microcomputer work has been based upon this foundation. Consequently we must begin by looking at some early mainframe work. From this we can learn something of the present possibilities for MCBA and particularly which tasks are likely to be most fruitful for investigation and development using the new technology. It is convenient to study this mainframe work topic by topic, examining each by chronological order of development. However, I recognize that not everyone likes history lessons, illuminating though they might be. If the reader is such a person then it will be convenient to move directly from this point to Section 1.15, referring back only where indicated in future chapters.

1.6 School timetabling

It will come as no surprise to learn that the construction of the school timetable was the first task to which computers were applied in school organization. There were still people around both in computing and education in the late 1960s who would tell you that 'it is a mere scheduling problem and has got to be dead simple for a computer'. Many were the Heads and Deputies who must have dreamed of presenting their requirements at the local computer centre and returning a day or so later to collect their timetable. Yet it has taken some of the best computing, mathematical and timetabling brains the greater part of twenty years to come to grips with the problem. Certainly we are not yet in the seventh heaven of the perfect computer solution.

As schools have grown, the annual timetable construction has become one of the most important aspects of school management and administration. The 1950s saw the end of the 'permanent' timetable framed behind the Headmaster's desk. Comprehensive reorganization with rising rolls implied six to ten weeks of arduous work by a senior member of staff attempting to satisfy complex educational requirements. Constraints were imposed by the available resources of manpower, rooms, equipment and time. Once again, the whole task was seen in two stages, the first interpreted as a 'management' function and the second as 'administrative' or even 'clerical'. In the first stage management decisions are being taken in terms of curriculum planning, the organization of option groups and the resource allocation of time, staff and rooms. The second stage was seen as purely 'administrative' – namely the completion of a jig-saw puzzle. Initially the computer's part was seen solely in the second stage with two objectives in mind. The first, and by far the most important, was to save the time of the jig-saw puzzle builder. The second was to allow the compilation of several timetables thus to enjoy the luxury of a choice of the optimum solution. The second objective was rarely, if ever, realized.

Not surprisingly, the first efforts to timetable by computer attempted to follow those methods used by the manual timetabler. In such a method the Head would be required to make a complete list of all the requirements in terms of which classes were to be taught by which teachers in which rooms. This data was then presented to the computer in the hope that a timetable could be generated. Generally two rules were followed by the program. The first was that scheduling should begin with those requirements for which there was least scope for manoeuvre (most manual timetablers will always insert the fixed points first, followed by the largest teams of teachers). The second rule was that where some degree of choice existed the lesson should be assigned to the slot where it was likely to cause the least problems. This method has been dubbed 'heuristic'. C. F. Lewis described such methods in his book *The school timetable* published in 1961 – one of the earliest books in this particular field.

A computer program using these methods was described by J. A. Appleby, D. V. Blake and E. A. Newman in *The Computer Journal* in 1960. Their program could handle double periods and special setting and room requirements as well as considering the distribution of subject lessons over the week. Although the program was never operational it is said to have solved a thirty-five period, twenty-six class problem in about ninety minutes on a slow machine – a considerable triumph for its day. This particular program is sometimes referred to as the Teddington system, and an extension of this approach was proposed by E. D. Barraclough in 1965. Known as the Newcastle system, it incorporated a more sophisticated algorithm with an improved mainframe computer. It is reported to have shown promise in field trials but again proved little more than an interesting experiment which allowed the researcher to formulate some measures of timetabling difficulty and quality.

The first non-heuristic approaches to the problems of school timetabling came, not from within schools, but from University based researchers who were more interested in the generalized mathematical nature of scheduling problems but who found, in the school timetable, a useful vehicle for their researches. It is said that C. C. Gotlieb first proposed some ideas relating to the solution of timetable problems using what is known as 'combinatorial mathematics' at a congress in Munich in 1962. In any event Gotlieb published a paper in 1964 with J. Csima, whose name is very much bound up with this line of development, entitled 'Tests on a computer method for constructing school timetables'. Csima himself wrote a doctoral dissertation in the University of Toronto, Canada, in 1965 entitled *Investigation on a timetable problem*. Combinatorial mathematics seems to derive its fundamentals from Boolean algebra and network analysis and is a territory which only the most advanced mathematicians might explore. This research did lead to an implementation in Canada known as the 'Ontario school scheduling program'. It has been said that although the theoretical basis of this program was rather weak, in practice it performed reasonably well.

A young researcher at Toronto during the time of the Csima–Gotlieb work was M. A. H. Dempster. During the early 1970s Dempster came to Oxford University and amongst other things continued his investigations into school timetabling using computers, this time in British schools. He devised what he called an 'interchange' system for creating the school timetable. It is, perhaps, a rather novel approach, but nevertheless based firmly on theories of the earlier combinatorial work. Essentially he started with a completed timetable which satisfied all the simple requirements. This 'initial' timetable might be that constructed for a previous year, or a simple block timetable, or one that is constructed without inserting all the constraints of teachers and rooms. This timetable would not satisfy all the necessary pre-assignments, but Dempster showed these could be incorporated by making 'interchanges' within this complete timetable.

Field trials of Dempster's system (marketed under the banner of Oxford Systems Associates, OSA) in 1975, highlighted some problems but also demonstrated that the system had great potential for 'interactive' timetabling by computer. This is a method whereby 'one-shot' solutions to the problem are not attempted, but the computer asks for decisions from the timetabler, at the same time feeding him with all the necessary information to take those decisions. This mode of operation for the OSA system was also suggested in some research conducted by Simon Pratt of the University of Bristol School of Education between 1977 and 1979. OSA continued development of the system along these lines until 1980 when, unhappily, the firm went into liquidation. The timetabling system was taken over by the Inner London Education Authority and is still being used by some of its schools. Favourable reports have been made on its use by the Operational Research Unit of Greater London Council (Wilson, 1979).

At the time of its demise, workers in OSA were investigating the possibility of transferring the interactive timetable system to a microcomputer for use on site in schools. The work was only in its embryonic stage but some of the ideas being discussed and the simulations undertaken appeared very exciting. Such a program, based firmly on its fifteen-year-old roots in theory and a great deal of practical experience, written by computer professionals, would have been a significant breakthrough right at the beginning of the microcomputer age. Unhappily this work seems to have been lost as an immediate practical proposition when OSA collapsed.

So much for the purely theoretical approach. Meanwhile, back at the heuristic ranch, other developments were taking place. In the late 1960s and early 1970s there had been several abortive attempts with programs which tried to combine both theoretical and heuristic methods. The Birmingham system (1968), the TIMACS system (London University 1970), the Price-Waterhouse System (1971) and the Scicon System (1972) all failed when it came to the practical problem of actually producing a complete school timetable. In 1972, however, some more permanent systems first appeared on the scene in the United Kingdom.

In 1966 a school timetabling system devised by H. Michalson began field trials in Norway and by 1970 his Nor-Data system was producing 100 schedules each year. Once knowledge about its results became public it quickly aroused interest in the UK. The Local Government Operational Research Unit (LGORU), a body with a long-standing interest in computer timetabling systems and their evaluation, sponsored a preliminary investigation and produced one of the first computer organized timetables in a British school. Inspired by this success LGORU, aided by the National Council for Educational Technology (then NCET, now just CET), set up the School Timetabling Application Group (STAG). The Nor-Data system became the main inspiration behind STAG's work.

The Nor-Data system of timetable construction was based in part on combinatorial mathematics and in part on heuristic rules containing some intuitive elements. For example, higher priority requirements are made to take precedence over those of lower priority. As STAG developed the use of the system in the UK environment, it became increasingly clear that the 'one-shot' method was not particularly useful. By 1974 the timetable was being tackled in stages and this new technique was evaluated by timetabling more than 100 secondary schools in the UK and Ireland. Through such developments STAG eventually concluded that ideally an interactive approach would provide maximum benefit to schools. By 1975 it was reported that the 'vast majority' of the 105 schools submitting data received timetables which were used operationally or which, 'had circumstances permitted', would have been used.

However, there were still problems. Some were not concerned with the practical operation of the computer program itself, but more with the logistics of producing a number of school timetables on a distant computer within a relatively short space of time. Although considerable efforts were made to train timetablers in the use of the system, they could not be left to their own devices to finish the job. Throughout the timetabling season, contact had to be maintained with the appropriate STAG adviser. Of course, with all schools wanting their timetables in July, and not having full staffing data until April, the bulk of timetable construction took place in May and June. It must have been a considerable headache to STAG's limited staff to advise a great number of scattered schools over such a period of intense activity. The frustrations of communication can be found in many computer aided timetablers' accounts of the mid-1970s and even STAG itself admitted in 1976 that 'none of the incompleted timetables can be attributed to failures in the computer system; rather it was problems of communication which prevented success in all cases'. In addition, if one mainframe computer installation was asked to cope with a large number of schools attempting to construct timetables in June the system could easily become overloaded. Some computer managers were unfamiliar with this kind of 'seasonal' activity, and did not receive it favourably. I remember asking on one occasion whether a County installation could cope with the timetables for sixty schools. 'Yes', said the Manager, 'providing I can do five each month!'

The problem of maintaining the momentum in the schools was serious, too. The promotion of a timetabler after two or three years experience, or disillusionment with results, gradually eroded the number of schools taking part. It would be interesting to know how many of those 105 schools cited in 1975 still continue to use the system. ILEA, through the Operational Research Unit of the Greater London Council experimented with Nor-Data in the four years from 1973 to 1976. Of the eleven schools using the system only three did so for more than one year (and those only for two). Of the fourteen timetables attempted only four were completed and of these only two were used. STAG, its development and research completed, vanished from the scene in the late 1970s, and this could have seen the end of the system apart from some persistent work by some LEAs. Nor-Data is still being used in an interactive mode. Recently, I was able to see it at work in Derbyshire. Reports are encouraging. Perhaps all is not lost.

Strangely enough, STAG had an initial hand in the introduction of the third contender in the computer timetabling stakes. In its early stages the group had examined the SPL (New Zealand) scheme. This had been developed by Dr C. Kent of a firm called Systems and Programs Ltd in New Zealand, and was in the early stages of its introduction into this country. Little is known about the details of its operation, but it appears to use a mixture of combinatorial and heuristic rules selecting periods to fit with the least degrees of freedom and gradually building these in to the initial blank timetables. STAG gave the system a trial in five schools, but for a variety of reasons – primarily because it rated the Nor-Data system as more promising – decided not to proceed further with it. However, the system was subsequently taken up and supported by the National Computing Centre. Under the Centre's guiding hand it was marketed as 'Timetabler', complete with training, consultancy and technical support, for purchase by LEAs to enable them to prepare their schools' timetables on their own computers. By 1978 it was said to have been purchased by eighteen Authorities and as a consequence to have been widely and successfully tested in practical application.

A strong user group met regularly to consider the use of the system, possible enhancements, and how to overcome any problems the users faced. The system works primarily by batch processing, but the data can be presented to the computer in stages, allowing completion of one section of the timetable before completion of the next. Like most other systems the data is subjected to a number of feasibility tests before construction of the timetable is attempted.

The SPL(NZ) system seems to have become the strongest runner in the race despite its many critics, and even though few details seem to be available of its success rate. Between 1975 and 1978 it was used by nineteen schools in ILEA and of twenty-five timetables eleven were completed and used, including one school where the program was used successfully for four consecutive years. During 1977, trials were carried out by LAMSAC on all three mainframe systems. In an inconclusive report (at least as far as effectiveness was concerned), SPL(NZ) was found to be less successful than the Nor-Data package. However, perhaps because of its marketing and training techniques, once supported by the National Computing Centre, and the strong interest of so many Local Authorities, it continues to satisfy its devotees.

In each case, then, the mainframe timetabling packages of the late 1970s have survived into the microcomputer age. It is still expensive to purchase these packages, and computer time for their operation will still be at a premium in many LEAs. Whether their speed and sophistication is sufficient to balance these disadvantages and to withstand the challenge of microcomputer programs in the 1980s remains to be seen.

So what have we learned from mainframe work on timetabling? Firstly, it must be clear that the 'one-shot' method is not a serious possibility. All work in the last twenty years points to the 'interactive' mode as the best way ahead. The microcomputer is ideally suited to this style of work, so what we now require is the software to make it possible. Secondly, we know that programs which simply mirror the working of the manual timetabler are unlikely to be very effective or efficient. It is likely that the best programs for the microcomputer will be those which lean to some extent on combinatorial mathematics. On this account, timetabling programs for microcomputers, when they arrive (and it is 'when' and not 'if') are more likely to be written by mathematical or computer professionals than by practising timetablers. Thirdly, we know from experience that interactive timetabling by computer demands a whole range of new skills from the timetabler. Working before the computer screen is a totally new experience when compared with the normal analogue methods using Lego bricks, pins or plastic grids. One practitioner described it as being a 'born again' timetabler! Many are those who will reject the microcomputer on this account. I suspect, however, that by the 1990s it will provide our main timetabling aid.

1.7 Option choices

During the 1960s, with the blossoming of the comprehensive school, it became fashionable to offer a wide choice of subjects to pupils right across the ability range. In its ultimate manifestation, pupils in a whole year group would undertake a number of 'compulsory' subjects (typically English, mathematics, physical education and religious education) while most remaining subjects were offered as options. If a free choice is given from as many as twenty or thirty subjects these must be arranged into five or six 'boxes' or 'option blocks' to allow as many of the choices as possible within the constraints of building a timetable. I can remember attending a number of courses from 1965 onwards which offered tuition and advice on the most appropriate way to construct these option blocks. The most complex I can recall involved a great deal of shuffling of multicoloured cards recording the pupils' choices in an effort to find the most appropriate combinations of subjects in blocks to fit the maximum number of choices.

Considering the complexity of the task it is surprising that little was written about attempting this task on computers until the mid 1970s. One of the first references to the help a computer might give is in an article by Frank Cowie in the journal *Computer Education* (no. 22, 1976). He describes experiences in Perth Grammar School over the previous three years and emphasizes how the sorting and listing problems can so quickly be dealt with by the computer.

An article in *The Teacher* (August, 1976) also extolled the virtues of using a computer to aid option choices in the comprehensive school. The scheme reported appeared to be more concerned with getting the right information to teachers and pupils than with constructing the blocks.

One of the earliest formal accounts of an option block system being organized by a computer was given by Peter Barker and Roger Williams in their paper entitled 'Computers in school administration' published in 1977. The authors describe a case study in which a program supplied output in the form of a listing of pupils with their chosen subjects. In addition it provided lists of pupils choosing particular subjects. The program allows this same information to be rearranged for use by guidance and curriculum design staff. Teaching sets can then be identified and, if constraints demand, reallocations of pupils can be made. Another version of the program printed the 'course option matrix' from a 'free choice' of subjects by the pupils, thus aiding the design of option blocks. It is suggested that a logical conclusion for such a program would be the printing of individual pupil timetables, but it is reported that 'to date the program has not reached this degree of sophistication'. Technically, even then, it was quite possible to do this. I recall that in the school where I worked in the early 1970s we regularly had a problem of communicating the new fourth year timetables to the pupils. A fairly simple program written for the local Polytechnic computer by the Head of Computer Science used a pupil and timetable database to produce the individual timetables. If the pupil data is already on file then only the timetable data needs adding to complete the necessary information. Nevertheless, Barker and Williams' paper has been useful in pointing the way ahead. They suggested that 'the potential of the package as a tool for the examination of curricular structures is considerable' and noted that 'users have been able to identify applications that are, at first sight, unrelated to the declared purpose of the package'. Those thrusting ahead with microcomputer packages should note the potential which these remarks reveal for management decision making.

Despite the paucity of published accounts in writing, considerable man-hours must have been spent trying to solve this problem on various mainframe computers during the mid-1970s. The 1978 LAMSAC report lists no fewer than eight packages all produced at different centres for different machines. This illustrates that peculiar phenomenon which has characterized program development in recent years – the simultaneous development of software for the same task and consequent 're-invention of the wheel'. Of the eight packages described four form the option blocks from the students' choices while the remaining four allocate students to predetermined blocks and test the efficiency of this arrangement. Only two of the packages would appear to be interactive and these are both of the latter type. An important feature studied in all packages was whether it allowed 'editing' of the original data. 'Editing' allows the easy amendment either of the block system under test or the original pupil data. Such editing is tedious for batch mode programs, since cards or paper tape must be repunched before a further run, but any interactive system worth its salt should allow immediate changes to the data at will. A microcomputer, or terminal with a screen, is particularly useful for this type of work. Both interactive systems studied appeared to allow such editing.

In constructing option blocks the timetabler or Director of Studies is faced with a considerable number of constraints. Some classes must be neither too large nor too small. Certain subjects must be taken in combination and in consequence must not appear in the same block. Other subjects require setting across the ability range and must have two or three classes per block. At the same time staffing limitations will probably require that any one block of subjects does not demand too many teachers. When one adds the complications of specialist rooms, time requirements and the constraints of the timetable itself, the number of variables to be considered becomes many. It will be an excellent program which can cope with all these constraints. Perhaps that's why so many of the programs rely on preconstruction of the blocks by the timetabler before they are tested against pupils' choices.

Again, for this task, the more powerful programs on mainframe machines would seem to have been written by computer professionals rather than teachers. At least two of the block construction programs referred to above have been translated for use on microcomputers although only one is now currently available commercially. Perhaps the trend away from options systems is making them redundant. Most programs currently available are of the design and test variety. Some of these are discussed in Chapters 2 and 4.

1.8 Pupil record systems

The 'Bible' on pupil record systems for mainframe computers should be the LAMSAC report published in 1974 entitled *Towards a computer based education management information system*. Most other writings on the subject refer back to this comprehensive document but in the eyes of those at the school chalk face, little would appear to have developed from it in the intervening years. However, it still holds a great many lessons for those beginning the task with microcomputers.

Incredibly, though, an account of an early foray in this field appeared in the *Times Educational Supplement* in July 1968. As far as I can see this was one of the earliest accounts of computer use in school administration outside of timetabling. The brief article by an unnamed author referred to the use of an Elliott 803 computer at Lanchester College to produce 'numerical summaries and sublists' from a limited pupil record database. The programs to produce the goods had been written by the author who was clearly a teacher. The school was an expanding one with a pastoral structure which demanded a great many lists. These included school, house, house tutor group, year group and form lists. The aim appeared to be to reduce clerical time in the production of these lists and the associated statistics. Many of the observations are still relevant today, particularly with regard to the maintenance of the database and the production of up-to-date information. In terms of achieving the project's aims the author makes the following statement:

In assessing the true savings in using such a computer system it is essential to appreciate that clerical labour is not entirely eliminated . . .(the work) however needs to be done only once whereas with a manual system a comparable clerical task needs to be done year by year.

It is this sort of saving which is still being sought as microcomputers begin to undertake the list making task today. No doubt the idea appealed to many in 1968 who were without the technology available to us. The unknown pioneer, in order, perhaps, to avoid being trampled in the stampede, concluded his article thus:

In the light of limited staff time and resources of the present computer the College will be unable to offer a service to schools in this work at the present time.

A report by the British Computer Society Schools Committee (BCSSC) in 1976 relied heavily on the earlier LAMSAC report for some of its suggestions, but it took a good look at the question of pupil records on an individual school basis. It notes that these records are central to the information requirements of schools and that the data will probably be held by a variety of people on a variety of media such as card index, record card, mark book, etc. For a large school in particular, the problems of recording, rearranging, retrieving and probably re-recording the information result in wasted manpower, needless delays and duplication of effort. The nature of a pupil database in schools will be examined later but suffice to say here that the report suggests three main categories of information, namely, general background, school progress, and the short term record. Clearly some of the data stored could be sensitive and the report suggests that the implementation of computerized pupil record systems is slow to progress not only on account of cost but also because of the social problems it presents. The schools cited, where there had been some implementation prior to

1976, all seemed to concentrate on list production or mark processing. It is noted that a worthwhile database retrieval system requires a powerful computer.

The report by Barker and Williams, referred to earlier, also makes brief reference to pupil record systems. It notes that lists of various types – by class, by house, by sex, by age, by entry number – whether in alphabetic or other order, are often required and simply mean rearranging the information in the admissions register. The computer can extract this information and produce it much more quickly than a secretary, but time saving is not the major advantage. The accuracy of the prepared information is much more valuable – the lists containing the same categories of information about each pupil, free from transcription errors. Aside from listing, however, the report suggests no further use for the pupil record database.

I have already indicated my opinion that the LAMSAC (1974) report should be a major source of reference for those involved in pupil record system production. Although it was written for Local Authority use and made its recommendations with the uses of large mainframe computers in mind, it poses a number of important questions equally applicable to those who are working in one school on a microcomputer system. Let me cite just a few of these:

What is the purpose of recording items of data?
Is it practical to collect the data?
Who should collect the data?
How frequently will the information need to be updated?
If it is very frequent, is this practical?
Will the validity of the data change with time?
Who should have access to the data?

These are questions which must be answered before any record system is designed for the microcomputer. I shall examine some of these issues at various points in later chapters.

The report goes on to consider what a pupil record database can provide. As we have seen, earlier writers could only suggest the reorganization of the data in various ways to provide necessary lists. However, the LAMSAC report suggests the following:

Information for administrative decisions
Information for counselling decisions
Information for planning decisions
Information for research

Under such wide-ranging headings, pupil listing only occupies a very small subheading under the 'administrative' section, which also includes subsections for the processing of examination results and the completion of statistical returns. The major headings suggest that the pupil database might be a great deal more use if reports are generated for 'management' use instead of just using the data for 'administrative' purposes. This is certainly an area which lacks any development so far in the school situation.

Social implications are also considered and the report makes the point that human variables are quite frequently ignored when computer systems are designed. These are the points which we must consider: the invasion of privacy for the individual; the time needed by teachers for data collection; the danger that senior staff may feel by-passed and their autonomy threatened; and the fear of change brought about by the use of computers.

If we can make the leap from the vastness of the LEA environment into the comparative microcosm of the single school, there is a great deal to be learned about the implementation of pupil record systems in this report.

1.9   Marks and reports

Once the idea of a pupil database is accepted, it is a natural extension to consider keeping an academic record as part of it. The LAMSAC suggestions contain a section relating to this, although individual marks are limited to results in certain standardized tests. Barker and Williams go a little further than this in suggesting the marking and analysis of objective test answers, especially where test results can be read directly from an answer card into the computer, or are in a form where data can be directly punched from the pupils' answer sheets. It is suggested that analysis of such marks when standardized, can be associated with the promotion or demotion of pupils, the provision of reports on achievement, and the availability of diagnostic data for the teacher on the performance of the individual and of the class.

In an interesting article written in the journal *Education for development* in 1977, Cliff David wrote of a program used to scale sets of marks for preparing assessment profiles of pupils. He suggested scaling to a mean of 50 and a standard deviation of 15. Teaching staff recorded raw marks on data sheets which were then transferred to punched cards by a key punch operator and submitted to the computer in batch mode. The output with both raw and scaled marks as well as ranked lists was used to assist in the assessment of pupils at all those times considered relevant.

An important point to note here is that the data preparation was carried out by specially employed personnel, not clerical staff or teachers. On a microcomputer it might have to be done by a teacher, with all the problems of time to do the job and the need to validate the input. In computer centres punched cards are usually validated before being used, by asking a second operator to repunch the data onto the same cards from the same data sheet. When errors are detected, new cards must be punched. Data validation on a microcomputer can considerably increase the preparation and entry times. I have been told of one school where teachers are required to present marks every three weeks. No doubt someone finds the results useful, but the thought of all that data preparation makes me shudder – especially as they were using an in-school minicomputer.

Cliff David goes on to consider how the recorded data could be used by the computer to produce reports for parents. He concluded that this could possibly save time for staff and suggests that the role of the computer could be enlarged to include not only marks but also comments. Data sheets were designed so that teaching staff could indicate, using a code system, the information they wished to be recorded on the report. The data sheets allowed for three lines of comments, each line having seven or eight different possibilities. So the coding A5, B4, C4 would be interpreted by the computer as:

Satisfactory
Shows interest
But finds the work difficult

Personalization was achieved by a handwritten report signed by the Form Tutor, and the Head Teacher. Nevertheless, the attitudes of the teaching staff, even after they had become familiar with the data sheets, had been varied. A few teachers were unhappy about computerized comments on the reports despite a built in opportunity for writing personal comments. This observation was confirmed in my own research work. Of all the potential applications of the microcomputer in administrative applications, this one is most disliked by teachers.

1.10   Attendance

Most reports require either a comment or a figure to be given to parents as an indication of their child's attendance at school. School education welfare officers seem to pore for hours over registers totting up absence records and trying to spot patterns of attendance. Barker and Williams discuss the feasibility of basing registration on a computer package. Once again there is a massive problem of data capture. In a large school it would probably take a secretary the best part of one day at the microcomputer to input the attendance data for just that day. It is suggested that light pens, or bar codes, or 'clocking in' might answer the data capture problem. True, the computer is able to maintain registers over extended periods without errors of addition and transcription (unlike many teachers!). There is clear potential, too, for the identification and matching of absence patterns. However, until a reasonably quick and efficient means of passing the data into its memory is found, it is unlikely that we can capitalize on the computer's efficiency.

1.11   Statistics

Any database should be able to yield cumulative statistics about its contents. The LAMSAC report indicates several statistical returns which might be produced from its proposed database. Three or four of these might be of interest to schools, such as returns of examination entries and results, data on school leavers, an analysis of subjects being studied and the annual Form 7 returns. Anyone who has wrestled with the problems of the latter in a large school would be grateful for computer assistance. I have known it tie up two secretaries for several days, and demand several evenings of form filling following days of data collection for a Deputy Head. One particularly innumerate Head was still completely muddled after almost two weeks' effort!

Peter Piddock wrote about the possibilities of using a computer to tackle this task in *Computer Education* as long ago as 1975. Interestingly enough he was a teacher in the same school as that described by Cliff David. The important point here is that the required data, namely the class and date of birth of each pupil was already contained in a datafile. It is doubtful if a computer will save much time in the task if this datafile is not already available. Form 7 comes in several parts and Piddock's article deals only with the basic data about division of pupils by age into the given date frames. Another portion of the form requires a more detailed breakdown of pupils aged over fifteen years by reference to courses of study, as well as by date frames. A recent article by Trudy Gallagher (*Educational Computing*, November 1982) discussed a program for 6th Form groups, but it is clear that course choices must be held in the database before analysis for this part of Form 7 is possible. If it is not, then an alternative is to ask the computer to identify the pupils in each date frame by name and to collect their courses data manually.

There are more possibilities for statistical analysis and returns which remain unexplored. It is Form 7, however, which has received greatest attention in the literature. Any worthwhile database interrogation package for school administration by microcomputer will have to cope with this task.

It is, perhaps, curious that little has been written about the task of using computers for examination administration or even the rather specialist subtask of results analysis. Geoffrey Lyons identified examination administration as a major administrative task for senior school staff as early as 1974, yet since then little, if anything, has been written about the need for more efficient methods of working in this area. Barker and Williams refer briefly to the monitoring of external examination results between departments, or even between schools, but suggest that a major problem with such applications is associated with the size of the database and the considerable problems of data capture. Yet the whole task seems made for the computer. In the school situation data has to be captured, collated and rearranged without transcription errors. By manual methods, even if the data is faultless or 'clean' at the capture stage, there is no guarantee that it will still be so after a manual rearrangement. With the computer, once the data is 'clean' it will remain so. The possibilities for using a computer listing for entries instead of the manually prepared entry form, offer considerable time savings, as well as absolute accuracy. Such techniques, with the built-in checks which are possible, should remove the nightmare of the accidental entry of a candidate for the wrong examination or, worse still, his total omission from the entry lists.

The analysis of public examination results is tedious to say the least. Yet with increasing public concern over results, the task has become more demanding annually, and now legislation demands that a tabulated list of results is made publicly available. Analyses have to be prepared in different forms for public consumption (both press formats, with candidates' names, and by subject for the legally required school prospectus), for internal use by department, and for external use by the Local Authority. I know that Local Authorities now have the facility for collecting their schools' results directly into their computer from the examination boards' databanks. However, such statistics rarely give a realistic picture, since they fail to show relationships in results between various syllabuses or distinguish between genuine pupil entries and all those private entries made by candidates using the school as a local examination centre. The use of an in-school computer allows the school much better control over the presentation of its results.

Perhaps we shall all make much more use of the analysis of statistical data in the management of our schools in future. Writing on management information systems in *Computer Education* in 1979, A. W. Howard suggested that: 'The biggest impact (for the future) will occur in smaller organizations who currently do not have their own computer.' This could be particularly true for schools as the use of microcomputers spreads, and also as they enter a more competitive age. For as Howard concluded: 'Organizations which have the best information retrieval will have a distinct advantage in an increasingly competitive world.'

Schools are presently facing pressures of contraction and other uncertainties. Under such conditions decision sequences may be foreshortened, at which time rapid access to, and analysis of, data will be especially important.

The remaining potential tasks for computers in school administration have received scant attention in writing. However, three short accounts are worth mentioning.

1.12 The school library

Writing in the journal *Conference* in 1980, Charles Moseley and Alan Greenwell of the Leys School give an excellent short account of the application of a microcomputer in the school library. They recommend the Cheltenham cataloguing system for filing details of books on disk, rather than the Dewey system, since 'cataloguing and finding can be more accurate'. It is worthwhile quoting in full the possibilities and advantages that such a system offers:

Feeding in author, title, accession number and shelf-mark allowed several options. We could print out all books by a certain author; all accessed between certain dates; all books in one class, or with a particular word in the title; the file could be added to, or books deleted; and, most important, we could print out a shelf-order for the whole or any part of the library. Eventually we shall use print-outs to make a replacement for the old card-index catalogue. The advantages were clear; checking of shelves is much faster and more accurate; books not in the print-out are removed and replaced correctly, and books missing can be searched for if they are not properly signed out, in the Houses. A full library check, which used to take up to three weeks, can now, we think, be done in two days with six people.

In the same sense there are wider possibilities for use of the computer in resource management and resource scheduling both inside and outside the school library and resources centre. These possibilities are discussed briefly in the 1976 BCSSC report.

1.13 Accounting

As early as 1973, D. Millard, in the journal *Conference*, gave a brief report of the introduction of computerized accounting at Felsted School. He suggested that the system was not labour saving but simply presented a bigger database and a more frequent and easy check between budget and expenditure. Although schools have an increasing number of different accounts to handle and budget (Lyons has suggested that such tasks can be of major significance to teachers) and good software packages have become generally available to conduct such tasks on microcomputers for small businesses, to my knowledge there have been no further reports from schools. Perhaps in the last ten years this task has passed over more to Bursars and Administrative Officers who are more satisfied with, and trained in, manual accounting systems.

1.14 Careers

The power of the computer to organize and hold large amounts of data in a form in which it can be readily accessed suggests that it might be used to match the aspirations, talents and interests of school pupils to particular careers. The 1976 BCSSC report cites several mainframe systems such as CASCAID (Computer Assisted Counselling Aid System) and CAPITAL (Computer Assisted Placement in the Area of London) which were around at that time. Perhaps this area of use falls into that grey area between administration and the curriculum. There are certainly those who argue that it is a matter for vocational guidance and counselling alone. The problem with this application is that it needs a very large database. While mainframe computers are able to offer a great deal of memory for this purpose the present generation of microcomputers is only able to provide a fraction of the information required for a full careers analysis. Significantly in this respect, a careers package for microcomputers recently introduced commercially demands that a disk with the pupils' responses to the profiling program is returned, at an extra fee, so that an analysis for each pupil can be provided. The size of the database, and keeping it up-to-date, are problems much more easily handled centrally.

1.15 Benefits and implications

Thus we have now examined the pedigree of MCBA. It stretches back not much more than twenty years and has gained momentum as we have moved towards the present day. Some of the developments may have been along blind alleys, but all have taught us something about the possibilities for today's microcomputers. However, there are other factors, aside from the potential tasks, which will affect our adoption of the microcomputer as a tool. Experience with mainframes has something to tell us here, too. In particular it is worthwhile considering two questions concerning computer applications: What are the general benefits? What are the social implications?

1.16 General benefits

Before any system is computerized it is worthwhile asking why it should be done this way. The 1974 LAMSAC report considered the advantages of applying computers to educational administration generally and came to the following conclusions:

1 The computer can store a lot of information which can be brought up-to-date quickly, be processed in various ways and be communicated over long distances if necessary.
2 The accuracy of data held by a computer can be maintained no matter how many different ways it is processed.
3 The computer can cope with very complex problems, so the production of complicated statistics or forecasts can be easily handled.

Overall, concluded the report, computerization offered a number of important benefits to an education service:

(i)   Since the computer will reject input data not to system requirements users are obliged to adopt standard procedures, rationalized documents and consistent codes, which make the accuracy and reliability of information more assured – a real benefit regardless of whether a computer is to be used or not.
(ii)   The computer offers the facility for saving clerical effort by taking on routine, often mundane tasks which are performed at the moment by human beings.
(iii) Once the records have been established on the computer and are being efficiently maintained, there is endless scope for analysing data, which is not possible under manual methods.
(iv)   Computers can be used to transfer information in standardized formats from one point to another without incurring a lot of clerical effort. This would facilitate the easy transfer of statistical information in the education service.
(v)   Finally, the computer offers the possibility of bringing control to areas formerly inadequately controlled because of the cost of setting up manual systems to do so.

Although these conclusions were drawn for a somewhat larger service, it seems that some, at least, would apply to the individual school's situation.

The 1976 BCSSS report examined the costs and benefits with the individual school in mind. It should be remembered that the processing of data off-site in a local computer centre would have been firmly in the mind of the Committee at that time. The need to identify the cost of any project was recognized although it was felt to be difficult to assess and presented the greatest problems when growing from a single school development. It seems that the authors considered that a sigificant increase in workload would result at local computer centres if all schools were to avail themselves of an administrative service.

The benefits, too, proved difficult to quantify. However, the authors considered that educational benefits were gained when:

teaching staff are released from routine administrative tasks;
where there is an improvement in the utilization of resources;
where the pupil or teacher is better informed; or where curriculum objectives are more readily met.

Perhaps the most important suggestion made by the report is that a realistic approach to initiating developments in the single school might be achieved by considering the following factors:

(a) What are the objectives?
(b) Is there any saving of teacher time?
(c) Is there any improvement in resource utilization?
(d) Does the teacher (or pupil) gain any added useful information?
(e) Is there a manual, alternative system? [Here asking presumably – is it better?]
(f) What are the implications of the system being used by a large number of schools within an Authority? [Here the worry was over too many schools – today, as we shall see later, it may be over too few schools, thereby causing problems over standardization.]
(g) Is the mode of access appropriate? There is a temptation to use on-line systems when batch processing may do.
(h) What sort of burden does the data preparation present?
(i) What would be the effect of the computer temporarily being unavailable?
(j) Is the system sufficiently confidential?
(k) Does the extent of usage justify the development time?
(l) Is it feasible to maintain a reliable, up-to-date database and who will be responsible for this maintenance?
(m) What are the consequences of erroneous output?

These questions are so important that the Head of any school about to implement MCBA must consider them. I shall return to them to provide some observations in Chapter 5.

Peter Barker and Roger Williams identified somewhat similar factors to the BCSSC in their report in 1977. They were:

. . .concerned only with programs that relate directly to the effective administration of the school with a view to providing a better education for its pupils: better in terms of the diagnostic information available to the staff, better in terms of efficient use of resources of staff, space and time, and better in terms of relieving the school office of unnecessary tasks, thus allowing the secretarial staff to act as support staff to teachers in ways more directly related to curricular needs.

Both these authors and the 1974 LAMSAC report had commented on the problems of data capture. If the task of collecting and entering data to a computer takes longer than conducting the whole task manually, then the computerized method is clearly inefficient. There is a considerable time factor affecting teachers in collecting data which must be taken into account when computers are used. Barker and Williams appeal for realism in this respect and summarize admirably some of the foregoing points as follows:

The main criteria for the acceptability of such packages (software) to schools are whether something can be done which has not been done before because doing it by hand would involve far too much labour, and also whether the computer can produce more quickly and accurately reports which were previously done by hand.

1.17 Social implications

Wherever computers begin to operate in close proximity to people's working or domestic lives, social concern always follows. In part the reason is due to anxiety about, or considerable resistance to, the changes that are brought about. However, it is also due in part to the human variables being ignored when the computer systems are implemented.

Where schools are concerned there appear to be three areas in which concern is likely to arise when microcomputers are used for administration:

1 The security and sensitivity of data
2 The time which servicing the systems might take
3 The changes which might be effected to the lives and jobs of people using the system

1 Security

The security and confidentiality of computer files is a matter which has been of great concern to commerce, industry and government for some time. People have been encouraged, sometimes unfairly, to distrust what the mass media have called 'the databank society'. The 1974 LAMSAC report categorizes these fears generally as follows:

- that information may be recorded about individuals without their permission or knowledge;
- that unauthorized access, whether accidental or intended, may be gained to personal information;
- that inaccurate or out-of-date information may cause injury to those about whom it is being held;
- that information previously held in separate locations may be brought together and correlated, enabling conclusions to be drawn to the detriment of the subjects of the information.

Pupil record systems could clearly be open to such misuse – indeed it is possible that many manual systems already are. Some teachers may already be concerned about this. In 1976 Geoffrey Lyons observed that:

many teachers feel hostile towards the keeping of confidential information . . .here there exists the basis of a conflict between those whose needs are to run the organization and those who see themselves in school primarily to teach.

When computers come on to the scene these feelings are exacerbated, possibly because of the ability of the computer to seek out or re-order the data so accurately and so quickly. In consequence pupil record systems have tended to concentrate on non-sensitive background data, and the 1976 BCSSC report was moved to comment: 'The actual implementation of pupil records is slow to progress on account of cost and the social problems it presents.'

So what can be done to allay these fears? Perhaps the most significant move towards examining the whole question of invasion of privacy at official level was the setting up by the Government of the Committee on Privacy, headed by the

Right Honourable Kenneth Younger, in May 1970. It is from the work of this committee that the general measures of the Data Protection Bill of the early 1980s has derived. This bill fell in its final stages when the 1983 General Election was called. However, the new Government has already stated its intention to re-introduce the bill into the new Parliament.

The Younger Committee proposed ten clear principles for the handling of private information on computers, and recommended that they should be enforced through professional codes of conduct. The ten principles, as listed in the 1974 LAMSAC report, are:

1   Information should be regarded as held for a specific purpose and not be used, without appropriate authorization, for other purposes.
2   Access to information should be confined to those authorized to have it for the purpose for which it was supplied.
3   The amount of information collected and held should be the minimum necessary for the achievement of the specified purpose.
4   In computerized systems handling information for statistical purposes, adequate provision should be made in their design and programs for separating identities from the rest of the data.
5   There should be arrangements whereby the subject could be told about the information held concerning him.
6   The level of security to be achieved should be specified in advance by the user and should include precautions against the deliberate abuse or misuse of information.
7   A monitoring system should be provided to facilitate the detection of any violation of the security system.
8   In the design of information systems, periods should be specified beyond which the information should not be retained.
9   Data held should be accurate. There should be machinery for the correction of inaccuracy and the updating of information.
10   Care should be taken in coding value judgements.

The 1974 LAMSAC report suggests that adherence to these principles would clearly allay fears about the invasion of privacy. It urges any LEA considering implementation of a pupil record system to adopt them. The report goes on to suggest that an education programme for all those involved might help to explain the reasons for the implementation of such a system and the safeguards involved. The distribution of an information booklet to all parents, and the holding of meetings in schools to discuss what is involved are suggested as ways to gain the full confidence of parents and pupils. Education staff at all levels must also understand the objectives of the system and the way it is to operate. Teachers must be made aware of what the computer can and cannot do. They must realize that computer programs are not infallible, that the computer does not control them or their pupils, and neither can it make judgements. It must be seen merely as a processor of information which is valuable in helping them with their job.

The implications for in-service training even in the individual school situation are alarming, and this is another matter to which we must return in Chapter 5. Suffice to say at this stage that here again is another area where schools can learn from one anothers' experience.

2 Time, and servicing the needs of the system

Everyone supposes that the use of a computer system will necessarily save time on any task. Barker and Williams suggested several uses of a computer which by manual methods would:

. . .involve school staff in considerable time and effort that could be better devoted to other activities; teaching and school organization is labour-intensive, and there is clearly no point in highly qualified and highly paid staff operating as little more than clerical assistants when certain tasks can be performed speedily and more often efficiently and effectively by a computer.

Not all teachers subscribe to the view that time is actually saved in this way. In 1974, the LAMSAC report suggested that 'teachers are worried about the extra work which they feel they may be forced to carry out to satisfy the computer's demands for information'.

The report goes on to suggest a number of aspects to this problem which should be considered:

1 Comparing a computer system to a manual record system the former should not create any more work than the latter if record cards are kept properly up-to-date. It is suggested that the individual teacher's clerical workload could actually be reduced if the record system was made to work efficiently. However:
2 Schools often see no real return for their data gathering, and the same may be true of teachers in individual schools. Real gains must be seen as a reward for data returns if potential criticism on this score is to be fully allayed.
3 If information about pupils is really important then more time should be made available to teachers to gather and record it. Most teachers would agree. There are wider implications in the allocation of this time to personnel involved in MCBA than just data collection. However, it would appear that the concern over time is potentially more easily soluble than the concern over privacy and security.

3 Change

Teachers as a group tend to be resistant to change, and it should not surprise us that the implementation of MCBA in a school is likely to be no exception, and may also involve the wider context of ancillary staff.

A. G. Oettinger in his book *Run computer, run! – the mythology of educational innovation*, eloquently presents the difficulties faced by the application of new technology in American schools during the late 1960s. He concluded that neither educational technology nor schools were, at that time, ready to consummate the revolution in learning, systematic planning and uniform standards that computers had the potential to bring. Major institutional change was called for before the new technology could contribute significantly. Whether the intervening fifteen years have allowed that change remains to be seen.

The same problem was discussed in the 1974 LAMSAC report:

This fear of the computer bringing about change in the procedures in an authority can only be allayed by the LEA's clarification of its intentions. The computer is only an instrument of change; human beings actually make the change.

The final problem which needs to be discussed is not a problem of the present time, but rather of the future when the computer system has been introduced. The introduction of a formal means of information processing, wherever informal methods exist at present, will bring a new dimension to people's work; it will emphasize the importance of information and require people to think about information.

Here again the answers might lie in in-service training.

1.18 Where we are now

The cumulative experience of the mainframe computer's application both in school administration and in the wider field of management and administration in business and commerce provides a valuable foundation for similar use of the microcomputer in schools. In particular it is notable that several of the potential tasks have already been explored in this wider context. Certainly issues have been raised to which I shall return in later chapters. If the introduction of the microcomputer to schools has brought us to the crossroads, then these experiences provide the picture of 'Where we are now'. We can now turn to examine where the microcomputer leads us.

2 Tasks for the microcomputer

or 'Where are we going?'

'If the computer says you're still in the 4th year
Smithers, then you're still in the 4th year!'

Tasks for the microcomputer

During the 1970s, progress towards the use of the computer in school management and administration was aided both by research and by individual initiatives in response to needs. Research which I conducted between 1979 and 1981 (Bird, 1982) revealed that the influx of microcomputers into schools had led to a rapid increase in their use for administrative purposes as teachers and administrators sought to explore their potential for various tasks. My research was also able to discern the tasks which were being attempted most often, thus giving guidance on what might prove the most useful lines of development with the new technology. In this chapter I shall examine these tasks loosely in the order of importance as identified by my study of almost 300 schools, beginning with the most popular task.

2.1 Pupil record systems – databases

In my research survey of schools the creation of some form of computer held record system commanded the greatest attention, although the nature of the records must have been somewhat primitive if the most commonly associated task is considered. This was the creation of the various lists of names which a school requires – form lists, set lists, year lists, alphabetical roll, and so on. For such tasks the set of records (or database as it should be properly known) only need consist of three items for each pupil – the surname, first name and class. Most schools will wish to include more data such as the date of birth, sex and year group. There is an argument for including the address, but this will not be necessary simply for printing lists of names.

What should be included in a pupil record database?
Certainly no more information than is required to satisfy the likely *uses* of the database. The need for the pupil's address, for example, should be critically examined, since it can take up a great deal of space in the record. Is it really required for any purpose? If siblings need to be identified or address labels printed then its inclusion might be justified. However, if there is no use for the address it should be left out. It is a waste of time to enter superfluous data into a computer.

The Head of one school told me that his secretary had to type the name of every pupil in the school almost fifty times during that child's compulsory schooling. His aim in adopting the microcomputer for listing purposes was to reduce this to just one typing, and that to be into the microcomputer database. If simple lists are all that this database is designed to create then names and class information are all that data entry requires. Few database uses will be this elementary. Many tasks described in the remainder of this chapter have some aspect which relates to the pupils and their records. Consequently the programs servicing these tasks will need access to a database which contains the necessary information. This implies a database somewhat larger than two items per pupil.

One of the most detailed investigations into a pupil information system and what its database should contain was carried out by a project team working for LAMSAC in the early 1970s. A report of the team's findings is contained in the 1974 report referred to several times in· Chapter 1. This investigation was considering the use of large mainframe computers by Local Authorities for the storage of a large volume of education information – much more than any individual school would ever find necessary. However, it raises some interesting questions about the size and nature of the pupil database and the information it can provide. Some of these questions, already outlined in Section 1.8, are worth considering from an individual school's point of view.

What is the value of the information stored?
Every piece of data recorded should have some purpose in terms of output.

Is it practical to collect the data?
In terms of a school database this will almost certainly mean that teachers have to glean the data and clerical staff feed it into the microcomputer. The use of the data thus collected should be cost-effective in terms of the time taken for its collection and entry.

Is the data accurate and will it remain so?
There has to be a check on the accuracy of the data entered into the microcomputer file of each pupil. This will demand more time and energy from clerical and teaching staff. Inevitably data will need to be corrected and updated. This must be taken into account in judging the cost-effectiveness of the process.

Questions are also raised in the LAMSAC report about the length of time which data should be retained in computer files and who should have access to it. The proposed Data Protection Act referred to in Section 1.8 may determine schools' policies both in these respects and in terms of what shall actually be stored.

The LAMSAC report proposes a comprehensive database containing what it calls the 'standard record' for each child. This record comprises eight sections each containing a number of 'fields'. A 'field' is a section of a record of known maximum length, in terms of letters or 'characters'. For example, one field of maximum length twenty characters could be identified for the surname, whilst another of one character could be set aside for the sex. It is not necessary to examine here every field suggested for the standard record, but merely some of the more important as examples.

It is useful to picture a computer datafile as a series of cards. Each card is a 'record', and each line on the card is a 'field' usually with a fixed length. The general structure proposed by the LAMSAC report is as follows:

1 IDENTIFICATION   Surname, other names, sex, date of
   8 fields in all)   birth, address, etc.
2 VITAL EXTERNAL LINKS   Name of mother, father, legal guardian
   (11 fields)   etc.

3	ACADEMIC PROGRESS (8 fields)	School(s) attended, form group, test and public exam results, etc.
4	HEALTH (6 fields)	Pre-school medicals, handicaps, restrictions on activities, etc.
5	HOME BACKGROUND (14 fields)	Nationality, place of birth, siblings, school meals, child care, etc.
6	CAREERS ADVICE (10 fields)	Interviews, interests, questionnaires, recommendations, NI number, etc.
7	POST-SCHOOL (2 fields)	Employment, Further Education
8	GENERAL (1 field)	Referral details

The report estimates that the average number of characters stored in such a record for each pupil would be 1500. It is most unlikely that any school would wish to store such a comprehensive database on its pupils, but if it did then one class of pupils per side of a mini-floppy disk [see Section 3.5] would be the maximum storage rate. The analysis of such stored data in any quantity would prove extremely difficult, if not impossible, on a microcomputer.

As might be expected, the LAMSAC report concentrates on benefits to a Local Authority in the using of such a database. However, it does identify some uses to the individual school. These are:

1 The production of class lists, etc.
2 The administration of public examination entries and analysis of results.
3 The production of a termly leavers list.
4 The return of Education Department statistics.
5 The compilation of statistical returns to central government:
   Form 7A – pupils by age and group
   Form 7(2) – candidates for CSE and GCE
   Form 7(d) – school leavers (with 10 per cent detailed)
   Form 8(a) – out-county pupils.

In examining such tasks we can, perhaps, gain some insight into the structure of the more limited databases which schools will be forced to use on the present generation of microcomputers.

2.2 A database for school microcomputers

In May 1980 Microcomputer Users in Education (MUSE) held a symposium at Oundle School on school administration by microcomputer. Here it was proposed that MUSE should produce a set of standards for database construction in this application. The reader is referred to the document published by MUSE later in1980 for the complete standards proposed, but it will suffice our purpose here to examine the proposed contents of the pupil record file to give some idea of the data which might be stored in such a database.

For a master file of pupil records it is suggested that the following contents might be essential and that the fields should be arranged in the following order. No attempt is made to define the size of the fields.

Field 1 Surname
Field 2 Forenames or initials
Field 3 Tag (to distinguish identical names – the DES pupil number is suggested)
Field 4 Date of birth (as YYMMDD – Year, Month, Day)
Field 5 Sex
Field 6 Form/Tutor group
Field 7 House

Considering the number of characters allocated to each field by the LAMSAC report, such information might require sixty to seventy characters per pupil. This would certainly allow a year group to be filed on one side of a mini-floppy disk. Even a whole school of under 1000 pupils might be held on one disk in this manner. The number of records which could be held completely in machine memory would vary from machine to machine. As an example, on the RML 380Z as supplied under the Department of Industry's 1981–2 scheme, and with the full memory used, about 400 records could be read into memory allowing for a program as well. This should be sufficient for a year group even in the largest schools.

The MUSE database standards document goes on to consider other potentially useful information which might be filed. However, it notes that such information might not be needed in every school and in consequence does not suggest any particular order for the fields. The fields as suggested in the document are:

8 Subjects being studied/options
9 Sets/groups
10 Date of entry
11 Siblings
12 Address – two fields (split parents?)
13 Previous school
14 Transfer grade
15 IQ
16 Next of kin – two fields
17 Extra curricular activities
18 Parish of residence
19 LEA
20 In/out County
21 Day/board/scholar/grant

22 Fees
23 Prefect
24 Religion
25 Date of leaving
26 Examination results
27 Mode of transport
28 Doctor
29 Medical
30 Special circumstances

Filing all this information would create a record containing about 500 characters for each pupil, restricting three classes to one side of a mini-floppy disk. The MUSE standards document appears to recognize this problem and suggests a master file containing the core data, from which other working files could be constructed. For example, a file to handle the examination entries and results of year group might require fields only for:

Field 1 Surname
Field 2 Forenames
Field 3 Date of birth
Field 4 Form
Field 5 Coded entries and results

The microcomputer could create a new disk file reading the first four fields from the master disk, leaving the coded entries and results to be entered as extra data under control of another program. This new disk would then contain the database for the examinations administration. Such techniques will be important in handling a database of any size on a microcomputer.

During the course of 1981 and 1982 some integrated pupil database management systems began to appear on the market for microcomputers. Some of these are described in more detail in Chapter 4, but it is notable that the databases contained somewhat similar information, reflecting that schools may have rather similar needs. The most common field categories seemed to be:

Field 1 Surname
Field 2 Forenames
Field 3 Date of birth
Field 4 Sex
Field 5 Admission number
Field 6 Address
Field 7 Parents' name
Field 8 Previous school
Field 9 Admission test scores
Field 10 Tutor group
Field 11 Subject information

The number of characters necessary to hold this information varied between 150 and 400 characters. Potentially this would allow between 180 and 480 pupil records to be stored on one side of each disk. Twin double-sided disk-drives would allow up to about 1500 pupil records to be immediately available to the microcomputer, although double density disks would subtantially increase this number. [The technical terms used here are explained in Section 3.5.] With such data available on disk there is considerable potential for a number of administrative and analytical tasks to be undertaken.

2.3   Pupil record systems – tasks

Lists

It is a pointless exercise to file large amounts of data on a microcomputer without making some practical use of it. As already noted, the LAMSAC report suggested some possible uses of a database for schools. Principal among these was the creation of the various lists which a school might require in its class organization of pupils. During my research this was among the most popular of tasks noted as being undertaken. Some lists which I saw being created from the database were:

1   School role (alphabetical)
2   Year roll (alphabetical)
3   House roll (alphabetical)
4   Tutor group lists
5   Subject set or class lists
6   Lists of pupils from contributory schools

Clearly there are many more applications, and the created lists may contain extra data. For example, form lists may contain age or date of birth and address for the information of Form Tutors, while other versions might just contain names for written entries of marks, grades or reports.

The creation of lists alone would not justify the time spent on compilation of the databases described earlier, so what other applications can be undertaken? If the address of parents is stored then the greatest use that can be made of this information is to print address labels for mass correspondence with large numbers of parents. This is likely to be useful in boarding schools or small day schools in the private sector where such correspondence is relatively common. In most maintained day schools, however, the postage bill precludes such mass circulation, and this is usually done by simply asking the pupils to carry circulars home. Since this was the only application of address use I noted in my research, it calls into question the whole notion of storing addresses in the normal day school, with the large task of data entry which is required. As I have previously noted, schools should examine very carefully the need to store addresses before the database is constructed.

Very similar remarks apply to the storage of telephone numbers in the database. Several of those commercially available have allowed for this data. However, it can be argued that only one record of this number is required in the school. Maybe the best place for this is on an office card index, unless the records are to be available on a microcomputer 'live' in the school office. So if the telephone number is not required, why waste valuable data space and input time storing it?

Form 7

Another popular task for the use of the database is the compilation of statistics required within the school, by the Local Education Authority and by the Department of Education and Science. Principal amongst these are the various versions of Form 7 (Schools) indicated earlier in this chapter.

Every school in England and Wales is obliged to complete Form 7A every January. This form defines intervals of calendar time between which the dates of birth of pupils will fall, requiring the total number of pupils (divided into boys and girls) to be shown for each interval. The usual method of obtaining the data for this form is to use the worksheets provided. Using one column for each registration group, the class register can be examined, tallying the various age groups into their respective divisions. This is repetitive and boring work, offering a high possibility of error, and usually carried out by a Deputy Head, Bursar or Secretary. This task is ideally suited to a microcomputer, especially when the necessary data (just sex, date of birth and form) is already stored on magnetic media. In fact it would be foolish not to make use of the database in this way, and every worthwhile suite of school administration programs should have this capability. The DES only requires that the totals in each division be returned (Form 7 Part B). However, some LEAs require the worksheet (Part A) to be returned for their own purposes, and the facility to reproduce this data does not always occur in program suites.

Another part of this form requires that pupils over the age of sixteen be divided not only according to age division and sex, but also by the nature of the course of study. Placing pupils within these divisions requires very precise information about the subjects which each pupil is studying. 'Mathematics' for example, would be insufficient. Information must be available within the database to determine whether this is A level, O level or CSE. It is unlikely that the database systems currently available for microcomputers either offer a program, or hold the details in the database to effect this task. It would certainly seem worthwhile to make the necessary provision for this in schools with large 6th Forms or for 6th Form Colleges.

Options choices – analysis and listing

Despite the current trend towards expanding the core curriculum, many schools still offer a choice of subjects to pupils at some stage in their five years of compulsory education. Typically a school might offer, in a twenty period week, a core curriculum of mathematics, English, religious education, careers, social and physical education occupying ten periods, whilst remaining subjects are divided into five blocks or pools (options) each occupying two periods.

There are two basic methods of arranging children within these pools. The first allows a complete freedom of choice from among the subjects offered (maybe twenty-five or thirty in a large school), then arranging subjects in the most appropriate way to satisfy, or at least maximize, the choices made. The second method arranges the subjects into blocks according to educational criteria and then offers pupils the choice of one subject from each block. Both methods are usually accompanied by a great deal of guidance and counselling, and the process to finalizing the choice can be a very slow one.

Meanwhile the timetabler is constrained by other criteria – the availability of specialist rooms and staff, the size of groups, and so on – and a count must be kept as the choices are made. Many schools use manual methods for this task, varying from the simple list of names (with messy erasures as changes are made) through to more sophisticated systems with boxes of coloured cards. With these it is possible to check visually the size of groups, and from the names on the cards define the membership of each. At the end of the process certain data will be required:

1   The timetabler/Director of Studies will need information on group size
2   Heads of Department or Faculty and class teachers will need lists of pupils in the expected groups
3   Year or House Heads, Form Tutors and pupils will need a list of the choices for each pupil

I have never seen a manual system which provides all this information easily, and in any case, all the information usually has to be passed through the school office for typing.

Clearly a microcomputer can be of great help here. The information on subject choices can be useful within the database for other purposes, but once stored there it can easily be amended at any stage. There are a number of administrative programs available which are dedicated to aiding the option choices procedure [see Section 4.7 and Appendix 1]. They usually have a facility to provide group sizes at any stage of the data entry. Some even give the group sizes as the data for each pupil is entered. Finally, when all the data has been entered and any late changes made, the database can be interrogated to provide any list which is required.

The method of choice which allows complete freedom to the pupil with subsequent construction of the option pools is a much more complex operation. There are logical aids to the process of block contruction. A clash matrix showing the numbers of pupils requiring each combination of pairs of subjects is essential. In his book *Timetabling*, Keith Johnson has shown how a microcomputer can be used in connection with the pupil database to undertake this tedious task. In addition, he also suggests how a designed option pool system can be tested against the pupils' choices to measure the degree of satisfaction provided. Such methods have a clear advantage over manual testing by allowing many more combinations to be examined than might otherwise be possible. However, Johnson's programs do not allow an automatic search for the 'best fit' of all the choices. It might be argued that this method would not in any case produce educationally sound groupings, but the task has long been a favourite among those experimenting with mainframe computers. I have seen one suite which can do this job on a microcomputer. It requires the input of its own individual data but, of course, once the blocks have been satisfactorily arranged and those pupils remaining unfitted have been found alternatives, the facilities for providing the pupil lists and class data required by the school are readily available.

Any suite of programs which provides information from a pupil record database should be expected to have facilities for listing pupil names by option groups in alphabetical order and giving the tutor class of origin; for giving the option group sizes showing numbers of boys and girls; and tutor class list showing the subject choices made by each pupil.

Reports on pupils

Once subject details are contained in the pupil record database these can provide a foundation for reporting and monitoring pupils' progress in various ways.

The processing of marks and grades was revealed to be a popular task in my 1981 survey. However, it was difficult to ascertain how widespread the use of such systems was in individual schools, and it is quite possible that in many of them programs were only being used on a limited basis within particular departments.

In a few schools it was claimed that test or homework scores were collected on a regular basis and fed into the microcomputer. After processing, the results were used to show whether a pupil's progress was declining, remaining steady, or improving. Sometimes the scores were used as a basis for reporting to parents. Such an application demands the entry of a considerable amount of data. As I commented in Chapter 1 on an earlier experiment, it seems to me doubtful whether the output can justify the time taken in this task compared with other more personal but less objective methods of assessing progress.

A large number of schools are using a method of reporting which demands the completion of individual slips by subject teachers which are collated into booklets for each pupil by the Form Tutor. Such a system demands a great deal more effort from teachers than the old 'report book', mainly because each individual slip has to have the pupil's name, form, set and subject written on it as well as the date of issue. Some schools have attempted to reduce the teachers' task by using the microcomputer to print all such standard information on the slips before the comment is written in by hand. The slips come off the printer by subject and by set in alphabetical order of pupils. The continuous stationery is distributed in blocks to Heads of Department, who simply divide the blocks into sets for distribution to teachers. From then on distribution and collation is as usual.

I know of one school which claims to save over 300 man-hours of work each year by using its microcomputer this way. Put into context that is one teacher's classroom work for a whole term. In addition there is the added advantage of a report which is neatly presented, with the name correctly spelled on each sheet and subject names given in full.

Some schools go further than this. There are those who use a report system based on a single card. Details are entered against each subject on the card in coded form. So, for example, a pupil might have C,4,1 recorded against mathematics. Elsewhere on the card the parent will find a key showing that C means 'average ability in this subject' and a range of, perhaps, fifteen comments in which 1 means 'always works keenly' and 4 means 'homework is satisfactory'. This is an efficient method of reporting requiring minimum effort from teachers. However it can become a little stereotyped. This can be taken a step further with the aid of a microcomputer. It is obviously quite possible to feed the coded data in and have full statements printed out. These could then be added to the slips described in the last paragraph.

The great danger is that virtually identical comments appear on each slip giving a very impersonal feel to the report. In this simple form I don't think that this approach has a great deal to commend it. As I have already noted, in my research this was one of the few computer administrative tasks rejected by the vast majority of teachers. However, recent advances using wordprocessing techniques with a greatly increased range of comments, holds the prospect for some progress in this field. An article by Phil Neal in the *Times Educational Supplement* (Neal, 1983), describes a successful scheme in which a wordprocessor was used to save time in the production of leavers' testimonials. It is clear in this report that some Form Tutors were worried and sceptical about this development, and that other teachers were concerned about possible reactions by parents. However, the benefits are well presented and, having seen some examples of the testimonials since publication of the article I must confess that some of my own previous scepticism on this issue has been overcome. More details of this scheme are given in Section 4.13(i).

Examination administration
In the last twenty years the complexity of this task has increased many-fold. The reasons for this include the greater importance placed upon examination success by society, the introduction of new examinations for the majority (particularly CSE), and the greater freedom given to schools in the choice of examination board, syllabuses and examination design. Twenty-five years ago it was the usual practice for schools to attach themselves to one General Certificate Board. Pupils were often divided into those who entered for exams (Grammar Schools or 'Grammar' stream) and those who did not. Only one syllabus per subject was taken by schools. Thus the administration of the school's external examination commitment was a relatively straightforward task, occupying perhaps only a small part of the Deputy Head's time.

Those concerned with the administration of external examinations during the 1970s and early 1980s will testify to its increasing complexity. It is not uncommon for the task to fill a large part of a Deputy Head's time these days, and if not assigned to such a senior person it would certainly fill all the non-teaching time of someone on a Scale 3 or Scale 4 post. One Deputy Head with considerable experience in this field recently told me that in the 'old days' the work could be reckoned to take a disproportionate amount of time only during that part of the Summer Term when candidates were sitting the exams. Now the 'season' covers two and a half months from early May to mid-July and the associated administrative routines cover the whole year.

Beginning in late November preparations must be made for the following Summer's entries by compiling the potential entry lists and advising Boards on expected numbers of candidates. Sometime between December and February most schools hold 'mock' examinations to give the candidates experience and to seek extra information on the most appropriate examination entry for them. In January the collection of data begins in earnest and is far from straightforward. In a large Department, say mathematics, in even a medium sized comprehensive school, it is not unusual to find 5th year candidates being entered for one of four different mathematics exams – or not being entered at all. Many of the candidates, and there will be several hundred of them in a large school (including 6th Form candidates), could be entering a mixture of CSE and GCE subjects covering several different Examination Boards. There are other additional complications. Some Local Authorities have entry policies which dictate that they will only pay for a fixed number of entries (usually eight) and for any entries above that number the candidate must pay. Some parents may disagree with the assessment for entry made by the school and press for a private entry or double entry (CSE and GCE). These must be handled differently by the school and one entry paid for by the parents. The hard-pressed examinations officer must keep track of all these variations as they occur and, above all, ensure that each pupil's entry is exactly right. Most pupils will only get one chance to sit these examinations, and an entry error not spotted at this stage could prove disastrous later.

When the examination season begins, the candidates must be marshalled to the right place on the right day. The correct papers and materials must be available and staff duly appointed to invigilate according to the Boards' regulations. There are always some late or absent pupils to chase, but more often it is the staff invigilators who are the worst offenders! At the end of every day the necessary paperwork must be completed before the scripts are despatched to their various destinations for marking. When the last exam desk is cleared away in July there is a very brief respite before the results start coming in. These days most tend to arrive either at the beginning or the end of the Summer holidays, so even these cherished days are not sacrosanct for the examinations officer.

In the old days, once this task had been accomplished the examinations officer could relax until the next entry season. Apart from some 'resits' in the Winter examinations, all would be quiet until the next Spring. Not so today. So intense is the interest in examination results that the examinations officer often has several different analyses to prepare – one for the local press, another for the legally required school prospectus, and yet another for the Head and Governors. And these might be just a few examples. Unfortunately, each analysis is likely to be slightly different in form and will require much detailed attention in compilation. Such is the management interest in results that more and more sophisticated techniques are being developed to aid analysis and compare the work of various departments and even individual teachers. It is likely that such developments will continue to complicate the examinations officer's task for some time to come even if the common examination at 16+ offers some hope for sanity before the end of the decade.

Given the complexities, yet the required accuracy of the examinations administration task, it is not surprising that this has been another favourite for implementation on the microcomputer. Many examinations officers have developed well-tried and trusted manual systems over the years, systems which many will be reluctant to change. Yet the pressures are such that now it is certainly worth exploring whether microcomputers can help.

In the acquisition of data alone the microcomputer can make a significant contribution. If names and dates of birth are already held in a pupil record database this can provide a useful source for the examinations officer's lists since this data is needed for each candidate on most Boards' entry forms. One examinations officer told me that the creation of such a list, in alphabetical order of all 5th and 6th year pupils in the school had been worth its weight in gold to him, saving many hours of work. The list showed the name, date of birth, and form within the school and was used to compile four different Boards' entry forms. Of course, such a list need not be created on paper. If it is created on a floppy disk, with the personal data required in three different fields and a fourth field being left vacant for entries and results, this will form a very useful mini-database for examinations work.

There are various ways of collecting pupils' examination entries, but most commonly the initial source is either via the pupil (checked by individual teachers) or via the class teachers (subsequently checked by individual pupils). I have worked with both methods but will describe one here where the initial entries are made by teachers.

Using the method described above, an alphabetical list of every pupil in the 5th and 6th years is produced by the microcomputer. Columns are added and the list is then photoduplicated and circulated to Heads of Department who have classes being prepared for subject examinations. Entries are made by ticking the candidate's name in the appropriate column, although it has been claimed that to enter a two digit code for the appropriate syllabus is more efficient for those entering the data on the computer and less prone to error.

Data entry to the microcomputer is made subject by subject. A simple program is used in which each candidate to be entered for a particular subject is identified by his 'computer number' as shown on the original alphabetical list. Each subject entry is held in coded form showing the Board, Level, Subject, whether school or private entry, and leaving space for the result.

Lists are then produced by the microcomputer, this time by tutor group, for checking of entries by pupils. Lists can also be arranged by subject for checking by teachers. This stage can produce a fair number of requests for changes, double entries and private entries. These amendments can be entered into the database using another small program. When all entries have been settled, the microcomputer produces a final printout for each candidate showing the nature of each entry and the amount of payment if necessary. This printout can also, if required, show the dates and times of each examination; or such a printout can be produced separately later.

Various lists can be produced for the examinations officer when the database is complete. The most useful is a list produced by Examination Board showing the candidates to be entered for each examination. These lists can be used later to complete the Boards' official entry forms, and in arranging seating in the examination hall. Some Boards already accept a reproduction of the entry form produced using the microcomputer's printer. This obviates the need for manual translation of data and eliminates another potential source of error.

Another possibility is that Examination Boards might collect entries on magnetic media rather than on paper. What this means in its simplest form is that once the entries have been made onto the microcomputer mini-floppy disk, a copy of the disk (copies are very easy to make) is sent to the Board where it is read by a similar microcomputer. The data is then transferred electronically to the Board's much larger machine and stored in its database. Eventually results might be declared by the reverse process thus absolving the school of the necessity to enter the results independently into its microcomputer. This method does demand, of course, that each school should use a database structure compatible with the demands of the Examination Board. The Oxford Delegacy of Local Examinations (ODLE) has already completed a pilot scheme using such techniques and intends to open this means of communication to all its centres in 1984. The ODLE plans to provide the programs to make this possible on any microcomputer used by their centres.

However, in normal circumstances, when results come through, these must be entered into the database, filling the space left for them when the database was created. It is then possible to produce a listing of each pupil's results. However, since the Boards already do this it is usually the Boards' slip that is sent to pupils as notification. The computer listing is more useful for the school's internal records. Any analysis required can be carried out with the appropriate programs. I have seen analyses by subject and by department showing the grades achieved; analyses of the outcome of double entries; analyses by feeder school, form tutor group, and so on, as well as the usual lists for the ever-hungry local press. It is, perhaps, here that we begin to move away from the idea of administration into the realms of management information. One Deputy Head told me that he believed his method of statistical analysis (comparing a department's performance with the average performance of each individual pupil) had played a major part in considerably improving the school's external examination results over the years. The method highlighted strengths and weaknesses both between and within Departments and had led to better understanding of the problems and fresh resolve in getting better results. His method demanded a great deal in terms of data collection and manual analysis. Yet a comparatively simple program would have produced the results from a computer database very quickly. It is the use of microcomputers in areas such as this which has been least explored so far.

There is one final point concerning examination invigilation by staff which it is worth making here. At least one of the timetable printing programs to which I shall refer in a Chapter 4 has a facility to strike out the 5th and 7th year timetables from its database, thus allowing space for examination invigilation commitments to be inserted and printed on a weekly basis around each individual's normal personal teaching timetable. At least they'll never be able to say again: 'Sorry. I didn't look at the invigilation notice board!'

Experienced examinations officers may question whether all this makes their life any easier. It may be just more complex in the technological sense in order to be more efficient. It is certainly a moot point. The answer depends, perhaps, on the individual.

At this point we move away from the uses in connection with pupil records to examine other applications of the microcomputer in school administration which do not demand access to this particular database.

2.4 School timetabling

Anyone who has undertaken the task of constructing a school timetable will have had the dream of simply presenting all their initial data to a computer and returning later in the day to collect the completed timetable. Experience with mainframe machines has shown that this dream is unlikely to be realized mainly because raw data, as generated by an initial curriculum design, is unlikely to have a first time solution in terms of a timetable. Indeed, it may not even be possible to derive any timetable from the data presented. In this sense the timetable problem is unique among those for which schools are likely to use a computer. Where computers have been successful in producing a school timetable this has not been achieved without a good deal of careful pre-examination of the data for obvious inconsistencies, and even then other compromises have had to be made along the way to completion. As I have already discussed in Chapter 1, the 1970s taught us the lesson that 'interaction' was essential if we were to harness even the most powerful and speedy of computers on this complex problem. Now that we have the facilities for interactive work with school-based microcomputers how close have we come to realizing the dream?

In 1979 G. Schmidt and T. Strohlein, in discussing the historical developments of timetabling by computer, were able to make the following prediction:

We feel that recent developments in computer technology and software engineering have not yet reached the area of timetable programming. A major evolution will, therefore, come in the near future. Timetable programs will probably move from remote handling in huge computing centres to minicomputer systems owned by the school and handled directly by teachers.

In 1983 that prediction is much closer to being realized, and at the time of writing several programs have appeared which offer the opportunity for interactive timetabling. In fact, the production of a timetable can be envisaged in three stages: curriculum design and pre-planning; construction; and checking and printing the final version. I shall examine how a microcomputer might help in each of these stages.

Curriculum design and pre-planning
The starting point for any timetable construction is curriculum design. The designed curriculum will be a practical expression of the fundamental philosophies of the school in terms of what subjects are to be offered to pupils, and how pupils are to be divided into classes at different stages of their development. Standard formats are available for the expression of the designed curriculum in tabular form. T. I. Davies suggested one method in 1969 and more recently B. Eustace and P. Wilcox (1980) have proposed a widely accepted alternative. The very nature of these formal tabular presentations suggests that they could be well handled by computer, containing as they do numerical and abbreviated subject data. The great advantage would be that this data could be then easily used in various forms of curriculum analysis facilitated by the microcomputer. Although there have been suggestions that work is being undertaken to accomplish this task, no software has come to my attention which is capable of doing it on any microcomputer.

For those whose curriculum design produces a blocking of subjects, teachers and time slots, further use of a microcomputer in the construction of a timetable may prove unnecessary. It is claimed by the supporters of the 'faculty' or 'blocked' timetable structure, that the construction of the timetable framework is so simple that aids other than paper, pencil and rubber are unnecessary. For the majority of planning and construction tasks this may well be true, but there are still the areas of manpower and curriculum analysis, timetable checking and printing which may be useful even to these devotees. They should be encouraged to examine the possibilities.

The design of a school curriculum is rarely left to one person. Usually it emerges from the melting pot of a debate which will involve most of the senior teaching staff in a school meeting under some title such as 'Academic Board', 'Curriculum Development Group' or 'Heads of Faculty Meeting'. Timetable construction from the curriculum design is a very different matter, however. This is very often delegated to one or two people. The first thing a timetabler will need to know is whether his teaching (manpower) resources are sufficient to cover the designed curriculum. In these days of contraction and financial constraint it seems to me that the majority of initial curriculum designs make demands in excess of the available manpower. Another question to be answered as school rolls and numbers of teaching staff fall is whether the demands of each subject can be met by the contributions of the specialist staff available. In a contracting situation the mere staffing of the curriculum is difficult enough to manage – the staffing of individual subjects by specialist teachers adds an extra dimension. Enough information must be available to a school's senior staff to take rational planning decisions during the timetabling and appointments seasons. Here the microcomputer can help by storing data on the manpower requirements of a curriculum in a database. Calculations produced from this data can suggest how manpower requirements might be fairly reduced and indicate which specialist areas are overstaffed and which are understaffed. As a Head, I find I need to update such information constantly, as resignations and appointments are dealt with. Yet the calculations are lengthy and tedious, needing to be undertaken from scratch at each change, as courses within the curriculum are introduced, re-arranged or abandoned. This is particularly true while the pupils' option choices are still being settled.

Software is available for microcomputers to undertake this task and is discussed in Chapter 4. Most programs are based on a sound theoretical foundation. The information they provide is not only useful for the many decisions which must be taken in timetable planning, but will also produce a final analysis of the curriculum when the timetable is complete. Since many LEAs require their schools to produce these calculations in the form proposed by T. I. Davies (1969) or similar, there is considerable time saved on the data collection and calculations usually involved with this task.

The use of the microcomputer in progressing from curriculum design to timetable construction in the way described, produces another genuine example of the way in which new technology can be used to aid management decision making as opposed to conducting purely administrative tasks.

When the curriculum design has been finally established, the pupils' option choices made and the teaching staff appointed, the timetabler is ready to begin construction. He has at his disposal an immense amount of data from which it is possible, theoretically, to construct a timetable. Inevitably, however, the data will contain inconsistencies which make it impossible to complete the task without changes being made. I have always felt that these inconsistencies fall onto three levels.

At the first level are those inconsistencies which are painfully obvious to the trained observer at first sight. Examples of such are the request for a teacher to operate two classes in the same block of sets, or for seventeen double periods in five seven-period days. Timetablers will easily spot these problems without the aid of a microcomputer.

At the second level are those inconsistencies which need some effort in analysis before being identified. For example, some departmental requests may appear quite feasible in terms of staff allocations, but analysis will show that the way teaching teams are arranged does not allow timetable construction within the normal number of periods in a school week. Manual methods are available to identify such inconsistencies. Keith Johnson (1980) uses a 'combing chart' on each departmental allocation. Neill Ransom, in his timetabling training material published by Educational Courses, uses a similar device which he calls a 'visual planner', while the STAG team called theirs a 'schematic diagram'. Whatever method is used, the analysis tends to be somewhat tedious and a microcomputer can certainly be used to help. Keith Johnson has already provided a program to make this possible and while data entry demands a fair amount of time and effort, the microcomputer can be safely left to conduct the analysis and produce accurate results. Decisions on resolving the inconsistencies are, of course, left to the timetabler.

In most timetables where pupils are given option choices in the 4th and 5th years, a careful analysis must be made of the teams of teachers required within each pool or block. Manual methods described as a 'conflict matrix' by Keith Johnson and an 'options clash table' by Neill Ransom are almost identical and will show clearly which pools cannot be timetabled simultaneously. Again, Keith Johnson has provided a program which takes the effort out of this chore. Once data entry has been made the microcomputer will produce printed output of the clash tables for future reference.

There are other second level inconsistency tests which can be applied. Keith Johnson has suggested rooming tests as well as an application of what he calls 'Zarraga's rule' concerning teams of teachers who are in parallel or in series for pure class activities. John Brookes (1979) deals thoroughly with the pre-planning stages of checking timetable resources. However, apart from the areas already indicated most other pre-planning checks have not yet been applied using microcomputers.

The third level of inconsistency in timetable data includes factors which do not seem to be identifiable until after construction has commenced. It is difficult to define exactly what these inconsistencies are and how they arise, since the manual timetabler tends to take ad hoc decisions to solve them as construction progresses. The computer organized timetable in its 'one-shot' mode ceases construction when solutions cannot be found with the data available. In this case, the data requirements are changed to 'inch-up' the timetable to 100 per cent completion. Here again ad hoc solutions are used without the nature of the blockage being fully identified. For some time it has been recognized that the interactive approach is the only solution to these difficulties, with the computer feeding sufficient information to the timetabler so that informed decisions are enabled as quickly as possible. This technique is now being exploited both in mainframe and microcomputer timetable construction.

Timetable construction
After all the planning there comes the time when the timetabler must start the construction in real earnest. The traditional timetabler is an individual, developing his own style and methods of working. Most will like long periods free from interruptions and distractions, and this will mean withdrawal from their normal duties for periods varying between three and ten weeks. (It is primarily to reduce this time input that computers have been considered as the logical alternative.) All timetablers have their favourite apparatus, too, to assist them with construction, and I have seen everything from the traditional roll of paper, pencil and rubber, through the home-made boards with pegs, trays and plastic pieces, to expensive commercially produced

apparatus using lego-like blocks or multicoloured pegboards. Every timetabler insists that his much-loved apparatus is the best. Perhaps that's why the microcomputer is slow to make its impact as the alternative.

Microcomputers have the advantages that they take up much less space and are much more efficient at recording and remembering decisions already taken. I recall an event in my timetabling days when I found, with an almost completed timetable, that two blocks of periods from an early decision on the class board had not been recorded on either the staff or room records. To rectify this situation meant extracting about one-third of the prepared timetable and lost about three days work. This would never have happened using the microcomputer as an electronic pegboard.

There are disadvantages, however. A considerable amount of work could be lost if decisions are being held in the computer memory when there is a power cut! The motto, of course, is to record decisions to magnetic media frequently. It has been argued that the microcomputer cannot be monopolized by the timetabler over his 'season'. If programs fulfil their promise he may not need it for that long. Another disadvantage is that screen size does not allow the display of more than a fraction of the data at any one time. You either have to get used to the idea of working with something that resembles a timetable under a microfiche reader, or to masses of paper generated by the printer as each successive stage is faithfully reproduced. These alternatives do not seem attractive to those used to working surrounded by pegboards and lego bricks, from which Picasso-like display they can extract the most relevant information at a moment's notice.

The use of the microcomputer as an electronic pegboard will demand new techniques, self discipline and training. Once mastered there will be bonuses to be gained. Already with most programs it is possible to list free staff or free rooms for any period of the week. Full information is available in seconds – certainly much faster than scanning two or three boards noting the results and possibly missing some details in the process. Beyond this it is possible to assign whole blocks of staff together as a team, or have that part of the schedule so far constructed checked to find where such a team could be assigned. Any assignments can be 'locked' electronically (for essential pre-assignments like outside swimming lessons or TV lessons) so that they are not moved by accident later on without a message being displayed. Usually with manual systems such 'lockings' are carried in the timetabler's head! This application can also be used with staff timetables so that particular days are 'locked-out' for part-timers.

More advanced programs which are now becoming available will, on request, find the activity with the least amount of freedom for scheduling and suggest placings for it. From this situation it is a small step to the automatic mode in which the 'tightest' activities are sought and scheduled in turn until no fit is found. Only then will the program need to seek further guidance from the timetabler. If it is necessary to 'unravel' the timetable to any extent to explore solutions, the microcomputer can be used to keep track of the unravelling process so that several different branches can be explored on the tree of possible solutions. This will allow the best alternatives to be selected. All this is already technically possible and programs using these techniques are either already available or are in the process of development for most of the microcomputers now commonly used in schools.

Whether it will ultimately be possible to hand the whole process over to a microcomputer must remain a matter for debate. Perhaps it will be possible to produce several different solutions from the same data with the interactive help of the timetabler. In this case we should certainly have better timetables and more efficient use of the timetabler's time. Timetablers must be prepared to learn the new skills. Perhaps the initial compromise is to work using both the microcomputer (to explore possibilities) and the physical apparatus (to create confidence and act as a physical data store).

Timetable checking, storing and printing

If the timetable is prepared by electronic means then all the data should immediately be available for printing, and no other method should be considered. Even where the timetable is prepared by blocking or other physical methods there are very good reasons why checking and printing should be carried out by the microcomputer.

The transfer of the timetable from apparatus to paper in a form in which it can be used by those for whom it is intended (pupils and teachers) is a tedious process and prone to errors. In many cases where it is transferred in handwritten form, legibility becomes a problem. In those cases where it is typewritten, legibility improves, but more errors may creep in if a third party such as a typist is involved. When a timetable is transferred to electronic storage, the program should ask a number of questions at each entry. Is this teacher already teaching? Is this class already being taught? Is this room already being used? The answers produced by the microcomputer to these questions will, collectively, erase almost all errors of data entry. In other words the data is self-validating. With the data safely stored it can be printed in any form required (class timetables, room timetables, staff timetables and so on). A good program will allow printing in a format to be decided by the school. It is unlikely that the computer printer will be able to produce all the copies to be required, but sufficiently good quality copy should be available for duplication by off-set litho or other photoreproduction. In my experience not a great deal of time will be saved. Typically it took two people about three days to dictate and write my school's timetable. Data entry to the microcomputer can be effected by the same two people in one school day. After that it is just a matter of watching the printer and overseeing the duplication. If a good quality printer is used you should have a very legible timetable containing more information than was previously possible. In my own case we can now provide individual timetables for staff and, in addition, everyone has a room timetable showing the staff and classes using each room for every period of the week.

```
                                          PAGE  8
   |     AH     |      JE     |     YYY    |      BN    |     MO     |     PHH    |
MON*| U6-1 :---->| 3P5 :---->| 4B8 :---->| 2P4 :---->| 4B4 :---->| 4B7 :---->|
1A/B|PH M12:---->|PH M11:---->|MA M2 :---->|MA L8 :---->|MA M3 :---->|MA M4 :---->|
----+------------+------------+------------+------------+------------+------------+
  2 | 4A3 :---->| 4A4 :---->|     :      |     |      |     :      | 2Q3 :---->|     : R4   |
A/B |PH M11:---->|PH M16:---->|     :      |     |      |     :      |MA M3 :---->|     :XX    |
----+------------+------------+------------+------------+------------+------------+
  3 | L6-1 :---->| 4B4 :---->| 1L2 :---->| 5B6 :---->| 5B2 :      | 1M11 :---->|
A/B |PH M12:---->|PH M11:---->|MA PL :---->|MA M1 :---->|MA U21:      |MA M4 :---->|
----+------------+------------+------------+------------+------------+------------+
  4 |     :      | 1Q+ :---->| R2  :      |     | U6-1 :---->|     : R3   | 3Q2 :---->|
A/B |     :      |JS L14:---->|XX   :      |     |MA S4 :---->|     :XX    |MA M4 :---->|
====+============+============+============+============+============+============+
TUES|     :      | 2P3 :---->| 3P6 :---->| 3P2 :---->| 2P4 :---->| 3P5 :---->|
1A/B|     :      |JS L14:---->|MA M2 :---->|MA M25:---->|MA M3 :---->|MA M4 :---->|
----+------------+------------+------------+------------+------------+------------+
  2 | U6-1 :---->| R2  :      | 5A4 :---->| 5A3 :---->| 2Q3 :---->| 5A2 :---->|
A/B |PH M12:---->|XX   :      |MA M2 :---->|MA U16:---->|MA M3 :---->|MA M17:---->|
----+------------+------------+------------+------------+------------+------------+
  3 | 3Q4 :---->| 3Q5 :---->|     : 4B8  | L6-1 :---->| 4B4 :---->| 4B7 :---->|
A/B |PH M11:---->|PH M16:---->|     :MA M18|MA S3 :---->|MA M3 :---->|MA M4 :---->|
----+------------+------------+------------+------------+------------+------------+
  4 | 3P2 :---->| 3P3 :---->| L6-1 :---->|     :      | L61A :---->| L6-3 :---->|
A/B |PH M11:---->|PH M16:---->|MA S2 :---->|     :      |MA M3 :---->|MA S4 :---->|
====+============+============+============+============+============+============+
WEDS|     :      | 2P5 :---->| U6-1 :---->|     :      | 4A4 :---->|     :      |
1A/B|     :      |JS L14:---->|MA S4 :---->|     :      |MA M4 :---->|     :      |
----+------------+------------+------------+------------+------------+------------+
  2 | 5A2 :---->| 5A3 :---->| 4B8 :---->| U6-1 :---->|     : 4B4  | 3Q2 :---->|
A/B |PH M11:---->|PH M16:---->|MA M2 :---->|MA S4 :---->|     :MA L9 |MA M4 :---->|
----+------------+------------+------------+------------+------------+------------+
  3 | U6-1 :---->| 3Q5 :---->| 1L2 :---->| 5B6 :---->| 5B2 :---->| 1M11 :---->|
A/B |PH M12:---->|CH M11:---->|MA L9 :---->|MA L21:---->|MA M3 :---->|MA M4 :---->|
----+------------+------------+------------+------------+------------+------------+
  4 | U6-1 :---->|     :      | 5A4 :---->| 5A3 :---->| 2Q3 :---->| 5A2 :---->|
A/B |PH M12:---->|     :      |MA L12:---->|MA U22:---->|MA M3 :---->|MA L14:---->|
====+============+============+============+============+============+============+
THUR| 5A2 :---->| 5A3 :---->| U6-1 :---->| 5B6 :---->| 5B2 :---->| R2  :      |
1A/B|PH M11:---->|PH M16:---->|MA S4 :---->|MA M4 :---->|MA M3 :---->|XX   :      |
----+------------+------------+------------+------------+------------+------------+
  2 | 3Q2 :---->| 3Q3 :---->|     : 4B8  | L6-1 :---->|     : 4B4  | 4B7 :---->|
A/B |PH M11:---->|PH M16:---->|     :MA U22|MA S3 :---->|     :MA U21|MA M4 :---->|
----+------------+------------+------------+------------+------------+------------+
  3 | L6-1 :---->| 1P-X :---->|     :      |     |      |     :      | 4A4 :---->| 3Q2 :---->|
A/B |PH M12:---->|JS L12:---->|     :      |     |      |     :      |MA M3 :---->|MA M17:---->|
----+------------+------------+------------+------------+------------+------------+
  4 | L6-1 :---->| 2P5 :---->| 3P6 :---->| 3P2 :---->|     :      | 3P5 :---->|
A/B |PH M12:---->|JS L14:---->|MA M2 :---->|MA U16:---->|     :      |MA M4 :---->|
====+============+============+============+============+============+============+
FRI*|     :      | 4B4 :---->| L6-1 :---->|     :      | L61A :---->| L6-3 :---->|
1A/B|     :      |PH M11:---->|MA U16:---->|     :      |MA M3 :---->|MA S4 :---->|
----+------------+------------+------------+------------+------------+------------+
  2 | L6-1 :---->| R3  :      | 3P6 :---->| 3P2 :---->| 5B2 :      | 3P5 :---->|
A/B |PH M12:---->|XX   :      |MA S8 :---->|MA M2 :---->|MA L6 :      |MA M4 :---->|
----+------------+------------+------------+------------+------------+------------+
  3 | 4A3 :---->| 4A4 :---->| 5A4 :---->| 5A3 :---->| 2P4 :---->| 5A2 :---->|
A/B |PH M11:---->|PH M16:---->|MA M2 :---->|MA U16:---->|MA M3 :---->|MA L8 :---->|
----+------------+------------+------------+------------+------------+------------+
  4 | 3P4 :---->| 3P5 :---->| 1L2 :---->|     :      | 4A4 :---->| 1M11 :---->|
A/B |PH M11:---->|CH M16:---->|MA M2 :---->|     :      |MA M27:---->|MA M24:---->|
----+------------+------------+------------+------------+------------+------------+
21/7/83   DATA VERSION  16
```

Figure 2.1 A page of a staff timetable printed using a microcomputer. This example was produced on daisywheel printer using data prepared by TTX (see p.133) and a special BASIC program.

61

There is another bonus. Every September, when the timetable gets under way, it seems that teachers want to make minor amendments to what has previously been scheduled – two teachers wish to exchange rooms, a Head of Department changes his mind about which classes to schedule to a probationer, or the Head of English wants to use the library in a slightly different way. All these changes mean that sheets of timetable amendments must be issued and for efficiency, senior members of staff and the school office will have to hand-write these onto the originals. This can lead to some problems later in the year if it is not carefully done. I have found that one hour's work can suitably amend the computer's database, after which revised copies of the timetable, suitably inscribed and dated, can be printed and made available. This is, I believe, an example of the microcomputer being used to improve efficiency in school organization as opposed to just saving time.

Other applications of the timetable database
Once the timetable data is stored electronically then there is no reason why the data cannot be used for some other applications. For example, all the data except for pupil numbers will be available for curriculum analysis, although at the moment I know of no program which undertakes the task in this way.

It is also possible to print individual timetables for pupils providing that details of their sets or classes are known. If these have been collected into the pupil database, for report printing purposes, there is no reason why this data cannot be linked with the timetable data to print individual timetables. This would resolve one annual problem of communication within the school.

Programs to print individual pupil's timetables have been around for some time, mainly on mainframe machines. A deterrent to their use has been the large amount of time necessary for data preparation and validation. Keith Johnson, in his book, gives an example of such a program (OPT6) but only for pupils whose option choice data is already held. However his timetable data is not provided by his timetable (TT) programs, but is created separately.

Even when data is available without the creation of a further database it is debatable whether the printing of individual timetables by microcomputer could be justified for all pupils in a large school. A large number of pupils and a slow printer may make the application impossible. In this case it may be better to limit this treatment to pupils with complex timetables in the 4th and 5th years.

The 1978 LAMSAC report summarized admirably the benefits which accrue from computer aided timetabling. These are:

Better use of resources (teachers, specialist rooms, etc.) saving of time for timetabling staff so that they may give more attention to other essential duties. A thoroughly checked timetable with full or part copies available for all concerned.
Less stress on the timetabler.
An option structure better suited to demand.
A teaching staff more informed on general timetabling possibilites and difficulties and the need for planning.

The school timetable, then, provides fertile ground for the application of microcomputer technology. It is probably in this field that the greatest developments will be seen during the 1980s.

2.5 Wordprocessing

Of all the applications investigated during my research in 1981 this one had the greatest potential by comparison with its surprisingly small degree of application at that time. The principal reasons for this may have been the lack of reasonably priced software and the fact that most respondents were teachers who had in mind more direct applications than those which concerned principally the school office. More will be said on wordprocessing software in Chapter 4.

Wordprocessing involves the creation, editing, storing and printing of textual documents by electronic means. It is usually used for text where redrafting is likely at regular intervals. On this account it hardly makes sense to prepare 'one-off' documents on wordprocessors. There are those, however, who would argue that you can 'personalize' documents via wordprocessors in ways which would not be practical in any other medium.

Let us consider a case in the school context. Suppose that a letter has to be sent to the parents of fifty pupils going on the school skiing trip to Switzerland. The normal method of preparing this letter is to write 'Dear Parents' and to print a standard letter using Roneo or off-set litho processes. At the very most, perhaps the address and parent's name might be written in by hand. To personalize the letter would require the preparation of the text on the wordprocessor. A list of parents' names and addresses is contained in a file held on the computer's disk. The letters are printed on the computer's printer one at a time while the addresses and names are read from this file and placed into the appropriate spaces within the letter. The time necessary for this is significantly longer than the standard process – time which I don't see can be justified in terms of the extra 'efficiency' gained.

Documents which I do see as suitable for wordprocessing in schools, are those which are lengthy yet have to go through several drafts before completion. One example of such are the papers for Mode 3 GCE or CSE examinations. We find these have to go through three or four modifications. One electronic creation of the text can save a great amount of time here and, usually, only one good copy of the final version is necessary for duplication. Other documents suitable for this treatment include those which come up for annual revision. The departmental syllabus, or scheme of work, is an example of such a document. It should be revised on an annual basis, but the office finds it such a chore to retype all of them. Once safely stored electronically, the text can have minor amendments made as required and the date changed each year. To all intents and purposes it appears to be a brand new document each September.

Perhaps most time saving occurs with lengthy tomes like the 'Staff guide'. In many schools this document has become so vast that it is impossible to retype every year. In consequence, each new guide has an envelope full of amendment sheets, or the office must constantly alter and re-use old Roneo stencils which have seen duty over several years. One such staff guide I know had pages 19a, 19b, and 19c, 20 and 21, but no pages 22 or 23! When stored electronically this text can be amended each year and repaged automatically by the system. It only means feeding the stencils through the computer's printer or, with off-set litho techniques, using continuous white stationery as a basis for master copies. The wordprocessors' 'text search' facility can aid the compilation of an index, too. This allows the document to be searched for the occurrence of certain words, although since each word required has to be entered separately this technique can still be tedious with long documents or a large index. Other documents suitable for wordprocessing treatment are the school's prospectus, the handbooks for new parents and pupils, for 4th year option choices, for careers work, and entry into the 6th form.

There are one to two other bonuses to wordprocessing apart from the greater efficiency of the school office. It is already technically possible to typeset text direct from electronic media. At the moment this demands special apparatus which will not be available in schools. But certain printers are beginning to equip themselves with the necessary technology. The text has to be typed onto the wordprocessor in the normal way at the school and saved on a mini-floppy disk. This disk is sent to the printer who sets the type directly from it. [An address is given in Appendix 2.] Even now this process is considerably cheaper than traditional typesetting methods and has the potential to produce first class quality work. While somewhat more expensive that the usual ink stencil or off-set litho processes, this electronic typesetting may prove ideal for those schools which need to produce high quality prospectuses and other such documents.

The second bonus for wordprocessing software lies in its use as a text editor. Technically a text editor is somewhat inferior to a wordprocessor and used mainly by those familiar with microcomputers to alter or maintain programs and datafiles. Most, but certainly not all, wordprocessors have a text editing capability and where they do so I have found that secretarial staff can handle the updating of databases much more efficiently than they can using an ordinary computer program. If, for example, a pupil's record needs to be deleted from a file, a secretary who is familiar with the wordprocessor can use its text search facility to find the pupil's record and actually witness its deletion on the screen. Equally easily, records can be changed while being viewed on the screen. A little more care has to be taken with the insertion of new records, but with proper training it can be done.

As already noted in Section 2.3, wordprocessors can be used in the production of testimonials, references and reports. In this case, simply typing these onto disks before printing is probably not the most efficient method of production. Typing and photocopying could be just as quick. With the use of standard phrases and paragraphs, if taken from a sufficiently broad selection, the wordprocessor has the capability to save teachers and secretaries a great deal of time.

At the moment the purchase of a program to convert some school microcomputers into a first class wordprocessor will call for the biggest investment in software which a school is likely to make. Provided that good professional software is purchased, backed up by a sound manual and, possibly, training for the staff who have to use it, it will be, in my opinion, a very valuable investment to make. There is the added spin-off that senior pupils on commerce courses could be given experience in this new office technology.

2.6 Accounts

One of the biggest uses made of microcomputers in small businesses is to keep track of customer accounts, bills and invoices. It is quite likely that independent schools who have to bill parents for school fees and, sometimes, a host of other extras, could make substantial use of a microcomputer in this respect. Some, I know, have already begun to do so, but in such cases it is usually on the initiative of the Bursar or Senior Administrator rather than a member of the academic staff.

Good commercial accounting software tends to be rather expensive and is not always ideally suited for immediate application in the school situation. However, there is a multitude of different programs for different microcomputers available. These will cover such diverse tasks as sales, purchases, VAT, invoicing, payroll, budgeting, balances and financial reports. They will be marketed under different names such as 'general ledger', 'integrated accounts', 'commercial accounts' or 'cash book'. Some come equipped with extra facilities such as a wordprocessor or the ability to undertake complex calculations.

The greatest advances have been made in those schools where the Bursar is convinced that a microcomputer application would bring added efficiency and has commissioned specialist software for the task from a local or recommended consultancy. In such cases the software is prepared to specification and training is usually offered to the operating personnel. The demands on the microcomputer are likely to be such that it must be dedicated to administrative use. Thus the application in these circumstances is far from cheap and it has to be a serious and reasoned decision to take this route. Some saving can be made if schools are prepared to use software which has been prepared by consultants for use elsewhere, since in this case no capital expenditure in preparation is required. To this end Bursars should always seek advice from those schools where microcomputers are already used in this way.

In maintained schools the situation is somewhat different. Here the handling of accounts tends to be minimized by the Local Education Authority's central accounting process – invariably a mainframe computerized system these days. Given the information feedback from this system, a sophisticated microcomputer based accounting system within the schools would seem to be unnecessary at the moment. Most administrative personnel seem to be happy with their internal bookkeeping systems for capitation transactions. The need to enter data to the microcomputer in addition to County requirements would seem to double their workload unnecessarily.

There are, however, two areas where I have seen microcomputer accounting systems at work in maintained schools. In both cases teachers rather than secretarial staff have been concerned with the maintenance of accounts. The first of these concerns what is generally known as the 'School fund'. It accounts for all monies which do not fall under Local Authority capitation. These include 'voluntary' contributions by pupils and parents, monies for school trips, accounts for concerts, plays and so on. The total turnover in such accounts can often be greater than that handled in the capitation account. Some teachers have found that the use of the microcomputer can save time here and auditors seem happy to accept the computer organized accounts.

The second application concerns the distribution of capitation between various departments or faculties within a school. Some schools have developed sophisticated formulae for the 'fair' distribution of these funds and a microcomputer program can save a considerable amount of time by carrying out the calculations quickly. I have also seen a set of programs extended to keep track of the consequential departmental spending. In circumstances where it is essential that schools and individual departments do not overspend their capitation accounts, it is important that the amounts committed to orders by the departments are known at any time of the financial year. The teacher or administrator responsible for this task often keeps accurate records to show current spending. However, some Heads of Department are not so careful! The keeping of accounts on a microcomputer allows monthly spending to be circulated to Heads of Department rather like a personal bank statement, and without a great deal more effort by the 'accountant'. These accounts announce the amount spent showing details, the amount committed to undelivered orders and the balance remaining. By virtue of the individual sub-account records, the 'accountant' is easily able to keep track of money remaining in the school account. Rather than a true accounting system I tend to regard this application as a further 'management information service' use of the microcomputer.

2.7 Stock control

Stock control programs abound in the application of microcomputers in commerce although these are likely to be much more complex than is necessary in schools, who do not sell a tangible product. Schools using stock control programs as identified in my research were using entirely 'in-house' generated software. Once again this use appeared to be entirely in the hands of teachers with some responsibility for the supply or circulation of materials in the school. Usage seems to vary from the monitoring of stationery supplies right through to keeping track of expensive audio-visual equipment. It would appear that few of these schemes are developed to any degree of sophistication at the moment. For the most part the updating of resource lists at regular intervals is something which could equally well be undertaken by wordprocessing programs.

2.8 The school library

Since many university libraries now use computer organized storage retrieval and security systems, it is not surprising that some schools should have considered and implemented such uses. It is too early yet to expect that school libraries will have a dedicated 'on-line' microcomputer system to identify books and non-book resources, although it is a logical extension of the normal card index or 'optiflex' systems. Some school libraries have, however, 'filed' their book stocks on floppy disk. From such a file a number of options are open. Books by certain authors, in certain classes (topics) or with a particular word in the title can be listed. Books can be printed out in shelf order for all or part of the library thus speeding shelf checking. Missing books are easily identified and those misplaced on shelves can be properly restored much more quickly.

Library cataloguing systems lend themselves to computerization. I have noted both Dewey and Cheltenham cataloguing systems at work. Data usually includes the catalogue system number, author's name and book title. A fair effort in initial file creation and file maintenance is required, but such effort may eventually have significant rewards. The library service in most schools is often very hard pressed.

Where a microcomputer is installed permanently in a school library or resources centre then its use can be enlarged beyond being an electronic book cataloguing system. It is possible to hold data on a wide variety of topics and this need not be held just on one disk. It is possible that a collection of disks could provide a large database on other sources of information within the resource centre. This could save time for the librarian in answering the question 'Where can I find out about . . .?'. Some microcomputers can be equipped to communicate with the Prestel database service via telephone lines, thus opening the opportunity to access considerable amounts of catalogued information. It is probable that, in a few years' time, no school library or resource centre will be considered complete without its microcomputer equipped for teletext and Prestel services. When this occurs the microcomputer will play an increasingly important role in the library's administration.

2.9 Other tasks

Some fifty other applications were reported to me by respondents in my research work. Most of these were concerned with record keeping of various kinds such as medical, discipline, transport, and sporting records for pupils as well as old pupils' and staff records. In the main these records seemed to be kept for list production or address label printing rather than for sorting on various fields, which is a more usual computer application.

Other minor applications included the keeping of career records and the results of UCCA applications in order to provide information for future generations of applicants. Finding out which universities and colleges offer the appropriate courses can be a major problem for would be applicants. Some schools have attempted to keep such details in a database held on magnetic media. However, the revision of this database on an annual basis is itself a major task. If this could be undertaken by a central agency for a small fee payable by subscribing schools then this application could save considerable time both for staff and pupils. I understand that the Careers Research Advisory Council (CRAC) have some programs which might be useful in this respect.

I am fairly certain that the applications examined in this chapter exhaust the possibilities for the microcomputer's use in the administration and management of schools at the moment. They include all those reported to me in a survey of almost 300 schools with experience in the field. These applications alone will be enough to keep us busy for some considerable time. No doubt other applications will materialize as time progresses, for nothing is constant in the world of microcomputers. I should like to see greater effort in the field of 'management' as opposed to 'administration', but the immediate advances are more likely to be made with 'clerical' tasks.

3 Microcomputer hardware for school administration

or 'How will we get there?' (Part 1)

'It's not exactly what I had in mind when I asked you to
go out and buy some hardware.'

3.1 'Will it be technical?'

This is a question I am often asked by participants in courses on microcomputers in school administration. My answer is always 'No', because I believe that everyone should be able to use a microcomputer as a simple piece of equipment, just as we use a television set, or a video cassette recorder, without knowing in detail exactly how it works. The more I get into discussions in these sessions, however, the more I realize how difficult it is to divorce the microcomputer's technical background entirely from its use. To carry the domestic equipment analogy a little further, there is not much point in going out to buy a television set without knowing that you need the appropriate aerial pointing at a transmitter before you can get a picture on it. Likewise it is difficult to explain the limitations of a particular microcomputer for school administration purposes without making some reference to its technical capablities.

There are other reasons, too, why I make no apologies for a chapter on 'hardware' – the bits and pieces of equipment which make up a microcomputer configuration. The microcomputer world is notorious for its 'jargon'. Words have been 'borrowed' or made up to describe things which have never existed before. This has been necessary to aid communication between people working in a rapidly expanding field. Yet, as in most languages, the words are easy to understand once you know their derivation. There is nothing wrong with making up words like this – the Welsh organized a national competition to find their word for 'television' – 'teledu'. Many of the words emerging in the new technological age will soon pass into common usage. So it is part of everyone's lifelong education to understand them. In looking at the hardware some of the more common terms will be needed and I can explain them as we go along. Another important reason for looking at hardware is because I believe the microcomputer will soon find a permanent place in school administration and management, just as the telephone and typewriter did many years ago, and the off-set litho and plain paper copier have done more recently. When the microcomputer is purchased for the school office, however, it is unlikely to be the Bursar or Media Resources Officer who takes the decision. It is much more likely that the Head or Deputy will be in the hot seat. There will be plenty of high pressure salespersons willing to come in to 'advise', but if experience with plain paper copiers is anything to go by, woe betide anyone who comes to a decision on their advice without at least a little technical knowledge.

What follows, then, is a layman's guide to the technical background of microcomputers, suitable for the busy Head or Deputy to assimilate. It certainly won't enlarge the knowledge of the electronics expert or computer 'buff', but they will know other sources where the material is expanded into a book (or books!) in its own right.

3.2   The heart of the matter

In Chapter 1 I explained the difference between a microprocessor, and a microcomputer. The microprocessor is the very heart of the computer system – a tiny 'chip' of silicon , which may contain the equivalent of over 10 000 electronic components. This is encapsulated in a plastic package from which a number of 'legs' or wires emerge. These are used for communication with the outside world. This package is often referred to as the CPU (central processing unit) and every microcomputer will have at least one; some of the more recent arrivals on the market have two or more. Despite their complexity these devices are incredibly cheap – at 1983 prices less than £5 for the most commonly used units.

So what does the microprocessor do? It works entirely with 'binary' numbers. Because of the influence of 'modern' mathematics in schools in the last twenty years most of us know what binary numbers are – numbers represented with just 0s and 1s where 2 is represented by 10, 3 by 11, 4 by 100, 5 by 101 and so on. Basically, the CPU receives a binary number and interprets it as an instruction, carries out that instruction, sends out the result of the instruction, fetches the next instruction, and so on. As befits a heart, the CPU has a regular cyclical 'beat': fetch instruction – examine; decide what to do – do it; output result; fetch instruction – and so on. To help it in this task the microprocessor has a number of devices in its circuits. Important among these is a built in 'clock' which controls the cycle of operations. The speed of this clock will give us some idea of the speed at which the CPU can work. Its speed is measured in millions of pulses per second (represented by megahertz or MHz). Typically these devices work at speeds of between 1 and 4 MHz – some of the newer devices at speeds up to 8 MHz. The speed of eight million operations each second almost defies the imagination. Another important component of the CPU is its arithmetic and logic unit (ALU). This unit allows the microprocessor to add, subtract or compare two binary numbers. Although the ALU can only accept very small binary numbers it is the main workhorse of the CPU and through it all the arithmetic of the computer is carried out. Multiplication and division are carried out by repeated addition or repeated subtraction; to evaluate something so complex as a square root very lengthy routines are undertaken. These are conducted so quickly that the time taken passes almost unnoticed by the user. Even letters of the alphabet can be handled and compared after being converted into unique binary numbers or 'binary code'.

More of what goes on inside this incredible device need not concern us here, but it is useful to know something of the binary numbers being handled. Very early microprocessors would only handle binary numbers which had four digits or less. These have now been entirely superseded and the most common microprocessors today will operate with numbers having eight binary digits. An example of such a number is:

10110010

This number happens to be represented by 178 in our normal denary notation, but that is not an important point. For people working with such numbers on a regular basis it became a little tiring to keep saying 'eight binary digits', so 'binary digits' got shortened to 'bits'. Consequently microprocessors are now referred to according to their type as '4-bit chips' or '8-bit chips'. Quite recently the '16-bit chip' has appeared on the market and some of the more powerful microcomputers now being introduced have such chips as their CPU. It won't surprise you to know that the '32-bit chip' is being discussed – that is the way of technology. You may well ask why, if the microprocessor can work as fast as you've been told, it's necessary to double up the size of the binary numbers it can handle. The short answer is that it handles arithmetic even more efficiently and makes extra 'memory' more easily available to the CPU. I shall have more to say about memory in the next section.

Were there just one microprocessor chip, life could well have been a great deal simpler. As always in the history of human endeavour, discoveries and technological advances happen in different places simultaneously, and so it was with the microprocessor. As a direct result of these parallel advances, microcomputer designers have always had a choice of CPUs. In a survey of 160 microcomputers on the market early in 1983, I found four main, although not entirely unrelated, 8-bit microprocessors in use, plus sundry other custom produced chips. Of these, by far the most popular was the Z80 designed by ZILOG Ltd (or its more recent version the Z80A). This accounted for over 60 per cent of the 8-bit market, whilst its main rivals, the 6502 (MOS Technology Inc.), and the 8085 (INTEL Corporation), could only account for about 20 per cent of the remainder. The 'instruction sets' (the binary numbers which convey instructions to the CPU) of these units are quite dissimilar. The same set of binary instructions sent to both the Z80 and the 6502 would have quite different effects. In consequence 'programs' or series of instructions written for one cannot be transferred to the other. Even where two microcomputers both have the Z80 chip as the CPU, this does not necessarily mean that programs are interchangeable as a result of other differences in the design of the two machines. This illustrates the difficulties over standardization which have beset the design and implementation of microcomputer systems. It has been suggested that manufacturers have a vested interest in non-standardization, because once they have you and your programs 'hooked' to their machine it can take a great deal of time or money or both for you to move to a competitor.

Microcomputers based on the 16-bit chips are only just beginning to become available. Early in 1983 there were sixteen models of microcomputer offering this technology and these were using four different chips. Of these the most popular was the 8088. The development of the Z80, known as the Z8000 was only in use in one machine. The 16-bit chips have been developments from 8-bit 'families'. This helps to keep the instruction sets compatible. However, to use the greater power there must be additions to the 'instruction set'. Consequently, programs for 8-bit machines will have to be rewritten to make full use of the 16-bit chip. Some machines currently offer dual 16-bit and 8-bit microprocessors, giving the power of the 16-bit chip with access to the large numbers of programs already written for the 8-bit chip.

3.3 Memory

Powerful though they are, microprocessors have little capacity to retain information other than for the immediate operations in hand. Instructions could be passed to the microprocessor directly from a keyboard. However, being able to process instructions at a million per second is a useless attribute if these instructions have to be fed by a human operator at a maximum of one per second!

To make full use of the computer's speed and ability to repeat a task the instructions from the CPU have to be stored in advance. A place also has to be found for the data which the CPU will process and answers which it needs to keep. These places to keep instructions, data and results are found in the computer's memory. Essentially 'memory' can be conceived as a number of 'cells'. Each cell is able to remember whether it is 'on' or 'off' – a zero or a one. A collection of eight cells are required to remember one 8-bit binary number. In the 1950s such memories were difficult to design, very costly, slow to operate, large, unreliable and expensive on energy. They had a nasty habit of becoming very hot! In the 1960s a great deal of use was made of 'core' stores. These comprised very small ceramic rings, containing a magnetic material and joined by wires. By comparison with today's 'memory' the stores were very large and very expensive to make. One board measuring 10 cm by 10 cm might contain 10 000 rings or cells. Memory cells no longer use ceramic rings and today over 64 000 single memory cells are routinely made on single chips of silicon a few millimetres square. Such chips are fast and reliable, cost very little, consume little energy and keep cool. At the present time chips with over 500 000 cells are being planned. The cost of large amounts of 'memory' has ceased to be a problem. Most microcomputers have the facilities for memory expansion so that chips in addition to those fitted to the machine when purchased can be utilized. Currently, one firm is offering a plug-in module for one well-known microcomputer with 128 000 memory cells for £20.

Like any physical entity, memory has to be measured. People who deal with numbers are always making up units. Anyone who has been through metrication will know how confusing it all is until you fully understand. Obviously, if instructions to microprocessors are contained in 8-bit numbers, you have to find storage space for 'so many' 8-bit numbers. Saying '8-bit number' is rather a mouthful, so some genius came up with the word 'byte' to describe it! Yes – it is spelled with a 'y' so we don't get totally confused! So:

One byte = one 8-bit number

The computer's memory is divided into groups of eight cells. Each group can be regarded as a 'pigeon-hole' which has an 'address', so each 'pigeon-hole' holds one 'byte'. The amount of memory can be measured in terms of the total number of bytes it can contain. Since this usually runs into thousands we can abbreviate this even more using the term kilo, which in metric terms means 'one thousand'. So:

One thousand bytes = one kilobyte = 1K
(Actually, for technical reasons 1024 bytes = 1K, but nobody bothers too much about this discrepancy!)

Most microcomputers which we are likely to use for administrative purposes will have at least 32K bytes of memory. Even this will provide some limitations, and it would be best to aim at the highest possible size of memory which for 8-bit microprocessors is 64K. Cunning ways are being found to go beyond this. Some 8-bit microprocessors are being programmed to use memory beyond their theoretical maximum of 64K and, in any case, 16-bit types can go well beyond this. Memory capacity is increasing at such a rate that in just a few years we shall be out of the range of K memories and into the next range, the megabyte. 'Mega' is the metric prefix for 'one million', so:

One million bytes = one thousand kilobytes = one megabyte
(Or 1 048 576 bytes = 1Mb if you wish to be pedantic!)

There seems to be some disagreement about the use of the 'b'. Sometimes one sees Kb for kilobytes, but more commonly it is just K. Mb is almost invariably used for megabytes.

To put this size of memory in context, 1Mb would hold the data for over 650 pupils with even the largest LEA database proposed in the last chapter. In the reasonable kind of school database proposed by MUSE over 14 000 pupils' records could be stored. Put another way, 1 Mb of memory could hold 300 pages of A4 text prepared on a wordprocessor.

3.4 RAM and ROM

There are two kinds of memory for microcomputers – RAM and ROM. Manufacturer's literature often refers to both in terms of the amount expressed in kilobytes.

Memory described in the previous section is the kind where program instructions and data are stored while the computer is in use. Any one of its many 'pigeon holes' or addresses can be accessed by the microprocessor either to seek information (known as 'reading' from the address) or to place information (known as 'writing' to the address). The addresses can be accessed at random by the microprocessor. Consequently this type of memory is known as 'random access memory' or RAM for short. The amount of RAM which you have in your microcomputer is very important when considering the use which you are going to make of it. Another important factor to remember about RAM is that the memory is 'volatile', that is, when you turn the power off, everything which you had stored there is lost.

The second kind of memory does not suffer from this disadvantage. It always contains the necessary instructions whether the machine is turned on or off. This also means that you can't alter the contents of the addresses either. The computer can only 'read' the instructions which are there. This type of memory is known as 'read only memory' or ROM for short. There might be one or more ROM chips in a microcomputer. The instructions will have been 'burned' onto the chip by the manufacturer to do a specific job. This might be to offer facilities for a special 'language' to be used, to get the machine to behave in a certain way immediately it's switched on, or to allow it to do a certain job, like wordprocessing. Certain machines, like the BBC microcomputer, have sockets in their circuit boards where ROM chips can be plugged in when you are able to afford enhancements to your machine. Other machines, like the ATARI, allow various cartridges containing ROM chips to be plugged into a slot to change the machine's use. Manufacturers' literature often give the amount of a microcomputers' ROM in terms of kilobytes. This figure is of little value unless you know what the ROM does. For example, a specification of 32K RAM plus 32K ROM is useless information unless you know that the ROM contains the language in which you wish to program or a wordprocessing facility which you wish to use. If these are two uses you wish to put your computer to, it means that none of your precious RAM will be taken up to hold these facilities and can be used to handle data.

Never be tempted to make a straight judgement between two machines on the basis of RAM either. Consider two machines – X and Y. X is advertised with 48K RAM and Y with 32K RAM. On the basis of memory alone X might appear more attractive until you realize that 20K of X's RAM will be taken up to hold a language facility before you can program it, whereas Y's language is entirely held in ROM.

3.5   The 'ins' and 'outs' of hardware

It's all very well to talk of microprocessors which work at the speed of light and memories which can store vast quantities of information, but where does the human being get into this? There have to be ways in which we can get data and programs into the machine and also get information out.

Keyboards

Despite the fact that it's technically possible to speak to a microcomputer and have it talk back to you, these are not yet useful facilities for school administration. Maybe in the future, when we have a machine which can interpret a vast range of words spoken in different dialects and produce from this a correctly spelled text, the need for the traditional office typist will disappear. This will not happen, I guess, while the Head's afternoon tea still has to be made! Meanwhile we are left with the standard keyboard as the most common way of communicating with our microcomputer. Programs or data for a microcomputer initially get into its memory this way 99 per cent of the time. Increasingly there are other possibilities with marked card and bar-code readers, as used by some hypermarkets to read prices from black and white line codes on the labels of goods. Nevertheless, keyboards are likely to remain the main data input and communication device between computer and human operator. As various styles and qualities of keyboard exist, care is needed in selection for purchase.

Almost all keyboards have the standard QWERTY layout. For those who have never typed, QWERTY is the order of the top row of letter keys on a typewriter reading from left to right. It has come to mean the 'standard' keyboard layout among the microcomputer community. After that there are some variations. The best keyboards are those where the keys are depressed positively just as on an electric typewriter. Other keyboards are laid out on a flat surface and are 'touch sensitive'. At first sight this seems attractive and labour saving – additionally so since this style tends to be cheaper. But such keyboards are not much use for normal typing, and are much maligned by secretaries because, so they tell me, the keys do not always react well to their touch. The fingers need to be 'rolled' across the 'key' to ensure contact. Some other keyboards appear to have normal keys, but they are in fact 'dummy' touch sensitive keyboards. The give-away is that when pressed the keys click like those on a calculator. Typists don't like these either – yet some are advertised for wordprocessing! It is false economy to make do with anything except a good quality keyboard. Those with an extra group of 'numeric' keys to facilitate data entry are useful. Top quality keyboards sometimes have other 'special' keys to control specific functions, in wordprocessing for example.

Many microcomputers come with an integral keyboard. This cuts down the risk of broken or twisted cable connections, but where there is also an integral screen the operator can be too close to the screen for comfort and without the opportunity to readjust the distance. If you are going to introduce a microcomputer into the school office let your secretary have an opportunity to comment on the keyboard first. If she rates it satisfactory you're off to a good start.

Screens

While the operator is typing instructions or data to the computer at the keyboard it's usual (though not essential) to have an indication that the computer is getting the message, and also some means for the computer to present prompts and other messages to the operator. At present the most common means for this purpose is the cathode ray tube. To most people that implies a 'television set', but this is far too narrow an interpretation and such a device is not ideally suited to administration applications.

Almost all microcomputers except the very smallest have an output to a cathode ray tube. In the case of most small and cheap microcomputers, for example the Sinclair ZX 81, that will be via an aerial type cable into a domestic television set. This is because that is the only type of cathode ray device commonly found in the home environment in which they were designed to operate. Thus, most microcomputers designed for home use will have this type of output, but some of the better and more expensive models will have other types of output which are far better suited to serious use. The disadvantage with domestic TV (UHF) output is that a television set's prime use is to receive broadcasted pictures and it has been designed accordingly. It receives information in a 'coded' form necessary for the pictures to travel from aerial to aerial through the aether. This information has to be 'decoded', after reception through the set's aerial cable. If the computer's signals are fed through the UHF reception plug on the TV set they have to be properly 'coded' before leaving the computer so that the TV set 'thinks' it is receiving a broadcast picture for decoding. This means that there is a great deal of loss in the picture quality – more so on colour TV sets than on monochrome, but even then enough to give the picture a very 'fuzzy' appearance. This quality loss can be acceptable to a home computer enthusiast working in front of a 22″ TV set, but is very frustrating to an office typist or someone not used to working with a computer, and particularly so in circumstances where very small letters or characters have to be used on the screen.

The answer to this picture quality loss is to send a 'pure' unencoded signal from the computer to the cathode ray tube. This pure signal is sometimes known as a 'standard video signal' and is, in fact, easier for the computer to put out than the encoded type. The trouble is that it needs a specially equipped cathode ray tube set to receive it. Such a set is called a 'monitor'. Monitors can be either monochrome or colour sets and often do not have sound facilities. Where the computer works with colour and good quality colour pictures are required on the monitor, there may be provision for another type of video output called RGB (red/green/blue). At the moment it would be unusual to require this facility for school administration purposes.

A good monochrome video monitor is essential if a microcomputer is to be used seriously for school administration. Sometimes monitors are called 'visual display units' (VDU), but such units usually have a built in keyboard. 'VDU eyestrain' is taken very seriously in the computer industry. Some users find that long hours spent in front of a screen can have adverse effects on the eyes. Consequently all possible efforts are made to protect operators in this respect. It is claimed that starkly contrasting black and white pictures are particularly damaging and consequently many monitors are now made with tinted screens and some with anti-glare filters. Green is a particularly common screen colour for this purpose, sometimes with yellow characters. Also orange and amber screens are made. The 'size' and 'resolution' of the screen will also be important. Size is usually measured diagonally across the screen in inches. A 12″ or 14″ monitor is usually adequate for office use. Most good monochrome monitors can be expected to have a resolution of 750 to 800 dots or 'pixels' (picture cells) across the screen.

Some microcomputers have a built-in monitor screen (e.g. Commodore PET and Sharp MZ80). These usually produce an excellent picture and do away with the need for trailing leads and cables. However, as I have previously indicated, since they are attached to the keyboard, the operator does not have the opportunity to adjust the distance between eyes and screen and this sometimes causes dissatisfaction. If you are going to buy a microcomputer for the school office it would help to let the likely users see the screen as well as the keyboard and to let their opinions be one element in making your decision.

Printers

For almost every application of the microcomputer in school administration you will need to have a written copy of the information which the microcomputer produces. This is referred to as 'hard copy' and will mean using a printer. Once again the range of machines and variations in technology available are alarming. Basically, there are four different types of printer:the thermal printer, the dot matrix printer, the ink jet printer and the daisywheel printer.

The thermal printer is the lowest cost and poorest quality method. 'Lowest cost' is used in terms of the original purchase only, since this type of printer uses a specially treated heat sensitive paper which, by comparison to plain paper, is expensive to buy. This type of printer is really only suited to home use, and is certainly not at all practical for any serious school administration purpose.

Dot matrix printers are the most common type found. Their technology involves rows of pins which are thrust out to strike a ribbon in the appropriate combination to form letters. They have the advantage that all sorts of different characters and letters can be formed besides those normally found on a typewriter. Consequently, quite complicated pictures like graphs and bar charts can be printed directly from the computer on paper. These printers are also very speedy. Typically they will work at between 100 and 200 characters per second (c.p.s.) and some of the most expensive and fastest will reach speeds of almost 350 c.p.s. Compare this with the six to ten characters per second which might be achieved by a competent typist working flat out and you will appreciate the speed of the machine. With printing heads able to print lines of text or characters either left to right or right to left (bi-directional) they are exceptionally quick at producing 'hard copy'. The one disadvantage of dot matrix printers is that the printed characters are not up to the standard of that produced on a good typewriter, although the quality comes very close on some of the more recent machines. In general the quality of the print is recognizable as having been produced by a dot matrix printer and is the kind of print that most people associate with computer output. To some extent the quality of print is governed by the size of the matrix of pins which form the letters. Some of the cheaper and earlier dot matrix printers employed a five by seven matrix. These days seven by nine or nine by fourteen arrangements are far more common. In general, the bigger the two numbers quoted in the matrix the better quality the print will be. Another factor to watch out for is whether the printer is able to print 'true lower case descenders'. This indicates whether the 'tails' on letters like p, q, and g appear below the line of characters or are held within it. If the descenders are held within the line of print the style appears very cramped and the text can be quite difficult to read. Essentially, it is only an aesthetic matter, but true lower case descenders are now offered on the majority of, but by no means all, dot matrix printers. One other trick that these printers can do is to produce enlarged or emboldened eye-catching type. This can be quite useful for some administrative purposes. It is said that by removing the ribbon, dot matrix printers can be made to cut stencils for ink duplicating. Personally, i've never tried this as I am concerned that stencil wax might clog the matrix head, but I do know people who have used this technique for documents requiring mass circulation.

Ink jet printers use tiny droplets of ink or particles of carbon to form the letters. These are built up on the paper by an electric discharge which runs from the small printing head through the paper to a plate behind it. In this way the number of moving parts in the printing head is significantly reduced, as is noise, which can be quite a problem for printers relying on impact for their print image. The cost of ink jet printers is roughly the same as dot matrix printers with equivalent features. The printing speed, too, is roughly the same – typically between 100 and 150 c.p.s. Because the characters are formed by the electrical discharge on a matrix principle the quality of print is little better than with the dot matrix type. However, the technology of the ink jet is comparatively new and significant improvements in print quality might be expected in the immediate future.

Dot matrix and ink jet printers offer speed cheaply and are strong and reliable workhorses. They are suitable for most school administration purposes except, in my opinion, for documents which are for public circulation such as standard booklets for visitors and parents. For this purpose I believe that you have to move one step further on in quality – to the 'daisywheel' printer.

Like the dot matrix printer, the daisywheel derives its name from the technology of its printing head. The characters are arranged around the rim of a wheel, each one being on its own 'petal' so that it can be taken out marginally from the plane of the wheel. This printwheel gives the impression of looking like a daisy flower of roughly 3″ diameter, hence the name, 'daisywheel'. The wheel is rotated by the print head until the correct character is before a small hammer. This strikes the 'petal' causing the character on it to be printed through a ribbon onto the paper. The resulting type looks just as though it had been produced by a good quality typewriter – indeed, many of the better electric typewriters are beginning to use this technology. The speed of the operation is amazing when you realize that the hammer cannot afford to strike whilst the wheel is being revolved. (Some of the early daisywheel printers had this fault – petals were soon knocked off the printwheel rendering it useless.) Even so, most daisywheel printers are not as fast as even the slowest dot matrix printers. Typically they will print at between 30 and 60 c.p.s. The fastest is only 80 c.p.s. while some of the cheapest and slowest operate at as little as 16 c.p.s. Apart from the quality of their type, daisywheel printers have few advantages over the faster dot matrix printers. They tend to be more expensive and slower in operation, and are also less readily able to cope with chart or graph production, or different sizes of type. It is possible to change the style of print by changing the daisywheel every time a new style is required. They are also able to produce emboldened type and to print in 'proportional spacing'. This style of print allows the printer to 'sense'

A

BLOGGSVILLE SECONDARY SCHOOL

Bloggsville 374281
Headmaster: R.Jefferies B.Sc., Ph.D.

Newtown Lane
Bloggsville
Ambershire

1 June 1984

Dear Parents,

SCHOOL TRIP TO PARIS

I am now in a position to be able to give you full details about
the trip which leaves on the 17th July.

Children should assemble at the school at 8.30 a.m. leaving all
luggage in the school's main foyer. Parents and children may
wait in the Main Hall until the coach arrives at 8.45 a.m.
Pupils travelling should remember to bring a packed lunch to be
eaten on the journey, and to be certain to carry the identity
cards which have been issued.

I expect the coach to leave at about 9.00 a.m. It will be
crossing to the continent via the Dover - Calais route.
Accommodation is at L'Hotel de Ville in La Rue de Chanson, Paris,
but any emergency communications may be made through the school
or via my home, telephone number Bloggsville 372071.

The party returns on July 22nd. The coach is expected to arrive
back at the school at about 9.30 p.m., but the time may vary
according to Channel crossing conditions. The school telephone
will be manned from 7.30 p.m. and I should be grateful if you
could make arrangements to collect your child promptly from the
school.

Yours sincerely,

B

BLOGGSVILLE SECONDARY SCHOOL

Bloggsville 374281
Headmaster: R.Jefferies B.Sc., Ph.D.

Newtown Lane
Bloggsville
Ambershire

1 June 1984

Dear Parents,

SCHOOL TRIP TO PARIS

I am now in a position to be able to give you full details about
the trip which leaves on the 17th July.

Children should assemble at the school at 8.30 a.m. leaving all
luggage in the school's main foyer. Parents and children may
wait in the Main Hall until the coach arrives at 8.45 a.m.
Pupils travelling should remember to bring a packed lunch to be
eaten on the journey, and to be certain to carry the identity
cards which have been issued.

I expect the coach to leave at about 9.00 a.m. It will be
crossing to the continent via the Dover - Calais route.
Accommodation is at L'Hotel de Ville in La Rue de Chanson, Paris,
but any emergency communications may be made through the school
or via my home, telephone number Bloggsville 372071.

The party returns on July 22nd. The coach is expected to arrive
back at the school at about 9.30 p.m., but the time may vary
according to Channel crossing conditions. The school telephone

will be manned from 7.30 p.m. and I should be grateful if you
could make arrangements to collect your child promptly from the
school.

Yours sincerely,

C

BLOGGSVILLE SECONDARY SCHOOL

Bloggsville 374281
Headmaster: R.Jefferies B.Sc., Ph.D.

Newtown Lane
Bloggsville
Ambershire

1 June 1984

Dear Parents,

SCHOOL TRIP TO PARIS

I am now in a position to be able to give you full details about
the trip which leaves on the 17th July.

Children should assemble at the school at 8.30 a.m. leaving all
luggage in the school's main foyer. Parents and children may
wait in the Main Hall until the coach arrives at 8.45 a.m.
Pupils travelling should remember to bring a packed lunch to be
eaten on the journey, and to be certain to carry the identity
cards which have been issued.

I expect the coach to leave at about 9.00 a.m. It will be
crossing to the continent via the Dover - Calais route.
Accommodation is at L'Hotel de Ville in La Rue de Chanson, Paris,
but any emergency communications may be made through the school
or via my home, telephone number Bloggsville 372071.

The party returns on July 22nd. The coach is expected to arrive
back at the school at about 9.30 p.m., but the time may vary
according to Channel crossing conditions. The school telephone
will be manned from 7.30 p.m. and I should be grateful if you
could make arrangements to collect your child promptly from the
school.

Yours sincerely,

Figure 3.1 Examples of the same school letter produced by a wordprocessor and
printed in various styles.
A Dot matrix print with true lower case descenders.
B Typical daisywheel print.
C Proportionally spaced print from a daisywheel printer.

each letter as it is printed, thus giving a different spacing to i than it gives to w. A very pleasing and professional looking print results. On the whole though, it is only worth paying the extra for these printers if you have a wordprocessing facility with a lot of public documents to produce. Certainly, if a printer has to be used for dual purposes between administration and computing in the curriculum, then the dot matrix type would be the wiser choice.

Some printers now on the market are referred to as 'thimble' printers. These are essentially the same as daisywheel printers with the printwheel shaped like a thimble instead of the more usual daisy flower. The remaining technology is similar and so remarks made about daisywheel printers also apply to thimble printers.

It is possible to connect some daisywheel typewriters to microcomputers so that they can operate under control of the computer as a printer. The typewriter has to be properly and professionally equipped to do this, but such a printer can form the compromise between a new office typewriter and a daisywheel printer. These are sometimes known as 'keyboard send and receive' (KSR) typewriters. However, they tend to be amongst the slowest models for printing. A local office equipment specialist supplier would probably be happy to advise you about the possibilites of connecting such a typewriter to your microcomputer.

There are some words of advice which apply to all printers of whatever type. If you are going to use them for administration then almost certainly there will be some lengthy printing runs for purposes such as form lists or timetable production. It doesn't make sense to have someone sitting beside the printer waiting to wind in the next A4 sheet. You will need some method of feeding continuous stationery under the print head. There are four ways of doing this:

(i) Roll/friction feed A continuous roll of paper is fed between the printer rollers which grip the paper and pull it through as in a typewriter. The printer must be equipped with facilities for holding the roll of paper. This method has the advantage of being simple and cheap. On long runs, however, the amount of paper put out can be difficult to handle. At best it has to be re-rolled or folded and neither method is very satisfactory for large runs on this paper. It is just possible to use ready folded (fan fold) stationery in this type of feed but there are sometimes problems in keeping the paper straight within the rollers for long runs. If your printer is not equipped for any other form of feed the paper roll may be the only method open to you.

(ii) Pinfeed This method can more easily use ready folded stationery and keep it straight since pins at both ends of the roller on the printer pull the paper through using holes on either side of the stationery. On some such printers only one size of paper can be used because the distance between the sprocket pins cannot be changed. Make sure that supplies of this size of paper are readily available at reasonable cost. Pinfeed printers are now being produced which will adjust for various paper widths by allowing one pin-wheel to slide along the roller.

(iii)   Tractor feed This type of paper feed usually sits above the normal rollers and has adjustable sprocket pin positions so that various widths of paper can be used. This is the most versatile method for feeding fan-fold stationery, which can usually be drawn out of one container and deposited into another. It is, however, the most expensive of the methods described so far since the purchase of a tractor can add considerably to the cost of a printer.

(iv)   Cut sheet feed In some wordprocessing applications it is not satisfactory to produce documents on continuous stationery. In this case you are left with no alternative but to feed the sheets manually as required. A cut sheet feeder solves this problem. It is a hopper which contains sheets of paper of the required size. This sits above the roller and supplies the sheets of paper to the printer automatically. Such apparatus is usually very expensive – often as much as the printer itself – and does not seem to be a cost-effective proposition for the school office at the moment.

Ribbons

All dot matrix and daisywheel printers will use a ribbon to reproduce the characters on paper. For most dot matrix printers this will be a fabric ribbon in a continuous loop. Many daisywheel printers will have the extra option of a carbon film ribbon; in some cases this may be the only option. Carbon film ribbon passes only once before the print head and is usually contained in a cassette, for ease of insertion into the printer and disposal after use.

With fabric ribbons the print is initially dark but becomes fainter with time in use. They are used primarily for rough drafts and other such documents for internal use. These ribbons cost a little more than the carbon film type but last much longer. The length of life depends on your level of acceptability of print quality. Carbon film ribbons provide dark, sharp print of consistent quality. This is the medium to use for public documents or for anything that is to be photoduplicated. Since cassette life is relatively short, a good stock should be kept in hand. It is worthwhile searching the specialist suppliers' catalogues (see Appendix 2) for discounts on quality purchases. Ribbon costs can be an expensive 'hidden extra' in running printers. When buying a printer the availability of fabric ribbons for a particular model could be a significant factor.

Cables

Finally, there is the problem of connecting your printer to the microcomputer. For this you will need a cable and the appropriate plugs. This is not as simple a matter as it sounds. In order to send the appropriate data to a printer, for printing, a microcomputer uses some electronic circuitry called an 'interface'. Through this 'interface' messages are exchanged with the printer. It is an exchange because the computer sends data for printing, but the printer also sends back messages like 'busy for the moment', 'no more paper available' or 'new ribbon needed'. In order to receive the data and send these messages the printer must also be equipped with the same type of interface as the computer.

If there was only one type of interface connections would be an easy matter. However, there are at least four in common use. These four rejoice in the names of the Centronics parallel interface, the RS232 serial interface (sometimes known as the V-24), the 20 mA current loop interface and the IEEE interface. The RS423 interface found on some microcomputers is very similar to, and compatible with, the RS232.

When buying a printer you need to make sure that it has the interface with which your computer is equipped. Some microcomputers are equipped with more than one type of interface. Printers usually only have one type as standard. Sometimes there are options for alternative interfaces to be fitted, but at extra cost. The two interfaces in microcomputer and printer must be connected by a cable with suitable plugs at both ends. These cables can be expensive to buy – prices vary from £20 to as much as £60. If you know someone who is useful with a soldering iron you may be tempted to make your own cable. In this case you will also need technical details about the connections to be made at either end. One set will come from the printer suppliers or makers and the other set from the microcomputer suppliers or makers. You will also need to purchase the appropriate plugs and cable. A source of supply may be difficult to find. The catalogues of some of the national suppliers listed in Appendix 2 may help. One company – Inmac – now offers a bespoke cable making sevice.

I have heard of so many problems with printers and cables that would not interface with each other properly that it prompts me to suggest that both computer and printer should be puchased from the same supplier. If possible, try to get the dealer to show both working together. This is the best way to avoid problems, and if they do occur you have someone on hand to help solve them.

Backup storage – cassettes and disks

Most of the programs and data that are going to be used for administrative purposes will be too large to be input from the keyboard each time the microcomputer is used. Yet, as we have seen, the RAM where programs and data are stored is emptied every time the computer is switched off. The problem is common to every computer application, even with large mainframes, and the normal solution is to use some form of magnetic medium on which to store programs and data until they are required again. Microcomputers use either ordinary audio cassette tape or some form of magnetic disk to act as this 'back-up' store.

Cassette tapes have the advantage that they are very cheap, are readily obtainable and that an audio cassette recorder is a very common and quite inexpensive piece of equipment. Even a medium size cassette can hold quite a lot of information, so the technology necessary to allow computers to place programs on cassette for future use was developed as home computers became fashionable. For most small and cheap computers this is the only way in which 'back-up' memory can be used.

It is worthwhile saying at this stage that when a computer transfers information from its memory onto a magnetic medium the process is described as 'writing to' tape, disk or whatever. The reverse process, where the computer takes information from the magnetic media and places it in memory is known as 'reading from'.

Despite their cheapness tapes have their disadvantages as back-up stores to microcomputers. Many types of microcomputer are notoriously unreliable at reading information from tapes. In all fairness it must said that this is not always a design fault in the microcomputer. It is just that the cassette player or tape in use is not perfectly suitable for this purpose. All the same it is very frustrating to have the microcomputer keep displaying 'ERROR' as it tries to read the information from tape. Some manufacturers, for example Atari, insist that their own specialist cassette player be used for the task. This might overcome the initial problem but does nothing to help with the very slow rate of transfer of information. A long program or datafile might take four or five minutes to read. In addition, the human operator has to find the approximate position of the file of information on tape otherwise the computer might have to wait thirty minutes or more while the cassette player trundles through the tape at its usual speed.

During my research in 1981, I discovered that some seventy-six of the 203 schools I surveyed were using cassettes as their only back-up store in school administration. However, these schools were in general, not quite so well advanced as those using alternative forms of permanent store, and it was much less frequent to find administrative or secretarial staff carrying out the work. For any extensive application of microcomputers in administration the use of cassettes is certainly not to be recommended.

There are other tape systems for microcomputers which overcome some of the problems associated with the domestic cassette system. They have such names as 'stringy floppy system', 'micro cassette drive' or 'tape streamer'. One particular characteristic of all these systems is that the tape is moved very much more quickly across the read and write heads. Consequently they can store or read information much more rapidly than cassettes, but since the cost is little cheaper than a disk system and is still less efficient, there is little to be gained by the use of such systems in school administration other than as back-up store to the more expensive disk units.

If you are going to conduct school administration seriously on a microcomputer, undertaking all the main tasks, and in particular timetabling or wordprocessing, then a disk system will be essential. The most common form of disk system found in schools uses the 'mini-floppy disk'. These flexible disks are 5.25″ in diameter and coated with a magnetic film, rather similar to a tape surface, on which recordings can be made. To protect the magnetic film the disk is housed permanently in an envelope with the surface only showing where the recording is to be made. The inside of the envelope is lined with a soft material which allows the disk to revolve easily inside the envelope and brushes the surface clean at the same time. In order to make recordings on the disk it has to be placed in a 'disk drive'. The drive contains mechanisms to grip and revolve the disk inside its envelope at a predetermined speed. The computer controls the movement of a recording head and determines on which part of the disk a program or data will be 'written'. All the operator has to do is to give the computer a 'file name' by which that particular program or data can be identified. When the information needs to be 'read' the computer will identify and find it quickly according to its 'file name'. Because the whole surface of the disk is available to the read/write head, a file can be found much more quickly on disk than on tape. Also the rate of transfer of information between disk and memory is very much faster than between tape and memory, and considerably more reliable.

Not surprisingly disk systems are much more expensive that cassette tape systems. A single disk drive will start at about £200, and there may well be extras (cables, interfaces and so on) on top of that. It is more usual, for school administration purposes, to have two disk drives so that programs and data can be more easily copied and to allow access to a greater disk surface area at any one time. Twin disk systems will cost from £350 upwards. The disks themselves cost between £1.50 and £4.00 each depending on make and type. Unfortunately, not every mini-floppy disk is suitable for every drive. Disk drive and computer manufacturers usually offer technical advice about the correct disk to use. This advice needs to be followed very carefully. Disk drives are very reliable, but if damaged or worn they can be very costly to repair.

How much information can you store on a mini-floppy disk? This depends on the nature of your system. Early and simple disk drives only stored information on one side of the disk (single-sided) but recently it has become much more usual to have 'double-sided' drives where both sides of the disk are in use for recording the data. Depending on the make of drive one side of a disk will be able to accommodate at least 70K bytes of information – enough, for example, for a fairly comprehensive database on a year group of pupils in a large school. Modern drives using better disks are able to pack the information much more efficiently. In this way mini-floppy disks can store up to 200K bytes per side in a 'double density' format. With just a pair of double-sided double density drives it is possible to have the data for all pupils 'on-line' (immediately accessible) to the microcomputer at any one time even in quite a large school.

The mini-floppy is not the only type of disk system available. Drives using the larger 8″ floppy disk, available for many so-called 'business systems', can also be obtained for the microcomputers commonly used in schools. Some would argue that these are necessary for any true administration system. In my research work I found only eleven out of the 203 schools using them, but it could be that their use will become much more common as dedicated systems come into use for school administration. Both drives and disks tend to be more expensive than the mini-floppy systems but they can, of course, store a great deal more information. Typically a double-sided disk will hold 350K bytes of information. Using double density this can be increased to 700K bytes. Currently, systems are being advertised which offer up to 1.2 Mb per disk. Such a system with just two of these drives can hold on-line a very large amount of information, such as a database for a school of 1600 pupils of the complexity of that proposed in the 1974 LAMSAC report and described in Chapter 2.

More is to come, however. Floppy disks appear to have reached the limit of their technology and just becoming popular with microcomputer systems is an entirely new concept, the 'hard' disk. This is a rigid disk which is fixed permanently into its drive. Sometimes these are referred to as 'Winchester' drives. They have a very much larger capacity than floppy disks. Hard disks currently available can hold up to 21 Mb. With such a system every piece of data which a school might need could be on-line – pupil data, timetable data, finance data, staff data, curriculum data – with room to spare. I already know of a few schools considering purchase of such systems, but so far their potential has not been really explored in school administration. The costs are still comparatively high – over £2000 for the highest capacities. Since the disks cannot be changed some provision has to be made to 'dump' some files onto other long term storage media to make room for new data. The special tape systems available for this purpose could add another £1000 to the costs. As with all new technology no doubt the costs will soon come down from their initial levels. When this happens the Winchester hard disk could become the common storage medium for school administration systems.

3.6   Choosing your hardware

Having examined the types of 'processing units' and 'peripherals' (add-on items like printers and disk drives) which are available it is now possible to be more specific about the hardware which is necessary to conduct school administration by microcomputer. There will always be limiting factors, the most important of which will almost certainly be the cost. However, other factors will affect decisions too, so I shall look at some of these as well.

Are you in the position of being able to afford a microcomputer specifically for administraton? If not, then one limitation is certain to be the need to retain compatibility with other microcomputers in the school. The microcomputer you are going to use will presumably be shared between administrative and instructional use. At some stage teachers or pupils will be using it as part of their normal teaching or learning work. As has already been noted, programs written for a microcomputer made by one manufacturer do not usually run on that of another. In addition, the way instructions are given via the keyboard may differ considerably. It can be very frustrating to learn a set of instructions for one machine only to find that you have to relearn them, or alter them for another. On the whole then, it is not a good idea to 'mix' your instructional microcomputers. Some Local Authorities absolutely forbid it, having standardized on one particular machine. In the case of dual use then, your administration microcomputer should be of the same make as any other instructional microcomputers you have, although it may have extra enhancements, like a bigger disk system or better printer. Both the experience of practitioners and my research have shown that if the number of administrative tasks undertaken rises above a very small level then the administrative use begins to come into conflict with the instructional use. It's my belief that 'instruction' should always come first and if the conflict arises than a separate machine for administration should be purchased. Properly sited, it can always be used as an extra teaching resource in slack periods. However, the resulting compatibility will always be a bonus, expecially if anything goes wrong with one system or the other. Remember one of the important questions posed by the 1976 BCSSC report referred to in Chapter 1 was: 'What would be the effect of the computer temporarily being unavailable?'

Another important factor will be the availability of programs or 'software' to enable the computer to carry out the administrative tasks you have chosen. I shall have a more detailed look at software in the next chapter, but it must be noted that without suitable software, the hardware, however expensive and potentially effective and efficient, is just useless apparatus. I know of schools that have purchased hardware without due consideration of the software only to suffer disappointment and frustration when suitable products could not be found.

It is useful to consider what other schools are doing about hardware because this will give some indication about likely availability of software for particular machines. For the 203 schools responding positively to my survey in 1981, the major machines in use for school administration are shown in Table 1 below. The questionnaire was sent to about 400 schools that had, during 1980, declared themselves to have a microcomputer and to be using it for administrative purposes. These 400 were gleaned from two surveys previously carried out by CET and *Educational Computing* magazine respectively.

Make	Total users for administrative purposes
RML 380Z	100
CBM PET	62
APPLE/ITT 2020	11
TRS–80	7
SWTPC	7
NASCOM	4
MSI 6800	3

Nine other machines were declared with one user only in each case.

Table 1   Microcomputers in use for school administration – 1981

Using this information it will come as no surprise to learn that there is far more software for school administration available for RML 380Z, the Commodore PET and the APPLE than for any others. In fact, the amount of software is roughly proportional to the number of machines in use. There are many reasons why these machines are so popular, not the least of which was that they were all very early models in the market. In particular, identification of the RML 380Z for the Department of Industry's (DOI) 'Microcomputers in Schools' scheme has considerably boosted its popularity. There are those who say that some of these machines are not ideal for general administration. What must be remembered, however, is that if you go out and buy the latest 'all-singing, all-dancing' business microcomputer for your school administration, you will almost certainly have to pioneer your software development whatever the salesperson says. More about this later!

Given these limiting factors, what hardware do you need to make a start with MCBA? My view is that there is a basic and absolute minimum to aim at:

A microcomputer with a proper typewriter style 'QWERTY' keyboard
At least 32K RAM, (remember the caveat about how much is practically available)
A monitor screen
A disk system
A printer

For greater sophistication one can go a little beyond this and be more specific. If wordprocessing is to be carried out in the school office, then consideration must be given to the number of characters which will be shown on the screen at once. Many microcomputers only allow forty characters by twenty-four lines or less. This is quite useless for serious wordprocessing since most lines of standard typewriting contain sixty to sixty-five characters per line. It is possible to do wordprocessing on the forty by twenty-four screen by breaking lines into two, or 'shunting' them across the screen. You can never see a whole section of the type this way, and office staff are much put off by it. Standard screens for wordprocessing are usually eighty by twenty-four or eighty by twenty-five, so choose a microcomputer capable of producing such a layout and a monochrome monitor which offers the necessary resolution.

A twin disk system is so much better than a single disk system. It has been described as the difference between a motor bike and a uni-cycle! If the disk system can use the 8″ as opposed to the more traditional mini-floppy disk then so much the better. But do remember the compatibility problems which might be raised both within the school and in sharing other people's software.

Enlarging on the question of printers is difficult – it depends what you want to do with them. If buying a printer specifically for school administration, you may have to compromise quality of print against speed. It makes good sense to buy something which is fairly 'heavy duty', either one of the more expensive faster dot matrix printers or a fast daisywheel printer. Whichever is chosen, it would be best to have a tractor feed too, if it is available as an extra.

If cash were no object and software no problem my ultimate would be:

A microcomputer using a 16-bit microprocessor (plus second 8-bit microprocessor) and with 128K RAM
2 x 600K floppy disk system
5Mb hard disk and tape streamer backup
14″ high resolution tinted monochrome monitor
Medium priced fast dot matrix printer for draft work
Good, fast daisywheel printer for quality printing work

Since all this would cost me about £8000 at current prices it's clearly a daydream. I'm convinced that the time will come when schools can afford such a system, but first we have to justify it by showing that such a system at maybe, one quarter of the cost, is worthwhile.

One last thought on choice of hardware – don't forget to allow for costs and availability of maintenance. Electronic components tend to be extremely reliable – mechanical ones a lot less so. It is highly likely that you could have problems both with disk drives and printers. It may be tempting to buy these items from a supplier at some distance who offers marginally favourable terms. But the local supplier might be the better long term bet. He may be able to offer a maintenance contract to carry out repairs on site. If not, he should always be available to see personally and to accept delivery of equipment which needs attention. Computers and their peripherals always have a habit of breaking down when they're most needed. Remember Johnson's First Law (Bloch, 1982): 'When any mechanical contrivance fails, it will do so at the most inconvenient possible time.'

Having examined hardware in general, the time has now come to examine some particular systems. In doing so at this stage I make no allowance for the availability of software or otherwise. I shall merely examine some microcomputers which are popular in schools and suggest the configurations which might be necessary for school administration work.

3.7   Specific systems

(i)   The RML 380Z

This microcomputer is manufactured by Research Machines of Mill Street, Oxford. It was one of the early microcomputers on the scene although it has been greatly enhanced in various ways since it first appeared in 1978. It is probably the microcomputer most commonly found in schools. Although a survey in 1980 appeared to identify the CBM PET as the most popular machine this was hotly debated at the time, but by 1982 the DOI schemes had probably established the 380Z firmly in first place.

It can be found in a variety of forms, although all of these use the Z80 microprocessor as CPU. Some early versions have as little as 16K RAM, but the maximum possible is 56K. It has 4K ROM which contains sufficient commands to enable the machine to carry out very simple tasks (like load from a cassette or disk) when it is switched on. The standard machine has probably become the 'DOI version' which was equipped with 32K RAM and a twin double-sided disk system offering 288K of disk storage. This particular version also had a high resolution graphics facility. Since it is unusual to require such facilities for administrative purposes the memory associated with the high resolution graphics can be used instead as extra RAM giving a useful total of 48K. Recently machines have been equipped with both parallel and serial printer interfaces. RML supply a small range of both dot matrix and daisywheel printers, together with cables, to connect to their microcomputer. It is not

Figure 3.2   The RML 380Z – a typical administration configuration.

Figure 3.3   The CBM 8032 professional microcomputer – a suitable model for administration.

always a very easy job to connect printers other than the ones RML supply. The company does offer good technical support, but it is probably easiest for those with no immediate source of technical advice to purchase peripherals direct from RML.

The standard screen on RML 380Z is forty by twenty-four and thus totally unsuited to wordprocessing. However, an enhancement is available to produce an eighty by twenty-four character screen. This is known as the Varitext board. It costs about £100 to have installed as an extra when the computer is built, but about £300 if the machine has to be returned for enhancement. The motto is obvious – plan ahead if you want wordprocessing on the RML!

With the Varitext board the user can switch from forty to eighty character operation both at the keyboard and via programs, so most software written for the forty column screen will run on the eighty column model. The computer, its keyboard, and the monitor all come as separate units, although the mini-floppy disk system is integral with the computer. When everything is connected to a printer there tends to be a surfeit of cables lying around. There is certainly a lot of disconnecting to do if the machine has to be moved. My view is that for successful administrative purposes it needs to be housed permanently somewhere near the school office.

Because of its popularity there is more school administration software for this machine than for any other. Most of it relies on the BASIC language however, and in the 380Z the interpreter for this has to be loaded into RAM before the programs are run, thus using up precious memory. Consequently some administrative tasks can be difficult on a machine with only 32K RAM.

A reasonable minimum for a total administration system with the RML 380Z is:

Twin double-sided mini-floppy disk system 56K RAM
Varitext option for forty or eighty column working
High resolution 12″ green screen monitor
A suitable printer

All software currently available for school administration should run on such a configuration and memory will be adequate for most purposes except, possibly, in very large schools – say in excess of 2000 pupils.

(ii)   Commodore PET/CBM series

This is another microcomputer which has been around since the very earliest days, probable explaining its popularity in schools and adoption as standard by a number of LEAs. Like every other microcomputer of its age it has undergone a number of enhancements during its short life, but found commonly in schools is the 4016 (forty columns by twenty-five line screen and 16K RAM) and the 4032 (identical, but with 32K RAM). All the computers in this range use the 6502 chip as CPU. The 4016 would appear to be a little short on memory for school administration, despite having its 20K BASIC and operating system in ROM, but the 4032 is quite adequate to the task when used with one of the several

Commodore disk units available. Several schools are successfully using this system. In the PET/CBM series the keyboard, computer, and 12″ screen are all in one integral unit. This configuration cuts down the wiring connections and makes the computer a little more portable, but some operators complain that the screen is too close when working at a normal typing distance. The disk drives are in separate units and offer 171K storage on a single drive or 343K on the dual drives with those units most commonly found in schools. Currently Commodore offers a 2.1Mb dual floppy disk drive and hard disk options with up to 7.5Mb storage. Because the disk operating system is in ROM, attaching a disk drive does not use any of the computer's RAM.

The problem with the 4000 range is that it is totally unsuited to wordprocessing, and in consequence not a good machine to dedicate to administration in the school office. To run the best wordprocessing programs on the PET range you will need the 8000 series. Unlike the RML 380Z, the 4000 series cannot be 'enhanced' to eighty column working by a hardware modification. There are two members of the 8000 series – the 8032 (eighty by twenty-five lines, 32K RAM) and the 8096 (identical but with 96K RAM). These machines are identical in many ways to the 4000 series. Some software written for the 4000 series will run on the 8000 series, but compatibility is not certain if certain routines involving the 4000 model's 9″ screen are used. The Commodore Customer Liaison Department [address in Appendix 2] will be able to advise a remedy in this case.

Commodore provides a small range of both dot matrix and daisywheel printers. They tend to use the IEEE-488 interface, but a Commodore dealer will usually advise you on the feasibility of interfacing other printers.

The latest addition to the upper end of the Commodore range is the Commodore 700 business computer. This uses the new 6509 chip as CPU, has 28K BASIC and operating system in ROM, with a massive 256K memory. The keyboard separates on a very tidy coiled cable from the eighty column by twenty-five lines, 12″ screen thus answering criticisms of the earlier PET models. Certain models have integral disk drives with a capacity of up to 680K although it is quite possible to interface this machine with other Commodore external disk units. Although it is a top-of-range machine, the price looks very competitive in relation to the 8096, and PET users would do well to check it out as an administration system, although software compatibility with other machines in the PET range cannot be assured.

An absolute minimum to aim for in a dedicated school administration system using the Commodore range would be:

The 8032 eighty column 32K RAM model
Dual disk drives as appropriate from the Commodore range
A suitable printer

(iii) The APPLE II
The APPLE is another microcomputer with a long track record – not nearly so common in schools as the two ranges previously mentioned, but very popular in

the business and commercial world. It is marketed by Apple Computers of Hemel Hempstead, a subsidiary of the American Apple Company, but has a large number of dealers throughout the UK.

On the face of it the APPLE would appear not to have undergone so many changes as some of it competitors, but this is probably due to its facility for slotting extra 'cards' (printed circuit boards with all the necessary electronic components for a specific purpose) into its circuitry, which has made it a very flexible machine. Like the PET it uses the 6502 chip as CPU, but here the similiarities end. The keyboard and computer are contained in a single case, but a separate monitor is required which can be of the user's choosing. Dealers are always willing to advise on a suitable one. The normal display is forty columns by twenty-four lines, but by the addition of an extra 'card' an eighty by twenty-four display can be achieved on which all usual wordprocessing functions are possible. Both forty and eighty column programs should run properly in a machine equipped with the eighty column card.

The standard memory configuration is 48K RAM plus a 12K BASIC held in ROM but for some time now it has been common, given the cheapness of memory chips, to expand the memory to 64K RAM. Latest details suggest that it is possible to expand the APPLE II to 256K RAM with the addition of suitable memory boards. The disk drives, too, come as separate units. The standard APPLE drives are single-sided single density only, offering 120K of storage. A pair of drives would seem essential for school administration and whatever configuration is used, the appropriate card for control of the drives must be fitted to the APPLE. By the same token it is possible to fit interfaces for most printers. Dealers seem to have their 'favourites' to recommend at any given time and it is probably safest to get your printer via an APPLE dealer to be certain of being equipped with the correct interface and cables.

The up-market version of the APPLE II is the APPLE III. Another 6502 CPU machine, it has a standard 128K memory (expandable to 256K) and and integral 140K floppy disk unit. Costing almost £2500 it would hardly seem worth mentioning, especially since there seems to be no compatibility of software with the APPLE II, were it not for one thing. A quite significant piece of software for school administration has been developed for the APPLE III by Deverill Computer Services Ltd of Poole, Dorset. Called SCHOLAR III (schools on-line administration and reporting) it covers most aspects of administration, reporting and accounting requirements of public schools, and is designed for operation by existing staff within a school bursar's department. The cost of a total system (including software and hardware) is likely to be in excess of £6000, but it could cost considerably more for a school to develop its own system. I have found Datalink Limited [address in Appendix 2] always very helpful to advise on such systems and I am sure they would be willing to help those who wish to know more.

An absolute minimum to aim for in a system using an APPLE II dedicated to school administration would be:

APPLE II with 48K RAM
Disk controller and eighty column card

Twin mini-floppy disk system
Monochrome 12″ green screen
A suitable printer

(iv) TRS-80

The TRS range is marketed by the Tandy Corporation of Walsall, itself a subsidiary of Radio Shack, an American company. It is used in a number of schools, colleges and local authorities and the Tandy Corporation has done a great deal of work through its area centres to train teachers on these microcomputers and bring them to the attention of educational establishments generally.

Most computers in the TRS-80 range are based on the Z-80 CPU. The TRS-80 Model I is most likely to be found in schools, although its manufacture has now been discontinued. Originally the Model I was equipped with 4K RAM and BASIC in 4K ROM using a cassette player as back-up memory. More recently, the 16K RAM version has been standard with twin mini-floppy disk drives offering up to 307K storage. It is expandable up to 48K RAM. The full keyboard is integral with the computer, but display is via a separate monitor, normally supplied by Tandy, and offering sixty-four columns by sixteen lines.

The most recent Tandy entry to the education market is the TRS-80 Model IV. This also uses the Z-80 CPU, but has 64K RAM as standard with an option of expanding to 128K. A 14K BASIC is held in ROM. The Model IV can be supplied without disk units, but there are integral spaces for two of these which are mini-floppy drives each offering 184K of storage. The 12″, high resolution green screen offers a variety of modes, such as eighty characters by twenty-four lines (Model IV mode) or sixty-four characters by sixteen lines (Model III mode). Software for Tandy microcomputers tends to be unique to a particular model, but there is an excellent range of general purpose software available from the corporation, which gives a great deal of support for conversion of software from one model to another where necessary. Even with the slight disadvantage of the sixty-four by sixteen screen such a computer is quite adequate for wordprocessing using one of Tandy's own software packages such as Scripsit.

Both RS232 serial and Centronics parallel printer interfaces are offered and Tandy supplies an excellent range of printers of both dot matrix and daisywheel types, most of which use the parallel interface and can be easily connected to other microcomputers. Their Daisywheel-II printer has proved particularly useful for quality work in schools. It is a sturdy and reliable machine which runs at a reasonably fast speed of 45 c.p.s. and has a range of excellent facilities which can be used under software control. Recently Tandy have introduced a slightly cheaper daisywheel printer, the Model 410. Apart from running at a slightly slower speed it would seem to have most of the facilities of the Daisywheel-II and might well be considered if the budget is tight.

Tandy has its own hard disk system as an add-on for the Model IV with storage of up to 5Mb. There is also a range of more expensive business computers available with good upward compatibility of software.

A useful minimum for school administration using the current Tandy range would seem to be:

TRS-80 Model IV
48K RAM
Integral twin mini-floppy disk system
An appropriate Tandy printer

(v) The BBC microcomputer

By comparison with the other microcomputers dealt with in this section, the BBC is a relative newcomer. It suffered from a great disadvantage initially, in that the amount of software which had been created for it, especially in school administration, was decidedly sparse. However, it is becoming a very popular microcomputer in schools and, now that appropriate software is more readily available, is worthy of a section here on the grounds that it is likely to be used increasingly for school administration over the next few years, especially where compatibility with other microcomputers in the school is an important factor.

The BBC microcomputer is made by Acorn Computers of Cambridge and was supplied up to 1983 in two models – Model A and Model B. It appears that Model A will be discontinued by 1984. Model A has BASIC in a 32K ROM with a standard 16K RAM, and although it is expandable to 32K RAM, the many other extras available on the Model B make this version more suitable for school administration purposes. The BBC microcomputer uses the 6502 chip as its CPU. Model B has 32K RAM as standard, but it will soon be possible to expand this by the addition of a second microprocessor to the machine. The keyboard is integral with the microcomputer case, and has ten special red 'function' keys which can be programmed to undertake various tasks. This is a particularly useful feature in such applications as wordprocessing. All other units come as 'add-ons', including the screen, which can be operated by the microcomputer at a number of different character resolutions including the useful eighty by twenty-five. Most users will be using the BBC microcomputer with a standard television set, but the quality of the display is much improved by using a video monitor. The standard video output from this computer only supplies a monochrome video signal in the interests of sharper picture quality, but this is quite adequate for school administration purposes. With only 32K RAM, back-up memory is essential and this is supplied either by cassette or by two disk drive options – a single drive offering 100K or twin disk drives offering 800K. The single drive appears to be designed for the domestic market and may not prove adequate for administration. However, the twin drive should be excellent for this purpose, but it is also very expensive. Some manufacturers have attempted to fill the gap between these two options and offer competitive prices, but care should be taken in adding drives in this way, since it may be difficult to acquire the disk operating manual or the essential systems programs disk if you purchase elsewhere. One manufacturer who offers a range of drives with software support is Cumana. These can be obtained through dealers, but in any case it would be prudent to seek some technical advice about connecting non-standard drives. Disk drives can only be driven by the BBC Model B if fitted with an extra ROM which contains the disk operating system (or DFS – disk filing system – as it is called on this machine).

Both serial and parallel interfaces are available for connection to a very wide range of printers. The BBC micro user guide contains advice about cable connections, although some extra technical support and advice might be useful.

The BBC microcomputer has some other unique features which make it attractive for business use. Some programs are available as 'firmware', that is, they come on a ROM chip which can be plugged into the circuit board. Of particular interest to us in this respect are wordprocessing packages. Having such a package fitted on a chip, the microcomputer can be instantly converted into a wordprocessor without taking up valuable RAM in the process. Another feature is the so called 'tube' – an electronic system which greatly enhances the expandability of the computer. Using this the second microprocessor can be added, for example, with 64K RAM and doubling the processing speed. Soon the BBC microcomputer will be expandable in this way up to 128K RAM. It is also possible to incorporate the machine into a simple 'network' system in which over 100 computers might share disk drive and printer facilities. Some schools are already installing such systems, with one loop to the school office being a distinct possibility for expansion.

Except as part of a network system the minimum configuration for school administration would seem to be:

BBC microcomputer Model B
Wordprocessing and DFS ROMs
A twin disk system
A suitable printer

3.8 Supplies

A final word is necessary here about supplies. Any computer installation is going to need a good supply of materials to keep it effective. This will include stocks of floppy disks and proper storage for them, materials to keep disk drives clean and free from dirt and dust, ribbons and daisywheels for the printer, listing paper in various sizes and maybe even specially printed stationery. Do remember that where programs and record files are concerned, it is essential to keep a second 'back-up' copy on disk safely at a different location from the copies in usual use. Loss of computer files can be devastating if you depend on them.

A list of some major national suppliers of such materials is contained in Appendix 2. Most will willingly send you a catalogue or price list on request and delivery times on telephoned orders of standard items are usually excellent.

4 Microcomputer software for school administration

or 'How will we get there?' (Part 2)

'God bless you sir – buy a lucky program.'

Microcomputer software for school administration

Microprocessors are the heart of microcomputers. To do any work at all they must be provided with a series of instructions telling them exactly what to do. A series of instructions will form a 'program' for the microprocessor and hence for its host microcomputer. Programs are referred to collectively as 'software'. They might be given as a printed list of commands to be typed on the keyboard, but more usually they will be provided on a disk or a tape from which they can be read automatically into the computer's memory. You can have the most expensive and powerful microcomputer available, but without 'software' it is totally useless – equivalent to owning a video cassette recorder, yet not being able to acquire any video tapes.

4.1   What is software?

Programs can be produced in a number of different forms. In order to understand these it is necessary to explore a little further exactly how the microcomputer works. In the previous chapter we learned that the microprocessor accepts instructions in the form of binary numbers. Although it is possible to program in this way, it would be extremely tedious and very prone to errors. Imagine having to write out lengthy series of instructions just using 0s and 1s! To avoid this other methods of programming have been developed. We don't need to look at them in detail, but it will help to know what some of the terms mean.

Imagine the microcomputer as a house with cellar, ground floor and first floor. The microprocessor is in the cellar. This is a dark and misty world where instructions are issued in binary numbers, sometimes called 'machine code' and which we don't need to penetrate. The ground floor is the level at which we normally enter. This is the world which we can call the 'operating system'. This environment is a relatively simple one in which there are a number of elementary commands, usually letters or short combinations of them which conduct routine housekeeping operations like instructing the computer to get a program from a tape, or to see if its associated disk drive or printer is ready to work. Microcomputers entered at this level usually have a 'cassette operating system' (COS for short – pronounced as in the trigonometry function) or a 'disk operating system' (DOS for short – for no obvious reason usually pronounced 'doss'). From this level instructions can be 'passed down' to the cellar in the form of an 'instruction set' – two or three letter commands unique to the particular type of microprocessor which is down there. Issuing commands in this way is the usual method of producing 'machine code' programs.

Even this level does not concern most operators. They need only be concerned to know how to reach the first floor as quickly as possible. This is the environment of the 'high level language'. It is easier to write a program of instructions for the microcomputer in your native language rather than using the computer's. In our case that language is English. In the last thirty years various 'languages' (I consider that they should more properly be described as 'dictionaries') have been developed which enable the computer to do the translation into machine code. These have been given various names, usually according to the use for which they are most suited – for example, COBOL (common business orientated language), FORTRAN (formula translator) and APL (a programming language). These particular languages were originally written for mainframe computers and are not commonly found in microcomputers. However, some are now available where disk systems and memory make this possible.

During the early 1960s a high level language was developed for teaching computer programming at the Dartmouth Naval College in the USA. It was called BASIC (beginner's all-purpose symbolic instruction code). Because of this original purpose, it has the advantage of being one of the simplest languages to learn and this is probably why, for better or worse, it was adopted almost universally for microcomputers some fifteen years later. There are many purists who don't like BASIC as a computer language, but its grip is such that it is unlikely to be removed from its dominant position in the forseeable future. There are some differences between high level languages in the way they function. Some do all the 'translation' to machine code in one go and then store the translated version. These are known as 'compilers'. Others translate the program line by line as required and never store the complete translation. These are known as 'interpreters'. The resulting differences will manifest themselves mainly in speed on operation. 'Machine code' programs are marginally faster than 'compiled' programs, which in turn are very much faster than 'interpreted' programs. The microprocessor is so fast anyway, that for many applications the difference is of little concern. But there are some applications where it is. Sorting a school roll into alphabetical order might take many minutes with an interpreted program, whereas the task might be completed in as many seconds by machine code. BASIC is an 'interpreter' and this is one feature that makes it far from ideal as a language for MCBA programs. However, there is another side to the question, as we shall see later! A 'compiler' version of BASIC is available for some microcomputers but it is not in very common use.

Many microcomputers whisk the operator directly to first floor level as soon as they are switched on. The BBC microcomputer is an example of such. When power is connected it is immediately 'in BASIC'. Here all that is necessary is to LOAD and RUN the program for the particular task – known as the 'applications software'. Some systems even make it easier than this. Once a particular disk is placed in the disk drive and a simple signal is given by the operator, automation takes over. All that the user notices is that the application immediately begins. Software and computer systems set up like this (known as 'turnkey' systems) are much better for the inexperienced user. Lists of instructions on how to get from ground to first floor are not needed, and all the 'interpretation' going on inside the machine is unseen by the user.

4.2 Developing software

One of the great problems in microcomputing is the way that software production invariably lags well behind the development of hardware. This is, perhaps, not surprising because no software development of any kind can begin until the characteristics of a particular piece of hardware are established, and even then priority will be given to the most important, most general and most financially rewarding applications. Neither is the problem new. The distinguished educational researcher, R. G. Havelock, writing in 1969 well before the age of the microcomputer said:

The production and marketing of the hardware of the new media has far outstripped the more important but less glamorous and less profitable software accomplishments. As a result we are living in a pseudo-technological environment surrounded by sophisticated equipment which is performing trivial tasks and standing idle most of the time . . ..

Many hardware companies make no attempt to supply any applications software, claiming that it is the user who can best decide how to put the machine to the most appropriate use. Applications software for school administration has followed this general trend. If the introduction of the microcomputer in British education can be established as 1978, then some two years later there was precious little software available for MCBA purposes. Since that time matters have improved somewhat for machines prominent in educational use, but most of these have been around since 1978 and a five year delay would seem unnecessarily long.

Faced with this software famine, and eager to make use of and learn about their new equipment, schools began to take the only other way out – to write their own programs for school administration. Historically there is some support for the view that this is the best line to take. Richard Green, in an article in *Computer Education* in 1979 argued that schools should produce their own programs for school administration. His views certainly find support in the American literature. W. M. Tondow had pointed out some ten years earlier that it was easier and more beneficial to innovate with software rather than to wait for someone else to do the job, and that in this case you would also have a system which more nearly matched the needs of the organization.

The difficulty is in knowing when 'innovation' stops and 're-inventing the wheel' begins. I have always argued that the innovative phase for software is over some two years after the introduction of the hardware, and that after this time it is completely unnecessary for schools to attempt new programs unless they are totally convinced that nothing exists which can satisfy their needs in whole or in part. In this view there is some support from R. W. Ewart in his pamphlet entitled *Computers in educational administration today and tomorrow*. He suggests that in any computerized administration system it is totally unnecessary to go back to the beginning. One should start by using the experience of others and building on their development of computer software.

In 1981 I established that only 12 per cent of schools were using any externally produced software. In the main, schools lacked any help or advice about their software problem and were taking the only possible way out in designing their own software. In doing so teachers were learning about their machines in a way which had other practical benefits. However, the result of this general lack of direction was that similar developments started taking place in complete isolation, thus wasting, by duplication, a lot of valuable teacher time. Additionally, there was no standardization on vital issues like database structure which could have benefits to larger units than just the single school. The CET document entitled *A guide to the selection of microcomputers* published in 1980 put it succinctly in saying that production of software by individual schools and teachers will be 'wasteful of that most precious resource – teacher's time'.

Yet there is still something in what Tondow had to say about innovation with software. He had suggested that in using someone else's programs there were disadvantages because the user might need to change his own system or distort his operation to match the software obtained. There are many who feel that software 'brought in' never does exactly what you require of it and is consequently disappointing. I believe that there has to be some compromise between innovation and the application of less than ideal but ready made software. This is where BASIC has the advantage over machine code programs to which I alluded earlier. I find that schools often want to modify administration programs they have purchased to meet their own circumstances. With BASIC programs it is quite likely that someone (staff or pupil) will be able to 'tailor' the program to more effective use. This is a technique which I have used with some success on a number of occasions. It is always nice to oblige when someone says of a program 'it's all very well, but it would be much better if it could . . .!' The 'tailoring' of machine code programs is very much more difficult and lucky is the school which has someone to do it. BASIC programs have a much better prospect of being able to produce the compromise solution – external software customized for internal use.

In an ideal world, I suppose it would be best to contract out your administration software requirements to professional developers who would produce machine code programs to your specifications. Such a policy would be excessively expensive, however, and so we are left with compromises.

At this time I think we are very much out of the innovative stage and it is essential to emphasize the message that to go back to the beginning is unnecessary. Software is now available for most tasks although it may need a little adapting to suit your purposes. It would seem totally unnecessary for a teacher to begin designing from scratch a completely new system for one school. Designing a new system for a number of schools or for a Local Authority is a different matter which I shall examine again in Chapter 6. But Heads who set aside valuable staff teaching time for systems design should re-examine their priorities. I agree with such time being set aside for managing the computer systems – particularly if administrative time can be saved elsewhere – indeed, I would see it as essential; but this is not design work.

There is one other warning I would give about internally designed systems. My research revealed that in 50 per cent of the schools involved in MCBA the applications programs were written and managed by one teacher. In many cases the programs were not 'documented' with a result that the school was totally dependent for certain aspects of its administration on that one person. The dangers are obvious – if that person leaves the school certain administrative procedures may collapse for a time while manual methods are re-established or while MCBA routines are sorted out. Good documentation is one factor which helps avoid this situation. Training and involvement of other staff is another essential ingredient which the prudent Head will invoke to avoid this problem.

4.3 Documentation

'Documentation' is the written set of instructions to the user which should accompany any piece of applications software. It usually forms a manual without which the user will find it very difficult to use the program. Documentation accompanying programs can vary from the sparse to the comprehensive. In general, it should aim to present enough detail to allow the user to run a program efficiently, and yet be sufficiently succinct to encourage the most inexperienced potential users. It should contain the following:

1 A general indication of the scope of the program in terms of the task attempted
2 An indication of what data must be collected so that it is to hand for use during the program run. A blank data collection form is useful for this
3 A description of the output available and any special facilities which the program might have
4 A note on the hardware configuration which will be necessary in order to run the program
5 A general run through the program indicating what responses might be necessary and what their effects might be, and a description of any general commands which might be available
6 Sample printouts, a breakdown of the program structure and its variables to facilitate amendment, and details of where help or advice may be sought if it becomes necessary

If you are considering the purchase of a program it may be possible to obtain a copy of the documentation for inspection purposes beforehand, or at the very least some extracts from it. This will help make an assessment of the program's usefulness to you. You may even have an opportunity to see a program running before you purchase it. In this case try to assess whether it is 'user friendly' and 'crash proof' (sometimes also known as 'idiot proof'). 'Crash proof' means that it is impossible for the program to cease functioning before you want it to, on account of the entry of some meaningless or inappropriate instruction.

4.4 User friendliness

'User friendly' means that the program is as easy as possible for the operator to use and offers, on the screen, lots of useful hints about the responses it requires as the program proceeds. The more complex the program, the more difficult this is for the programmer to achieve. As a new user you should get the feeling that the program is trying to help you along. Some programs even allow you to type 'HELP' at any time to get some guidance as to what to do next if uncertain about a response.

I always feel that the most 'user friendly' programs will put you right into program operation at 'first floor' level without the need to name any program. They are 'turnkey' controlled. On one computer I've used this was achieved on closing the disk drive door, and on another by just pressing key 'B', after inserting the program disk. This is not an easy effect for the programmer to achieve because of the many different configurations of hardware on which a program might run. Some are able to achieve it for any combination just by asking you to run a particular program on the disk the first time you use it – thereafter everything is automatic. If the software you are using is a collection of programs – called a 'suite' of programs – to carry out different aspects of a school task, the most 'user friendly' programs will usually display a 'menu' of options open to you as soon as the program begins.

For example, suppose your suite handles a pupil record system. I would expect a really friendly system to behave something like this. Having placed your disk in drive A and closed the door (or perhaps having pressed a single key) the disk drive switches on and after a short pause the screen displays a message:

BLOGGS
SCHOOL RECORD SYSTEM

Place your 'records' disk or a blank disk if no records have yet been created, in Drive B.

Press any key to continue.

Having complied with the instruction the following might then appear on the screen:

OPTIONS OPEN TO YOU:

Create new records 1
Add to records 2
Delete records 3
Amend records 4
Interrogate records 5
Form 7 details 6
Print lists 7
Print timetables 8
End program 9
Choose your option (1 – 9 only)

Upon selecting your option the program moves, perhaps to another menu enlarging on the opportunities within that particular choice. Such a program is said to be 'Menu driven'. Being menu driven doesn't necessarily make a suite better than one that's not, but it often gives the operator more confidence than having to select and load any one of perhaps a dozen programs from an unseen list.

I once saw a records suite which, upon loading and running the first program, simply gave the prompt:

```
YEAR?
```

As it was 1982 the operator typed this and pressed RETURN to be faced with:

```
WHICH 1982TH YEAR CLASS?
```

This is a good example of a very unhelpful and unfriendly start. Another program I know, not an administrative one it's true, starts with:

```
OUT = IN?
```

The answer 'NO', which seems obvious, is not what the computer is after!

And what about a program being 'idiot proof'? This is not quite so derogatory to the operator as it might seem since if the program is not 'idiot proof' then, by and large, it's the programmer who has not done a reasonable job.

If, for example, in response to the title page of the BLOGGS SCHOOL RECORD SYSTEM you thought you had put the disk in Drive B, but in fact hadn't, the version which says:

```
Sorry, no disk in Drive B – try again
```

is idiot proof, but:

```
DOS Error type A at line 60
Ready:
```

means idiot programmer! And if, in response to the menu, you press a letter key instead of a number key, the message:

```
Numbers 1 to 9 only please – try again
```

is idiot proof, but:

```
Fatal Error 23 at line 170
Ready:
```

means idiot programmer.

What has happened with the 'idiot programmer' alternatives is that due to a very trivial error the program has 'crashed' or failed to work properly. The messages shown in these cases will cause concern to those people unfamiliar with the machine and send them rushing for advice. They are really only helpful to the programmer and it is relatively easy for him to avoid such things in the 'production' version. As one secretary said to me – 'I knew I'd break it – it'll only say "Ready" or "What?"'!

The really sound program from this respect is one you can't crash even if you try hard – and there's no harm in trying when you're assessing.

Another small point connected with user friendliness is worth mentioning here. This concerns the need for users to be able to save data on disk at regular intervals. Particularly where there is a large amount of data to be put in – when creating new files for a record system or entering data for a timetable, for example – users may not wish to complete the task in one session. Indeed, it may waste a lot of time if the user is not able to do so. At one school a small BASIC program was being used to print the school's timetable. The program did not allow storage of the data until all had been entered. Rather foolishly the timetabler did not arrange to use the full capacity of the microcomputer's memory. Having laboured for seven hours to input the data, the message 'Out of memory. Ready.' appeared on the screen. The program had crashed, losing all the data. I'm told that the roar of exasperation could be heard throughout the school! With provision to file data on a regular basis this need never have happened. User friendly programs which collect considerable amounts of data should have this feature, and users should remember to use it.

4.5 Buying software

So much for the background to choosing your software. In the rest of this chapter I intend to describe some of the packages which I know to be available. Please don't regard my descriptions as an assurance that the packages will work for you, or use them as a 'best buy' guide. If a program interests you then write to the author for more details – addresses are given in Appendix 1. Authors usually won't send you a copy of the program to assess – the risks of piracy are far too great – although some may send a demonstration disk. However, someone near you may be using the program already, and if you're going to spend a lot of money it may be well worth travelling some way to see a demonstration. Try to satisfy yourself on the following details before purchase:

1 Will it 'run' on my machine?
2 Will it do the job I require of it?
3 Is there documentation?

4   Can it be used easily by the appropriate people on my staff?
5   Is it worth the price being asked?

Unless all five questions can be answered positively there must be some doubt about proceeding with a purchase. If the answers are positive only you and your colleagues can decide whether the software is right for your school.

It is pleasing to note that so much software has now become available for school administration that it is impossible to review all of it in this chapter. I shall confine myself to a sample of those programs I have used or seen, and for which documentation has been made available to me. An exhaustive list of all the software I have been able to identify for MCBA is included in Appendix 1, which also gives details of how the packages described here may be purchased. I have tried to cover here programs for all the most popular machines and to deal with the programs under task headings in the same order as in Chapter 2. Collectively they give a feeling for the full range available.

4.6   Record systems

(i)   The Lakes school administrative suite (Alex Redhead)
This was one of the earliest school administration programs available for the RML 380Z. It was written using RML DBAS9 disk BASIC, but the most recent version of the suite will run under BASIC Version 5 using either a 56K dual disk drive or a DOI style 32K machine.

The key program called REG stores a limited number of details of all the pupils in a school in a simple database. Pupil records are filed in the database according to their registration group, and subdivided according to sex. Consequently it is not necessary to store these details in each pupil record.

Each pupil record has eight fields or lines as follows:

1   Surname
2   First name
3   Coded data containing: the title of parent(s) (Mr and Mrs, Mr, Mrs or guardian of another name); date of birth; telephone number
     4,5,and 6 are lines for addresses
7   Name of guardian if different from 1
8   Coded data concerning course choice

The number of disks used to store the data will vary from school to school, but I have found it possible to store two year groups of 260 pupils on one side of a floppy disk. Using both sides of a double-sided disk system a pupil roll of about 2000 can be held 'on-line'.

The most recent version of this suite of programs is menu driven. The nature of each program and its use is described in the limited documentation, the programs themselves have prompts to guide the operator as the program runs. The individual programs conduct the following tasks:

1   Compile the database files

2   Print file details for checking
3   Print form lists with surname and first name
4   Update the database
5   Give the ages and average ages of pupils up to a specified year and month
6   Print full alphabetical lists from the files
7   Print address labels
8   Print option choices by subject and by tutor group. The programs will need amendment to detail the subjects studied at a particular school, although 'tailoring' routines provided will minimize this task
9   List the Form 7 data (years 1 to 5 only)
10 Print a clash table of option choices from up to fifty subjects

The structure of the database is so simple, as is the program construction, that it is easy both to tailor programs to an individual school's use and to write new programs. For example, the documentation suggests that programs can be written to give numbers of children taking three, two, one or no sciences, or to produce report headings in the various subjects.

A secretary will experience few problems in using the system, particularly if the master disk is provided with an autostart system as the documentation suggests. At the end of each year the file names (form names) need to be revised, and the documentation suggests that the disk operating system needs to be used to do this. A secretary may not be so happy with this task, which will need the attention of someone relatively familiar with the computer's systems software. However, using BASIC Version 5.0 a simple program could be written to accomplish this task in a fairly easy manner.

(ii)   The O'Neill school administration suite (Ian O'Neill)

This suite of programs is written for the Commodore PET series 4000 with at least 32K memory, 4040 disk drives and PET compatible printer. It is intended for use in 11-16 schools with up to 300 pupils in each year group. Written primarily in BASIC, it is user friendly and geared for ease of use by both school secretaries and teachers rather than by what the author describes as 'program modifiers'.

There are sixteen programs in the suite, but these are driven from a main menu, so the use of each program is unseen to the user. Data on pupils are held in ten files, five on each of two mini-floppy disks. One disk is for boys, and the other for girls and both are divided into the five files by virtue of year group. This structure aids file maintenance as each year group moves up through the school.

Each pupil record has twenty-six fields each of which is limited to a minimum and maximum number of characters (letters or numbers). The fields contain the following information, with maximum field lengths shown in brackets:

1   Surname .... (15)
2   First name .... (12)
3   Year/stream .... (1)
4   Tutor group .... (3)
5   Address .... (56)
6   Home telephone number .... (11)

7	Father's work telephone number	(11)
8	Mother's work telephone number	(11)
9	Admission number	(4)
10	Date of birth	(6)
11	Previous school	(2)
12	Date of entry	(6)
13-18	Six fields for test scores	each (3)
19-26	Eight fields for option/course choices	each (3)

If some of the last fourteen fields are not required for their intended purpose they may be regarded as 'spares' and used for alternative data. The documentation suggests for example, that field 26 might be used to store 'area of residence'. Pupils can then be sorted by a program according to their 'area of residence', and all the pupils living in one particular area could be listed, for example. In this way the programs allow schools a fair degree of flexibility in use.

There is one additional datafile which stores the name of every tutor group, the form tutors' names and the numbers of the registration rooms.

The suite allows the user to carry out as many as twenty-eight different functions, although on account of the flexibility for list production the actual total is probably considerably more than this. In the summary the user can:

1 Create the datafiles from scratch
2 Maintain the datafiles as and when the need arises, both for individual pupils, and for groups of pupils requiring the same alterations
3 Print out pupil records and address labels
4 Print out lists of: the whole school; one year group; one or more tutor groups or forms; option groups; other groups of pupils with any filed information required; and of form tutors and registration rooms
5 Print statistical information for DES Form 7 and lists of pupils born on certain days of month
6 Print the statistics of the composition of option groups and tutor groups
7 Update the files in preparation for a new school year
8 Sort the files alphabetically by name or by tutor group order
9 Examine a particular pupil's record on the screen

The documentation accompanying this suite is extensive and detailed and is intended for use by those with little or no previous experience of computing and computers. In addition to the main documentation there is a loose leaf guide for teachers to produce 'selected lists' of their choice which includes instructions on using the computer's keyboard and disks. The screen displays appear particularly well designed and any teacher or school secretary should be quite happy using this system after only a short period spent studying the manual and practising at the keyboard.

Ian O'Neill has also collaborated with David Jewell to produce a suite of programs for a pupil record database on the RML 380Z. It is not identical with the PET suite, neither is it so self contained since a text editor is necessary to create the files.

(iii) Pupil list administration (Christopher Glover)

This suite was written for RML 380Z with twin double-sided disk drives. The programs wil run using RML BASIC Version 5.0. The optimum memory is 48K RAM but 32K will suffice for less than 300 pupils per year group.

The suite is built around a number of files, central to which are the pupil datafiles. Pupil records are filed by year groups and the program allows for years 1 to 7. Each pupil record has five fields as follows:

1   First name
2   Surname
3   Form
4   Sex (B or G)
5   Date of birth

Although the file structure itself does not limit the number of characters in each field some of the programs within the suite do. For example, the first name is limited to eleven characters and the surname to fifteen characters, although in practice restriction is unlikely to cause problems. Other files required by the suite are the form tutor file, which holds form names, form tutor's names and form room numbers, and the Faculty/Department file which identifies the faculty or department within which a member of staff teaches. Programs are provided within the suite to create all these datafiles. Two other sub-files – the form file and the set file – are created by programs within the suite. The form file is created automatically from the original pupil record datafile. The set file is created from the form file by adding the set data for each subject.

There are twenty-one programs in the suite. These are menu driven and as a result the whole suite is very straightforward to operate. Programs are available to undertake the following:

1   Create pupil record files from scratch (in one session, or several if necessary)
2   Amend records and files in various ways, including insertion of birthdates where these were not known at file creation time
3   Sort year groups into alphabetical order
4   Print alphabetical lists of pupils in a year group together with forms, and totals for the year
5   Print alphabetical form lists, with totals for boys and girls
6   Sort the set files into boys and girls alphabetically
7   Print set lists, whether singly, or all those in a year group, or simply give the total number of pupils independently
8   Extract Form 7 data both in September and January, and print a list of pupils not in their normal school year
9   Transfer records from one academic year to the next, with provision for simple amendment of form descriptions throughout a file

Secretarial staff can easily use this suite to input the initial data, and to maintain it subsequently. Another bonus for the suite is that the file structure links neatly with the examination administration suite by Garry Norman and Christopher Glover. Indeed, for ease of use of the latter it would be essential to use the pupil record files for examination record file creation. I believe that suites of programs used in schools should be linked in this way so as to avoid the creation of a large number of independent databases. The Glover and Norman suites make this possible for at least two tasks.

(iv) Database management systems

Some schools have successfully used general purpose database management systems (DBMS) to organize their pupils' records on microcomputers. Such programs can be used to store and interrogate collections of data. They can be used equally well to store details of a library of books, a collection of stamps or the activities of a group of bellringers as they can to deal with the pupil record task.

Users are able to define the features of each individual collection of records. The number of fields is given, each field is named and its length specified. In some of the more sophisticated systems even the layout of the screen showing the names of the fields and their length can be defined, considerably easing data entry. A school could define its pupil record database as follows:

Field	Name	Length
1	Surname	15
2	Forename	20
3	Sex	1
4	Address	40
5	Date of birth	6
6	Form	4
7	Previous school	25
8	Admission number	5

Once these details are collected for all pupils in the school and have been entered into the microcomputer, they are filed on disk by the program to form a database. This database can then be interrogated using features built into the DBMS program. For example, it would be possible to print formlists from the records defined above by instructing the program to output the following information to the printer:

Search for all pupils in 4M27 (field 6), girls first, then boys (field 3), arrange both groups in alphabetical order, print surname (field 1) and forename (field 2).

This instruction would have to be suitably coded as required by the particular DBMS program.

DBMS programs are particularly useful for seeking information and lists on a combination of fields, a feature which may not be available in a dedicated program. They are also more versatile in that schools are better able to define their own database. They usually have more features for sorting and ordering, too. However, they are rather more difficult to use than dedicated programs and tend to be less user friendly. They also tend to be less automatic in the production of a large number of lists.

Two examples of database management systems often found in schools for teaching purposes are MicroQUERY and MicroLEEP. More sophisticated and expensive packages are DataStar (380Z and APPLE) and Manager (PET).

(v) QADMIN (David Blow, Malcolm Fraser and John Porter)

Database management systems can be adapted for specific purposes, and an excellent example of this technique is QADMIN. This allows the creation of a pupil record database as disk files in one of two formats, either that used by MicroQUERY, or by its near relation QUEST. Once the datafiles have been created the powerful interrogation and editing features of the particular DBMS can be used. QADMIN eases the database creation problem by providing facilities to define the fields within each record. The first five fields of the record are fixed as:

1   Name
2   Admission number
3   Date of birth
4   Form
5   Sex

Thereafter the remaining thirteen fields can be defined by the school, allowing a record system to be devised to match the school's own 'personality'.

The QADMIN suite currently makes provision for the following tasks to be undertaken on the RML 380Z or BBC microcomputers:

1   Update form and tutor data
2   Print an alphabetic list
3   Print form lists
4   Print option lists
5   Print pupil profile forms
6   Print individual examination entries
7   Print individual examination timetables

Because the files are in the format required by MicroQUERY or QUEST a large number of other lists and statistical data could be generated using the facilities of these packages.

4.7   Option choices systems

(i)   Option choices – Programs OPT1-6 (Keith Johnson)

Of all the administration programs available these will be among the best known, largely because they first appeared in Keith Johnson's book *Timetabling* in 1980. Originally written for the PET cassette based machine, they have been translated for use on a number of other microcomputers – in particular the RML 380Z, APPLE, BBC and Tandy TRS-80 – in most cases using floppy disks as well as cassettes. The versions for these various microcomputers can be obtained from various sources, details of which are available in Appendix 1.

The programs are well documented in *Timetabling*. The database comprises a single field with the following information about each pupil:

Sex   B or G (optional)
Name   Any length
Course choice   Coded – single letter per subject

The programs are not menu driven. Each one of the six programs is loaded and run as it is required.

OPT1 compiles the database of pupils' choices for recording on disk or tape. It also prepares a clash table which will guide design of the option blocks by manual methods described in the book.

OPT2 considers the pupils' choices recorded by OPT1 and compares them with any option pools designed after consideration of the clash table. It outputs results showing which pupil choices cannot be fitted and an indication of the percentage satisfaction for the group of pupils as a whole. This program might be run several times to consider several different option schemes. OPT2 has been improved in several ways since publication of the original listing in the book.

OPT3 allows the database to be amended to accommodate changes, and to give subjects in the correct pool order. Inevitably, with a large number of pupils, some choices will have to be amended to give a final and complete fit.

OPT4 prints out the membership of each option group after all the choices have been made. The lists can include such information as teacher, room and timetable. The names are automatically sorted into alphabetical order (with girls and boys printed separately if the appropriate information on sex was entered under OPT1).

OPT5 performs the same task as OPT4, but was intended for use on machines where memory capacity is limited. This program neither sorts alphabetically nor separates boys' and girls' names.

OPT6 produces a list for handing out to each pupil showing the final options allocated and the teachers, rooms and times of the week for each lesson.

OPT7 is a more recent program which can be used to interrogate the data tape or disk produced by OPT1 or OPT3 in order to find the names of pupils with specific subject combinations. It is useful for identifying the pupils causing clashes on the OPT1 clash table.

The programs were designed to be used by a timetabler, or Director of Studies, who knows how to load programs into a microcomputer. Nevertheless, data entry can be accomplished by a secretary after some elementary instruction, particularly on a disk system. With the amount of data to be entered with program OPT1 a competent typist could save a considerable amount of time. The programs are written in BASIC and are relatively straightforward. It would be a fairly simple exercise to link this suite to other BASIC programs which store pupils' records, and timetable details, to avoid repetitive entry of data.

(ii) Fourth year options (Michael Lovett)

Written in BASIC Version 5.0A for RML 380Z, this suite follows the general lines of the Keith Johnson programs. Indeed, the terminology and algorithm of the clash table and option fitting parts of the package are acknowledged as having been drawn from that suite. However, there the similarity ends, for the twenty-five programs in the suite are menu driven and have a considerable number of sophisticated features in terms of output.

The programs require at least 32K bytes of memory and two double-sided mini-floppy disk drives. An EASISTART program is included on the supplied disks which, after use, allow the user to enter the program menu by a single keystroke after inserting the disks.

The programs use a database organized into a number of different files so that, unless changes are made, data has only to be entered once. A great deal of the file handling is made automatic by the programs, and thus the use of the data files is largely 'transparent', or unseen by the user. The main files within the database are the year file and parameter file.

The year file contains the name, form, sex, group, and coded subject choice data for each pupil. The data is held in the file in a single 'string', or row of characters, which is subdivided by the software into fields. The coded subject data may not contain more than nine subjects for any one pupil. The group, form and sex data fields are limited to one character each. Surname and first name are not limited in length.

The parameter file contains details of the format of the curriculum being used in terms of the number of bands, option blocks, maximum number of pupils, format of the school day, and details of the subjects on the curriculum. It also contains information about the type of 380Z and printer being used. Other files of information contain details of the pupils' subject preferences, a year file sorted into alphabetical order, the subject code letters and a staff names file. The staff file allows for up to ninety-nine teachers.

The suite of programs will undertake the following tasks:

1   The input and editing of pupils' names and subject choices
2   The input and editing of curriculum and other data required by the parameter file
3   The input and editing of relevant timetable details
4   The input and editing of staff numbers and names
5   Production of a clash matrix
6   Fitting pupils to trial option schemes
7   Filing details of pupils' final choices
8   Printing both core and options curriculum details
9   Printing class lists

10   Printing class totals
11   Printing form lists showing option and core choices
12   Printing details of final choices to be sent to parents
13   Printing pupils' timetables
14   Printing pupils' location charts
15   Printing alphabetical lists of all pupils
16   Printing staff names in alphabetical or numerical order

The documentation is very thorough and well produced: it includes a useful booklet containing nine data preparation forms to be used in conjunction with the suite. The disks supplied also contain files of trial data. With these the user can become familiar with the programs without the chore of additional data preparation.

The practical application of this suite will be in the hands of the timetabler, Director of Studies or Head of Year. However, data preparation for the initial year file will be speedier if done by a typist, who should be able to accomplish this task after minimum instructions on loading the program suite menu. Thereafter the prime user will edit files and test option systems, perhaps bringing back the secretary to oversee the final list production.

Since the programs are written in BASIC and the year file structure is uncomplicated it should be a relatively simple task to write a program to produce the year file for use with this suite from any existing pupil record database.

(iii)   School option block structuring and pupil allocation system (Cleveland County Council Research and Intelligence Unit)

This system was derived from a similar suite used on a mainframe computer by many of Cleveland's schools. It has been rewritten in BASIC for the RML 380Z twin mini-disk 48K machine (or 32K with the high resolution graphics board called as an extra 16K memory) and differs in a number of important ways from the programs previously described.

Firstly, the programs use a version of BASIC known as XDB. This was an interpreter originally issued by RML as an 'extended disk BASIC'. It has the important attribute of 'random' file handling which is not found in other RML BASIC interpreters. These only have 'sequential' file handling, which means that every record in a file has to be read in order to access a particular record. With 'random' file handling a record can be identified by its particular position within the file and therefore, as the name suggests, records can be accessed 'at random'.

Secondly, the programs use the pupil choices to construct the option blocks in such a way as to satisfy as many of the pupil choices as possible. This facility is unusual in a microcomputer options suite, where the construction of the option blocks for trial is usually left to the timetabler. In this suite the optimum solution is suggested, although the timetabler can still make amendments to the suggested block system and have the new version evaluated.

The programs in the suite are not menu driven and various programs have to be loaded. These collectively cope with the several tasks which the suite undertakes. One of these programs allows the user to create the two necessary datafiles. The first datafile contains details of the option block system and is arranged as follows:

RECORD 1 contains:
(i)   a title
(ii) the number of blocks
(iii) the number of courses
(iv) the number of pupils

Each subsequent record contains:
(i)   a course code (maximum 4 characters)
(ii) a course name (maximum 10 characters)
(iii) the number of sets for the course

The second datafile contains details of the pupils, with each record containing:
(i)   a name (up to 25 characters)
(ii) their coded course choices

The main program in the suite conducts the following tasks:

1   Reads data from the files
2   Produces a clash matrix
3   Allows incompatible and preblocked courses to be specified
4   Compiles the optimum block structure
5   Evaluates the block structure in terms of each pupil's choices
6   Allows changes to be made to the block structure for re-evaluation

A second program in the suite conducts a diagnostic test to check the feasibility of each pupil's choices and to identify some reasons why certain choices cannot be met. This allows the timetabler to locate 'problem blocks' far more quickly than might otherwise be possible.

Other programs allow class sizes to be balanced, pupils to be allocated to classes, and class lists to be printed. A 'block timetable' can also be edited and printed for each pupil although in practice this really means a listing of the blocked courses for each pupil. There is also a program which sorts pupils into alphabetical order. Secretarial assistance with the suite will probably be confined to pupil data entry.

Some 'program moderators' have been at work on the suite and I have seen at least one version which is menu driven. Robin Ingledew (see Appendix 1) has a program which links this suite with his Random access files package.

4.8   Examination administration

(i)   Examination entries and analysis programs (Garry Norman and Christopher Glover)

This suite of ten programs was written for the RML 380Z twin single-sided mini-floppy disk system with 32K memory. Such a configuration should be able to handle a year group entry of 250 pupils. More memory would cope with a greater number of pupils. The programs are designed for use with BASIC Version 5 and are menu driven.

The suite makes use of three files of data. The entry file holds details about the pupil, his form and pattern of entries, and coded data concerning the subjects entered. The 'pattern of entry' details held are:

1   Number of school entries
2   Number of parental entries
3   Number of previous entries

The subject codes file holds details concerning subjects which are 'paired' for double entry purposes, the Board number, Board name and candidate entry fee for each Board used, and the subject name, Board number and subject entry fee for each subject. The results file holds the pupils' names, number of entries and results against each subject. These files are constructed using programs within the suite.

The first three programs in the suite conduct specific tasks according to their names. ENTRIES reads the pupils' names from an alphabetical file of the year group and requests an input of the subject codes for each pupil from the keyboard. From this data it creates the entry datafile. An alphabetical file of the year group is most conveniently created using the Pupil list administration suite by Chris Glover described in Section 4.6(iii). This method will considerably cut down the amount of typing necessary by forming a valuable link with the standard pupil database. However, as the structure of the file is given in the documentation it is possible to create it using a suitable text editor (such as TXED from RML) or a wordprocessing program (such as WordStar).

EXAMFEES prints a bill for each pupil who has fees owing, itemizing school entries and private entries separately. It works to a formula where the maximum number of County paid entries is eight, and sorts all the entries so that where charges are made to parents they will be for the cheapest subjects. A double entry on parental request is charged to the parents irrespective of the total number of entries. A summary of the amounts due from pupils is also produced. RESULTS reads the entry datafile and presents the name of each pupil and his subjects on the screen. It then invites an input of the results from the keyboard. These can be input over several sessions if necessary, and in Board order. The program also allows for deletion of a pupil or deletion of a subject.

Other programs in the suite deal with lists of school entries and parental entries in each subject; statements of entries for each pupil; and the amendment of either of the pupil datafiles.

The remaining programs in the suite are all concerned with results analysis. The tasks undertaken are as follows:

1   Printout of individual pupil's results
2   Summary total of the number of pupils with a given number of O level and/or CSE Grade 1 passes

3   An analysis of results by subject, printing the totals in each grade and results of individual pupils in that subject (for Heads of Department)
4   In each subject where there are double entries, a double entry analysis matrix is printed
5   Prints a condensed form of the results summary subject by subject (as might be required by the Head), and an overall analysis of the total number of O level and CSE grades for all subjects

(ii)   The Kingsdown Examination entry system (Gareth Cole)

This suite of thirty-one programs is written for the RML 380Z twin double-sided mini-floppy disk system using 48K memory (or 32K with high resolution graphics board called as an extra 16K memory). The BASIC interpreter used is BASIC Version 5. In this configuration the program can deal with some 350 student entries – even more with 56K memory.

The documentation describes how to create an 'auto-start' system on the program disk. In this case the user will be able to run all programs by selection from a central menu. Alternatively, the user may choose to run each program in the suite individually.

The programs use a database with just one file which contains the necessary details for each candidate and to which subject entries can be added as required. Each candidate record has four fields:

1   Sex, candidate's name
2   Date of birth
3   Tutorial group
4   Coded subject entries in a string with six characters per entry

In field 4 each group of six characters, when broken down, contains the following information:

Character 1   Level of examination, e.g. O, A, CSE.
Character 2   Examination Board
Characters 3 and 4 The subject code
Character 5   School or private entry
Character 6   Result or 'estimated' grade

This six character code is interpreted and expanded by information contained within each program.

The suite can be used to conduct the following tasks:

1   Set up the file of names and candidate data – over several sessions if necessary
2   Add the subject entries when available
3   Change any data in the file, including the addition or deletion of candidates
4   List candidates by tutor group, showing entries, and estimated grades if required
5   List candidates by subject of entry
6   Make various lists by Boards, for the transfer of data to Boards forms.

119

7   Send entries direct by disk or printout for the South Western Examination Board and the London Board
8   Enter results by Board and Level
9   List results by candidate
10   List candidates' results in a form suitable for press release
11   Carry out and print an analysis of results by subject and by grade

In addition several programs for 'utility' tasks are included such as:

12   Produce lists to check names and dates of birth of candidates
13   Produce forms for staff to indicate subject entries
14   To check the data on file
15   To create a backup copy of the data on a second disk

This comprehensive suite of programs is adequately documented and is aimed at the Examinations Officer with only limited knowledge of the microcomputer. A secretary could certainly be used for the data entry stage, and also for the production of many of the output lists. However, the data for expansion of the subject entry field codes is contained within the programs and these may need amending to suit a particular school. Although this process is described in the documentation, a little programming knowledge for this task would be an advantage.

(iii) GCE/CSE external examination package (Robin Ingledew)

This package has a central suite of ten programs which deals with the normal routines for entry and checking of data, the insertion of grades once results are published, and some statistical analysis of results. Significant additions to this package are contained in two other suites. One creates examination timetables in chronological order for all candidates, the other produces completed entry schedules in formats accepted by certain Boards. The programs are written for the RML 380Z with twin mini-floppy disk drives. The main programs are menu driven. In other cases, the documentation provided enables the user to identify programs to be loaded for specific tasks.

The programs operate upon two files – the subject file and the pupil data file. The subject file simply contains the names of all subjects to be examined in a form convenient to the user. Distinction between GCE and CSE is obtained by including these initials in the title. Distinctions between Boards is achieved by grouping subjects from the same Board together within the file. The pupil data file contains information about each candidate in the following fields:

1   Surname
2   Forename(s)
3   Tutor group
4   Sex
5   Date of birth
6   Examination data in the form code, grade, code, grade . . . etc.
     All grades are initially set as 'dummy' values by the program pending arrival

of the results. The position of the subject in the subject file is used as its examination code.

Programs are provided which create both these files. This task can be accomplished in one session, or more if necessary. It is assumed that grades will not be available when the files are created and a separate program is provided to insert these when the results are known. All data input programs allow addition, amendment or deletion of data.

The remaining programs in the suite conduct the following tasks:

1 List of candidates for each subject
2 List of pupils with all their details, including entries, for checking. It is also possible to produce a letter to go to parents with this information
3 List double entries in any specified pairs of subjects

After results have been entered the following tasks can then be accomplished:

4 List the candidates who took O level only, CSE only, both or neither, by sex
5 Conduct an analysis by subject of the number of candidates gaining each grade, together with percentage of entry and of year group; and total number of each grade overall for GCE and CSE
6 List the pupils gaining 0,1,2. . .O level or CSE Grade 1 passes with cumulative totals
7 List the pupils gaining at least one O level pass or CSE grade 1 with the number of Os followed by CSE grade 1s in brackets

The first extension, the EXAM TIMETABLES package, operates upon the same two central files and requires one more file (rawdates) which contains details for each examination such as the title of the paper, the session dates and starting times, the duration and the venue. These are sorted into chronological order by a program and from the resulting sorted file (xamdates) the following information can be produced:

8 A timetable for each pupil for the examination period in which only exams taken by that pupil appear
9 A school timetable for the examination period containing details of each session, including the total number of candidates
10 Lists of pupils with examination timetable clashes, showing details

The second extension, the ENTRY SCHEDULE package, produces entry schedules on the printer which may be sent directly to the appropriate Board. In the initial package the Boards serviced were:

The North Regional Examinations Board
The Joint Matriculation Board O level
The University of London Board O, A, and S levels

Provided users follow the methods outlined in the documentation carefully, these packages can be used by any Examinations Officer with a minimum knowledge of the microcomputer. The programs are user friendly and considerable effort has been made to check data input to avoid errors. Keyboard skills could be useful for rapid data entry.

(iv) Examination entries (Keith and Chris Johnson)

This comprises two programs which are intended to analyse public examinations results. They are designed for use after results are received and offer a comparison of the school's results department by department. CSE, O level and joint 16+ examinations can be analysed together, dealing with up to forty subjects for 300 pupils. Originally the programs were written for a 32K PET with a disk unit or cassette recorder, but versions are in preparation for other microcomputers.

EXAM 1 is the input program. This accepts names and results either as one batch or in several batches. If necessary names can be entered first with grades following later. This facility allows for the names file to be created by the microcomputer from another database. The entry of results from the keyboard is made fairly rapid by the routines used and facilities are built in for the amendment of incorrect data. The database can be recorded either onto disk or onto tape. It will contain the following information:

Sex (optional)
Name
Forenames (optional)
Form

and the coded subject results data.

EXAM 2 is the output program and undertakes a considerable number of tasks. It is menu driven with the following options:

0 Results of a named pupil
1 Results of all pupils
2 Results of all pupils in a named subject
3 Pupils who have 'passed' in a named subject
4 Pupils gaining a named grade in a named subject
5 Pupils gaining at least a named grade in a named subject
6 Pupils with exactly a named number of 'passes'
7 Pupils with at least a named number of 'passes'
8 Bar graphs of departments' results
9 Comparative analysis of departments' results

Items 0-8 are clearly useful for such purposes as:

conveying information both to candidates and teachers
making preliminary judgements concerning double-entry policy
making preliminary judgements on departmental results
judging the overall performance of the cohort of candidates

If the sex of each candidate is recorded in the database then analysis for boys and girls can be made separately.

```
LAURA NORDER H. S.                          I CIRCUMSTANCES
                                            I (FAVOURABLE +)
1982 5TH YEAR                               I (NEUTRAL 0)
                                            I (NEUTRAL 0)
        I       I NO. I       L___PASSES____ L_GRADE SCORES_ I(UNFAVOURABLE -)I
        INUMBERI 'O' I       I   I % INI    I   I % INI      I       INEW/I    I
        I OF    IEQUIVIGRADE I   IOTHERI    I   IOTHERI      IGROUPI/OLDISTAFFI
DEPTIPUPILSIPASS ISCORE I % ISUBJ*IDIFF I % ISUBJ*IDIFF I SIZEISYLLI ILL I
ENG. I 132 I 45 I 461 I 34I 25 I+ 9 I 50I 46 I+ 4 I  -  I + I  +  I
LIT. I  68 I 40 I 296 I 59I 36 I+23 I 62I 52 I+10 I  -  I + I  +  I
HIST I  52 I  9 I 132 I 17I 40 I-23 I 36I 54 I-18 I  0  I - I  -  I
GEOG I  73 I 15 I 206 I 21I 31 I-10 I 40I 50 I-10 I  0  I + I  +  I
MUS. I  11 I  6 I  49 I 55I 50 I+ 5 I 64I 58 I+ 6 I  +  I 0 I  0  I
FREN I  46 I 12 I 159 I 26I 51 I-25 I 49I 56 I-7  I  +  I + I  +  I
F.ST I  25 I  1 I  87 I  4I  5 I-1  I 50I 37 I+13 I  -  I + I  0  I
SPAN I   8 I  8 I  42 I100I 88 I+12 I 75I 75 I0   I  +  I + I  0  I
MATH I  80 I 18 I 236 I 23I 36 I-13 I 42I 52 I-10 I  0  I + I  0  I
ARIT I  35 I    I  41 I   I 10 I-10 I 17I 40 I-23 I  0  I + I  0  I
     1     2     3     4   5     6    7   8     9    10    11   12    13   14
```

Figure 4.1 Output from menu item 9 of program EXAM 2.

Menu item 9 provides a considerable amount of information. A table having one line for each department is produced giving the following information in ten columns:

1 The department name
2 The number of candidates
3 The number of O level equivalent passes
4 The 'grade score'

To compute the 'grade score', values can be assigned to the examination grades. Most usual are these:

GCE grade	A	B	C	D	E		
CSE grade			1	2	3	4	5
Value	7	6	5	4	3	2	1

The 'grade score' is the total of all values scored by candidates in that particular subject.

The next three columns relate to passes:

5 Percentage pass rate
6 Percentage pass rate of the same candidates in all the other subjects that they took

123

7   The difference between the previous two columns

The final three columns relate to the grade scores:

8   Percentage of total possible grade scores
9   Percentage of all the total possible grade scores by the same candidates in other subjects that they took. This is a measure of the ability of the candidates entered by each department
10 The difference between the previous columns. This is a measure of the success of each department

The statistics can be further adjusted by typing in the Board's overall results when these are published. I consider that these statistics have the potential to convey a great deal of useful management information, and the documentation discusses ways in which this can be used. Although data could be entered by a secretary, the mode of entry makes it possible for those without keyboard skills to do it equally quickly. The examinations officer will probably be the prime user of the program whereas the Head should certainly be the prime scrutineer of the analysis and instigator of the discussions which will inevitably follow. These programs clearly bridge the boundary of the clerical task into the realm of management reporting.

4.9   Timetable planning

(i)   ANALYSIS – A manpower analysis of a curriculum (Patrick Bird)
This program produces management information for the Head, Deputy Head, Director of Studies and Heads of Department during the process of passing from curriculum design to timetable construction. It was written in BASIC primarily for the RML 380Z with at least 32K memory and one single-sided mini-floppy disk drive. Versions are also available for the APPLE (by Peter Broome) and BBC Model B microcomputers. The program uses two well-known techniques for curriculum analysis. One is the method suggested by T. I. Davies in *School organization* which has been used widely since its publication in 1969, and subsequently has been further extended via the HMI COSMOS courses. The other is a closely related method used in ILEA which has been described in the booklet *Displaying the curriculum*, published in 1979. This method uses 'teacher-periods' instead of 'curriculum units' as the base unit, and is perhaps easier to interpret in the individual school. The program makes an evaluation of the manpower distribution using both methods. These techniques are normally used after completion of the timetable, but the program uses them in the planning mode to identify deficiencies or excesses in various parts of a designed curriculum.

Once a curriculum has been designed, it has to be expanded into teaching groups. At this stage the designers and other senior staff will not know whether the curriculum can be properly staffed by the available pool of teachers or whether, in finer detail, the subject specialist staff in each discipline can meet the demands of the curriculum. It is unusual at an early stage, to have a designed curriculum which exactly matches the staff input. Occasionally the staff has been underused, but more often the curriculum requires more teaching time than is available.

The curriculum designer is invited to input data concerning the number of pupils in each year group, the number of periods in a week and the full-time staff equivalent. This is followed by inputting data to a grid which shows the number of periods required by each year group in each specialist area of the curriculum. In addition, the number of periods which can be given by the specialist staff in each of these areas (once 'free' time has been removed) is required. Once entered this data can be corrected or amended and can be stored on disk for future use.

The analysis can be seen both on the VDU screen and on the printer. A typical output is shown in Figure 4.2. This might be circulated to senior staff and departmental heads for debate. From the total deficit of fifteen periods under the 'demand' column, it may be deduced that the designed curriculum cannot be staffed. A number of strategies now present themselves:

1 Get more staff
2 Ask whether some staff will teach more periods to fill the gap. The significance of the 'demand' contact ratio should not be missed here. If this rises too high (say beyond 0.82) then certain other difficulties might emerge, with scheduling staff or rooming the timetable, for example
3 Cut back on some courses. Again, watch the contact ratio
4 A combination of 2 and 3

If strategies 2, 3 or 4 are considered, then the statistics in the remaining analyses come into play. The bonus distribution, applied pupil–teacher ratio and average class size in each year group must be considered. In the example given, the 3rd and 4th years must be considered as prime targets for cut-back on account of the high bonuses employed. On the other hand, reasons not manifest in the data might be identified as a special case for retaining this provision. Decisions must be taken based on all the facts.

There are other matters in the example to which the Head might have to give attention. English is grossly understaffed; history is considerably overstaffed. If there are no staff changes then the historians will have to make a contribution elsewhere and English must be taught by non-specialists. Clearly if a historian resigns then an English teacher should be recruited as a replacement. There are other minor imbalances too, which the Director of Studies and his senior colleagues must resolve. As decisions are taken, the Director of Studies can call his data from disk and amend it accordingly, issuing new outputs as required. Eventually, when the timetable is constructed, the situation will be reached where the curriculum demands are in balance with manpower supply. Some users like the 'difference' column to be all zeros at this point, but unless teachers have been switched to genuine

```
CURRICULUM ANALYSIS FOR BLOGGSVILLE SCHOOL DATED 21/2/83
******************************** CURRENT DATA ********************************
```

```
-------------------------DEPT/YEAR DISTRIBUTION DATA--------------------
```

DEPT	YR1	YR2	YR3	YR4	YR5	YR6	YR7	SUPPLY	DEMAND	DIFF.
HEC	12	12	12	12	12	0	0	57	60	-3
CDT	8	8	12	18	18	2	4	73	70	3
ART	20	20	12	12	10	4	2	72	80	-8
MUS	10	10	4	2	2	2	2	33	32	1
DRA	4	4	4	4	2	0	0	16	18	-2
CAR	0	0	6	5	5	0	0	16	16	0
COM	0	0	0	10	10	4	0	20	24	-4
ECO	0	0	0	2	2	6	4	14	14	0
HIS	0	10	10	6	6	4	4	52	40	12
GEO	0	8	8	14	10	4	4	46	48	-2
SED	24	0	0	9	9	8	4	54	54	0
RE	0	10	10	7	7	4	3	43	41	2
ENG	24	24	24	27	27	14	8	132	148	-16
MLA	16	18	18	8	8	8	3	80	79	1
MAT	24	24	24	27	27	14	10	148	150	-2
SC	24	24	36	30	30	14	12	173	170	3
REM	29	18	18	12	12	0	0	95	89	6
PE	16	16	24	24	16	2	0	92	98	-6
TOTALS	211	206	222	229	213	90	60	1216	1231	-15

```
-------------------------------------------------------------------

-----------------------------MAIN DATA-----------------------------

PUPILS    YR1    YR2    YR3    YR4    YR5    YR6    YR7    TOTAL
ON ROLL   260    262    257    259    252    62     36     1388
FULL-TIME STAFF EQUIVALENT    = 76.5
NO. OF PERIODS PER WEEK       = 20

-------------------------------------------------------------------
```

second subjects I prefer the output to show pluses and minuses, as this indicates, to an extent, the amount of 'non-specialist' teaching taking place.

If the County requires a final 'curriculum analysis' then it can be reproduced directly from the final data on the printer. This program is designed to be used by a timetabler or Director of Studies to produce reports for the management team. A high order of keyboard skills is not required. The only knowledge required of the user concerning the computer, is how to load and run a program.

(ii) TTl-6 (Keith Johnson)
These programs complement the programs OPTl-6 described in Section 4.7(i), being the second set of six programs published in *Timetabling*. They have been made available for a range of microcomputers including the PET, RML 380Z, APPLE, BBC and TRS-80.

126

****************************** ANALYSIS RESULTS ******************************

```
                    DEMAND CONTACT RATIO = .804
                    TARGET CONTACT RATIO = .794
                    --------------------------
```

PUPIL/PERIOD ANALYSIS

YEAR	ROLL	FORM ENTRY	BASIC T.P.	ACTUAL T.P.	BONUS T.P.	BONUS AS % OF BASIC	P.T.R.
1	260	8.7	174	211	37	21.3	19.6
2	262	8.7	174	206	32	18.4	20.2
3	257	8.6	171	222	51	29.8	18.4
4	259	8.6	171	229	58	33.9	18
5	252	8.4	168	213	45	26.8	18.8
6TH	98	3.3	66	150	84	127.3	10.4
TOTAL	1388	46.3	926	1231	305	32.9	17.9

T.I.DAVIES/COSMOS STANDARD ANALYSIS

YEAR	PUPILS	BASIC UNITS	TEACHER PERIODS	CURRICULUM UNITS	BONUS	AVERAGE GROUP SIZE	STAFF USED	PUPIL TEACHER RATIO
	Z	$Z/3$	P	$Y=9P/W$	$Y-Z/3$	$9Z/Y$	$T=Y/9C$	$R=Z/T$
1	260	86.66	211	94.95	8.28	24.64	13.28	19.57
2	262	87.33	206	92.7	5.36	25.43	12.97	20.2
3	257	85.66	222	99.9	14.23	23.15	13.97	18.39
4	259	86.33	229	103.05	16.72	22.62	14.42	17.96
5	252	84	213	95.85	11.84	23.66	13.41	18.79
TOTAL	1290	430	1081	486.45	56.45	23.86	68.07	18.95
SIXTH FORM				$Y=$ 6.25P/W			$T=$ 5Z/Y Y/6.25C	
6	62	20.66	90	28.12	7.46	11.02	5.66	10.95
7	36	12	60	18.75	6.75	9.6	3.77	9.54
TOTAL	98	32.66	150	46.87	14.2	10.45	9.44	10.38

****

(C)PJB1982V3.0

Figure 4.2 Typical output from the program ANALYSIS.

Each of the six programs in this series is dependant of the others. Unlike many other suites these programs do not operate on any kind of common database and, indeed, none of them stores data in a file for future use. Each program operates on the data entered with a 'one-off' computation. This provides the timetabler with a printout of a great deal of useful information both for scheduling and for circulating the completed timetable.

TTI conducts a staff deployment analysis. The program requires data as follows:

1 The number of periods in the school week
2 The number of full-time equivalent staff
3 The number of teaching spaces available (optional)

4   The number of teachers required by the 6th Form (if there is one)
5   The number of pupils in each 'band', or other year group division, and the number of periods the group requires each week

The printout provides information on:

1   The contact ratio
2   The relative bonus for the curriculum
3   The rooming fraction
4   The staffing ratios
5   The distribution of curriculum bonuses (between year groups and across year groups)

These are accompanied by useful notes on how these figures may be interpreted. In addition, analyses are given for each group which show the way curriculum units and bonuses are distributed, together with average class sizes. The most recent version of TT1 prints an extra graph of relative bonuses which is particularly useful information for schools with falling rolls.

TT2 constructs and prints a 'combing chart'. For each department (or for the whole school) this program will evaluate whether the teaching allocation made to each teacher can be timetabled within the weekly time frame, given the teams within which teachers are requested to work and the way in which classes must be blocked. This is an essential pre-timetabling check.

TT3 constructs and prints a 'conflict matrix' for teacher teams in 4th and 5th, and possibly 6th Form option blocks. The matrix will show which teams have common members (intersect) and which are mutually exclusive (disjoint). Clearly only disjoint teams can be scheduled at the same time.

TT4 looks for ways to increase timetabling flexibility using 'Zarraga's rule'. This program compares teacher teams where teachers are 'in parallel' (e.g. in option pools) with classes where teachers are 'in series' (e.g. lower school classes which remain together for a considerable period). The information produced may indicate changes which will give increased scheduling flexibility.

TT5 operates as a timetable memory for use while scheduling. If teams of teachers are being inserted, the program will discover when all are free. It also offers a strategy to find the most useful periods to 'free' a teacher if there are no periods when the whole team is available. The information for each search is not filed so new data must be entered each time a problem requires investigation.

TT6 prints individual timetables for staff, classes and rooms when the scheduling is completed. There is no provision for data storage on disk or tape so data entry and printing must be accomplished in one run, and 32K memory is sufficient only for smaller schools.

4.10   Timetable scheduling and printing

Until recently it has not been possible to employ the power of the microcomputer in actually scheduling timetables. However, programs are now appearing which make a significant contribution in this field. An adequate description of progams for such a complex task demands much more space than can conveniently be allocated here. I can do little more than give a general indication of the potential of the programs and the facilities which they offer.

(i)   TT7, TT8 and TT9 (Keith Johnson)
This suite of three interrelated programs has been written in machine code for a 32K PET equipped with either cassette or disk for the storage of data files. The programs can be used alone but are best used side by side with a physical timetabling apparatus so that the machine can carry out at very high speed the tedious repetitive processing, and provide quickly a variety of information relevant to decisions which must be taken. Thus the timetabler is left free of minutiae to weigh judgement on the human factors.

The programs will cope with the following maximum entities:

80 forms/bands
120 teachers/specialist rooms
56 period week
10 day week

Classes can be indicated by four characters, but must be represented on the screen by a single symbol. Teachers are defined by a two character name. Rooms are less easily dealt with by the programs, although a tactic is defined to ensure that specialist rooms are not overloaded.

The programs have four modes of operation:

1   Semi-interactive – activities (or lessons) are entered in sets of up to nine at a time. These can be sorted into an order of difficulty and the program will find the 'best' possible position for the insertion of each.

2   Fully-interactive – all data currently entered for insertion (which may be the whole school or part of it) are examined to find the five tightest activities. These are then listed, with recommended positions for 'best' fit. After the timetabler has decided on a placement, the program looks to find the new five tightest activities and so on.

3   Semi-automatic – the program proceeds as in 2 but fits activities in order of difficulty without asking for a decision from the timetabler. It continues in this way until it finds an activity which cannot be fitted, whereupon it stops and asks the timetabler what can be done about this.

4   Fully-automatic – this proceeds as in 3 but if an activity cannot be fitted it is set aside and printed out for the timetabler's attention later. The whole timetable for a seven form entry school can be processed in this way in about three hours, thus offering the possibility of examining several different structures obtained by changing the curriculum or staffing of various groups.

The programs use a series of twelve commands which either provide information for the timetabler or conduct the various tasks.

Double, triple and quadruple periods can be handled and a technique called 'day-blocking' looks after the distribution of periods. For example, if one activity requires five single periods these will always be fitted into five separate days if possible. The timetabler can also call for information on the 'degrees of freedom' of several activities to seek out the order of difficulty for them before making an entry. Techniques are also described in the documentation which allow for pre-assignments, blocking of time for part-time staff, staggered lunch breaks, asymmetric days, and the constraints or flexibility offered by the 6th Form.

The 'steering' of the programs is determined to some extent by the order of data entry. In this the timetabler can be guided by:

1 Information on priority and degrees of freedom
2 The number of teacher periods involved in an activity
3 The conflict matrix from program TT3

The programs operate on three datafiles which are created sequentially as timetable compilation progresses. Scheduling can be stopped at any stage and the current status recorded. If files are kept on separate disks or tapes, the timetabler can backtrack to any stage for a new attempt.

At any stage the program can print out either staff timetables or class timetables. The documentation gives full details of the use of the programs, with examples. It is planned to add another program to the series – TT10 – which will accept the final timetable data to provide the various printouts which schools require.

(ii)   ROSTAR III (Paralax)

ROSTAR was originally written for timetabling in Dutch schools where it operated with some success before being modified for use in the UK. Originally written for APPLE II with 48K RAM, and the 16K RAM extension card, it will also run on the APPLE IIe. An eighty column card is a recommended extra which will be useful, although the program will run in forty column mode. Whichever microcomputer is used it will require two floppy disk drives, and a suitable printer. The Epson MX100 is recommended because it can handle wide paper.

ROSTAR is a comprehensive, fully interactive timetabling program. It has the added advantage that, using a special set of extra programs, it can also handle the option choices task for individual pupils and link the resulting database directly to the timetable.

The options section of ROSTAR is usually used before timetabling begins. In ROSTAR III the name given to options is 'clusters', so consequently the first program in this section is CLUSTER INPUT, with which pupils' names, sex and choices are entered. The program includes an editing routine by which any errors may be corrected, or changes made, while the process is viewed simultaneously on the screen. The option blocks are then arranged, on the basis of the choices, by a program called CLUSTER MAKER. This program has an automatic mode, although the process is interactive so that the timetabler can change the assignments of subjects to blocks as required when these are unsatisfactory. When the blocks have been completely settled they can be entered directly into the main timetable. It is this process which adds to ROSTAR's power as a timetabling tool, linking databases in two of the main MCBA tasks. Another important feature is that the data concerning the blocks can be filed for future use. This is particularly useful when the 4th Year becomes the 5th Year in the next timetable.

The timetabling suite has four main programs: CALC, FORMAT, INPUT and EDIT. CALC is a preliminary program which allows definition of the dimensions of the school in terms of the numbers of classes, teachers, rooms and subjects. It also sets up the files which will be needed to store all the information on disk.

FORMAT allows the timetabler to determine the layout of all the individual timetables, both on the screen and on the printer.

INPUT allows the characteristics of a particular school to be defined in a model. Under control of the program, codes are entered for classes, teachers subjects and rooms. 'Rooms' will include any lesson location such as the games field or pool. Using this data INPUT automatically makes up two other data files:

1 The lesson table specifies the number of lessons to be taken by each group of pupils in each subject on their curriculum. A 'group' can be assumed to mean any number of pupils from a class to a whole year group
2 The teacher table specifies the teacher's 'own' room and the maximum number of periods which can be worked each week. It also includes the teacher's full name to match against his 'code'

Having specified the model of the school, the EDIT program takes over. This shows on the screen the timetables of the particular class, teacher and room being worked on at any time. The timetabler can move through the timetables entering or deleting lessons as required. All entries are checked for consistency as they are made. This is particularly useful for pre-blocking certain lessons. In the auto-select mode EDIT fills in the timetable for a whole class and assigns teachers and rooms as appropriate. However, even in this mode the timetabler always has the option of choosing different teachers or rooms, or altering the placing of the lesson within the week.

When all its scheduling work is done ROSTAR offers a variety of printouts, including:

1 Class, teacher and room codes as created by INPUT
2 An individual timetable for every class, teacher and room
3 A list of pupils' option choices
4 A list of the subjects chosen in each option block showing the numbers of pupils choosing each subject
5 A list of the names of pupils choosing each subject
6 A master timetable for the whole school indexed by class, teacher or room

The number of entities (rooms, teachers, classes) which ROSTAR III can handle will be determined by the CALC program according to the memory capacity of the particular version of the APPLE involved, so it is difficult to specify limits for the size of school which might be timetabled. However, it appears that a 64K APPLE will be able to deal with a maximum 125 each of teachers, classes and rooms, and twenty-nine subjects.

The introduction of ROSTAR into the UK has been beset with difficulties and frustrations since it was first advertised by a company called Pegasus in early 1982. In particular, the long awaited version for the RML 380Z has still not materialized. However, those who have used or seen ROSTAR in the UK are extremely enthusiastic about it. Potentially it is one of the most powerful programs presently available for timetabling on a microcomputer, but a great deal more experience of it in real, practical use will be required before these powers can be fully assessed.

(iii) T/TABLE (Timetable Systems)

T/TABLE is a suite of three programs written in BASIC Version 5 for the RML 380Z with twin mini-floppy disk systems, together with a number of smaller 'satellite' programs. Basically the programs deal with three phases of timetabling – construction, rooming and printing. Pre-planning is not included and the manual makes it clear that such pre-planning as the timetabler feels necessary should be undertaken before use of the programs begins. The suite is not menu driven. However, on account of the sequential nature of the operations a good deal of automation is provided in terms of the loading of the various main and sub-programs and the filing and reading of data to and from disk. Data can be filed at any stage of the process for future reference. The timetabler is also left to decide upon the order of scheduling and there are some useful sequences which provide information quickly, allow rapid scheduling and check data for consistency. This allows the timetabler to exercise judgement to a greater extent than is possible using manual methods.

The preparation of data requires only the codes for teaching staff (two or three characters) and the same information about 'linear groups'. Linear groups are defined as classes which remain together as a unit for a substantial part of the timetable cycle, although taught by different teachers, such as lower school mixed ability groups.

Scheduling lessons involves the use of thirteen single letter commands. Collectively these commands allow:

1 Data to be amended
2 Information on the current status of the timetable to be displayed
3 Information about the availability of a teacher or groups of teachers to be sought
4 Definition of a linear group teacher team
5 Allocation of activities by the timetabler
6 Solutions to difficult allocations to be sought

7 Data to be filed

It is possible to pre-allocate and 'lock-in' certain activities and all data and activity allocations are checked for consistency on entry.

When scheduling is complete, the next program is automatically loaded so that the timetable may be 'roomed-up'. This program will deal with up to 100 rooms each displayed by two or three characters. Teachers can be assigned a special room, or a series of up to five rooms in order of priority. The program then allocates rooms to the various teachers according to this input. Eighty per cent or more of the timetabled lessons will have rooms allocated to them in a fraction of a second. Another program then handles the examination and modification of the room timetables created at this stage, and completes the process. This program has ten commands, six of which are in common with those used on the allocation stage of the suite. The remaining four allow:

1 Allocation of a room to an already timetabled lesson at one or more specified periods
2 Removal of a room previously allocated to a lesson at one or more specified periods
3 Listing of unallocated rooms at a specified period or for the whole timetable period
4 Loading of the timetable printing program

The timetable printing program prints the completed timetable from the final data file. Apart from some latitude with the paging, timetables are printed in a fixed format. The following timetables can be printed:

1 The staff timetable
2 The room timetable
3 A year timetable
4 Individual teacher timetables
5 Individual linear group timetables
6 Individual room timetables
7 A timetable of available rooms

(iv) TTX (Peter Andrews)

TTX (and its slightly less powerful ancestor – TT) is a program to assist the construction of the school timetable using the RML 380Z. The author assumes that actual construction will take place on some form of traditional physical apparatus. The microcomputer is used to maintain a copy of the timetable as it is constructed and to check the consistency of data. If an entry conflicts with data previously entered, information about the clash is displayed. The program has a number of extra facilities such as the ability to allocate rooms automatically and to prepare and print invigilation timetables during examinations. Also, it allows the user to define a format for the output suitable for individual schools.

Versions of TTX are available for use with both disk and cassette on the

380Z. The program is written in machine code and is exceptionally fast in the way in which it handles everything from data input to screen and printer output. The limits of the program are largely dictated by the amount of memory available. A school of eighty staff, sixty forms, seventy rooms and thirty subjects will just fit into a 32K system. The maximum number of staff, forms, rooms and subjects is 125 in each case, given sufficient memory. The basic display is for an eight period day with a five or six day week. However, the program will happily cope with any number of lessons up to eight. I know of at least one school which uses the program for a ten day week by making two separate files of data.

After entry of the basic lists of 'fixed' data – the codes for forms, staff, rooms and subjects – the program moves to its main entry phase. In this mode, sections of the staff or form timetables, or an individual teacher's timetable for the whole week, can be displayed on the screen. The timetabler may move rapidly from one to another by issuing the appropriate two character command. Activities are entered simply by typing the day/period, staff code, room code and subject code separated by spaces in any order and pressing RETURN. Such entries are displayed in the bottom six lines of the screen. Inconsistencies are immediately checked and the screen display updated. Data entry can be speedy as various options are available for compressing the inputs. The normal keyboard skills are of no great advantage. It is likely that secretarial assistance will not be required.

An automatic procedure can be called to allocate rooms to the completed schedule. This will allocate fixed rooms to those staff identified as having them. On a second scan through the staff, it identifies all those left without a room and provides sufficient information for the timetabler to select one.

Twenty-five simple commands allow the timetabler to conduct a number of tasks. Most important among these are:

1 Listing the empty rooms for the currently stated or next period
2 Listing the free staff for the currently stated period
3 Writing the current data onto disk or cassette
4 Amending or adding to the 'fixed' data
5 Counting the periods allocated to each teacher
6 Printing the various timetables

The standard printouts of Form, Staff, Room and Individual staff timetables will be adequate for the school where each of these entities can be identified by a two character code. Restriction in this way allows the printout to be made on any reasonably fast eighty column printer. However, two character identification codes are insufficient for many large schools and TTX acknowledges this by providing facilities for the school to format its own output. This is achieved by writing programs in BASIC using a specially adapted BASIC Version 5. Instructions on how to make this adaptation are given in detail in the TTX manual. Within reason schools using this system should be able to produce their timetables on the printer in exactly the same way as those previously produced by typewriter or written by hand.

Another useful facility provided by TTX allows for the timetable to be modified during school examinations. The entries for those classes taking examinations are deleted and alternative entries made to indicate the examination room and member of staff responsible for invigilation. These entries are checked in the same way as normal timetable entries. Printed individual staff timetables will now show both their normal teaching duties and examination invigilation.

One advantage of storing timetables electronically is that they can easily be updated. It is not unusual for a considerable number of amendments to be made when the timetable gets under way in September. Heads of Department can have second thoughts about both teacher and room allocation to various classes. Such amendments can easily be made using TTX. Even where a teacher changes during the course of a year the name can be changed throughout the timetable virtually at a stroke. An updated printed version of the timetable can easily be produced either for key personnel or for all staff as is required.

TTX is a program aimed at the timetabler. It is well documented but some familiarity with the 380Z is assumed, and a working knowledge of RML BASIC will be required to produce programs which will format the printed timetable to the school's own specification.

4.11   Cover for absent staff

Of all the tasks which Deputy Heads have to undertake, the one which is most regular, onerous and arouses greatest suspicion is arranging the cover for the classes of absent colleagues. Most computer programs used for the task seek to ensure that the arrangements made are scrupulously fair. The record keeping necessary to make this so is painlessly undertaken and all necessary lists are quickly produced by the printer. I include one such offering here as an example.

STAFF ABSENCE COVER (Alan Dean)
This program is written in BASIC for the PET 3032 or 4032, with 4040 disk drive and a CBM printer. As with any stand-alone program like this, data for the full staff timetable must be entered into file first. Once entered, this data will remain good until the timetable is changed, although amendments may be made at any time. A school timetable can be printed from this data if required.

The program is designed for use by the teacher with responsiblity for organizing the cover. However, if this person is not able to visit the microcomputer each morning, the task can be undertaken by passing a completed datasheet to a suitable operator, who simply has to enter the data and return the appropriate lists.

The process of arranging cover for a particular day can begin as soon as there is enough data to hand – perhaps the afternoon before. As long as the appropriate date is entered, the microcomputer will file the data for that particular day. More cover can be arranged by running extra data for the day on the microcomputer at any time, and the files of information are thereupon updated. However, once a particular day's operation has been concluded, that file can be erased, keeping only the cumulative totals for each member of staff for future reference.

The program has features which deal with most of the vagaries of the task. For example:

1 Restrictions on use can be placed on staff who are not available for cover, even though they are free
2 Absent teachers are assumed to be unavailable
3 Supply teacher cover can be input
4 Absence for any part of a day can be covered
5 Other events, like examinations, can have cover arranged for them

The monitoring and control phase of the program is complex, but it uses six different factors to decide on the best substitute teacher for any lesson. The parameters which control these factors can be changed by the user to suit any given school's situation. In addition to sharing the burden 'equally' as determined by the six factors, some 'fine tuning' routines are available which:

1 Avoid over use of part-time teachers
2 Give temporary respite to a less-than-fit colleague
3 Ensure that staff are only used more than once a day in exceptional circumstances

When evaluation of the substitutions is complete, personal slips and noticeboard copies are printed for distribution. The printer will also provide a summary of the way teachers have been used over a period of operation as a check on the fairness of the system.

4.12 Timetabling parents' evenings

This is another scheduling problem to which some programmers have given attention. In order to avoid unseemly queues and frustration as large numbers of parents all try to see a few teachers at the same time, many schools have turned to the organized timetable as a solution. If this is to be produced centrally, then a large amount of data will need to be processed. A computer program such as that described here may provide the answer.

PARENTS' EVENING SCHEDULING (Tony Thornley)
This program is written in BASIC for the APPLE II Plus (32K version) with a mini-floppy disk drive (DOS 3.3) and a printer. It can be used by untrained staff, although familiarity with the microcomputer will help. For data entry with

```
            2.    PRINT PARENT DATA


                    BLOGGSVILLE
                    SCHOOL
            Parents Evening   4.10.83
            *************************
(1)
S Bristow    1A
Your appointments are :

            0600    MR SALTER    Physics
            0610    MR APPLETON   English
            0620    MR BURGESS   History
            0630    MR HEPPELL    Geography
            0650    MR PARRY    Mathematics
            0710    MR BLACKMAN    Games
            0720    MR BLACK     Art
```

Please note that appointments are for five minutes only. This is
to allow as many people as possible to see each member of staff.
Please bring your child's report with you.

```
            1.    PRINT STAFF DATA


                    BLOGGSVILLE
                    SCHOOL
            Parents Evening 4.10.83
            *************************
(3)
                    MR BURGESS       History

0600   A Smythe   1A              0635   M Titcombe   1A
0605                              0640
0610   H Wilson   1C              0645   J Hunt   1B
0615                              0650   M Hobbs   1C
0620   S Bristow 1A              0655
0625                              0700   J Taylor 1A
0630   G Hall   1B                0705   D Exell 1B
```

Figure 4.3 Typical example of both types of output from the Parents' Evening
Scheduling program.

a large number of pupils, the assistance of a secretary would certainly be useful.

The program operates on two main datafiles, one containing the staff data
and the other the parent data. Once set up, the staff datafile can be kept, with
minor amendments, for use throughout the year, but a new parent datafile must
be created for each parents' evening. Alternatively, some time can be saved by
reading pupil's names from a pupil database, and adding times and staff

137

information to this. It is possible to vary the length of the appointment time and to set the times of the earliest and latest appointments possible. In addition, this data can be amended for individual staff, and rooms and subjects can be added to the staff data if required.

Each pupil takes home a standard reply slip for her parents to complete. This shows her name, tutor group, the times when her parents can come, and the names of the staff they wish to see. When returned, the details on these slips have to be entered into the microcomputer. When this is accomplished check lists can be printed showing the requirements of each pupil and the number of parents who wish to see each member of staff. If any member of staff has more than the maximum possible number of appointments at this stage, the names of the pupils will be printed out so that the list can be cut down to a reasonable length. It is also possible for staff to add the names of parents who they wish to see, or request double time appointments.

On its first run the program sorts the data and informs the operator of any obvious problems – for example where a member of staff is not available when a parent wishes to see him. Some problems can be resolved at this stage. If so, the necessary changes can be made before the final run. It is on this run that the schedule program arranges the appointments. Some problems may still be encountered, and these can be indicated both on the screen and on the printer. Once again, the user has the option of making his own adjustments to the final appointments list.

Finally, the timetables are printed. The first type gives notification to the parents of the appointment times showing teacher, subject and rooms as appropriate. There is also a facility for useful additional messages to be printed. The second type is for staff showing the times at which the various parents are expected. A staff comment sheet can be printed out for each pupil, which staff may use to make important memos during the discussions.

The scheduling is accomplished by sorting both staff and parents into priority order. In the staff's case this is by the number of free time blocks they will have on the completed schedule. For parents it is firstly by the length of time they have available (shorter time, higher priority) and then according to the total loading of the members of staff they wish to see.

In practice, the program is said to produce far better schedules than can be achieved either manually, or by allowing children to arrange their own appointments. As the program puts parents before staff, parent satisfaction is likely to be high. Staff usually find their timetables reasonable.

4.13 Wordprocessing

A chapter the length of this one could be written on wordprocessing software alone. A recent survey of professional programs for microcomputers identified almost forty programs for this task ranging in price from £50 – £700. One thing is certain, no-one will ever convince me that this is an area where a school can produce its own software in preference to the purchase of a professional system.

There will be some limitations imposed by the hardware you wish to use and the price you are able to pay, but there is almost certain to be a program which will suit you. Before you choose, it is vital so see a system working. No dealer is likely to let you take a program away 'on approval'. The copying risks are far too great. However, you should be able to see a system in operation in a local dealer's showroom, or even better, in a neighbouring school. Given the immensity of the task, I shall confine myself to remarks on the general functions you might expect to find in any wordprocessing program, and brief comments on some programs for microcomputers commonly in use for school administration.

Wordprocessing enables the typing of text into the microcomputer's memory and eventually to permanent storage on magnetic media, commonly a mini-floppy disk. Although permanent storage can be made on cassette, I don't consider this a suitable medium for use in the school office. When text is being typed in it should be displayed on the VDU, preferably in the format in which it will eventually be printed. Displays which have only forty characters across the screen are unsuitable for this task and any system worth its salt will use an eighty character width. A good system will also have a facility called 'automatic word wrap' which means that a carriage return is unnecessary at the end of a line. Any word that stretches beyond the fixed right margin is automatically transferred to the next line. Some programs automatically 'right justify' the remaining words on the line – spreading them out so that the right margin on the page appears straight down the edge of the text.

As far as margins, tabs and page lengths are concerned, these should be adjustable both before text is inserted and while insertion is proceeding. A good program should always allow reformatting of text to different margins and line spacings. The best programs allow the user to see this on the screen. Less useful are those which allow this reformatting only when text is finally sent to the printer by means of commands 'embedded' in the text.

In order to edit text, the program must allow a cursor to be moved quickly to various parts of a document so that at any point text can be deleted, inserted or corrected. The speed at which a cursor can be moved about the text file is important for efficiency of use. A more sophisticated feature of editing is the 'block move'. With this feature whole portions of text can be marked to be copied or moved to another point within the document. Another useful feature is 'search and replace'. This automatically seeks out one character, a word or some text throughout the document and replaces it with another – useful if you want to replace one name by another or seek out a word which may have been misspelt many times in a document. Some programs actually have a spelling checker which will scan the text for you and stop at or list all the spellings it does not recognize. The recognized words will be contained in a dictionary which might be anything between 10 000 and 90 000 words long. Some of these dictionaries can be custom compiled to allow for your own special requirements. This spelling check is usually run as a separate routine after the text has been completed. Some of the words identified may just be obscure words, but others will be genuine mistakes quickly recognized for correction.

Some programs have a facility for 'list processing'. This is the ability to read data from a list and place it in identified spaces within a document – for example, names and addresses in an invitation letter to governors or parents. This facility is useful for compiling pupils' reports and testimonials.

An important feature, which is not always easy to identify in a demonstration, is the way in which the program stores long documents. Some programs demand that when the computer's memory is full, all this portion of the text is filed on disk. This can be annoying in long documents if the memory is only sufficient for three or four pages of A4. Although provision is usually made for linking the files together for printing, it is much more difficult to move text about and to see the structure of the finished document without printing it. Far better are those programs which move text automatically to disk as the memory fills, thus keeping the document as one long file. This is known as 'continuous processing', and such programs are much easier for secretaries to use, provided that they are able to keep an eye on the disk space available.

Many wordprocessing programs will only run on specific makes of microcomputers. I give a brief selection for the most popular microcomputers here with some indication of how the program differs from the norms previously described.

RML 380Z

(i) WordStar I consider that this is the best program for wordprocessing on the 380Z. It can be purchased direct from RML's software department at a very reasonable price and has all the features necessary for efficient and effective office wordprocessing. It is available for a great many microcomputers which use the Z80 chip and CP/M disk operating system, and has been described as the 'industry standard' wordprocessing package. Your 380Z will need to be equipped with the Varitext 40/80 board (COS 4) and at least 48K RAM (preferably 56K) to run this program.

A bonus with WordStar is its ability to display a great many instructions on the screen to aid the typist, even when text is being typed in. This avoids the need for continual reference to the lengthy manual. When the typist is familiar with the commands these displays can be switched off.

WordStar files text continually on disk. Files must be no longer than half the remaining disk space, so one long file should occupy only half a disk to leave space for editing. This will give a limit of twelve to fourteen pages of A4 single-spaced text on a mini-floppy disk. Used properly, a double-sided mini-floppy disk system will allow space for up to forty pages of A4 text to be prepared and edited. By moving files, up to fifty-six A4 pages could be kept on a double-sided disk for long term storage. In order to do 'list processing' you will have to purchase an extra program called MailMerge to use with WordStar. Likewise, to check spelling you will have to buy SpellStar.

WordStar is so popular in the commercial world that there are plenty of training manuals and training courses available, some with accompanying audio cassette and disk exercises. *WordStar made easy* by W. A. Ettlin is a very useful primer.

There will possibly be training courses available for secretaries at FE Colleges in your area. Private 'on-site' courses are sometimes offered. One possible source making a special offer for schools is given in Appendix 2.

A package by Phil Neal exploits the powers of WordStar with MailMerge to produce pupils' reports and testimonials quickly. Basically, standard paragraphs are drawn from files and formatted to provide personalized documents. It is reported that in trials teachers were able to produce thirty very detailed subject reports in about twenty minutes. The information for about 1200 reports can be entered into the computer in one day. The package contains a pamphlet explaining the system, and disks which have files with suggested comments for testimonials and reports. Further details are included in Appendix 1.

(ii) TXED RML's own text editor is one alternative to WordStar for wordprocessing on the 380Z. In concept TXED seems to have been designed with computer program editing primarily in mind. However, it does have many of the features of a wordprocessor and certainly has some devotees among 380Z users.

TXED has two immediate advantages over WordStar. It is considerably cheaper and will work on the forty character by twenty-four line standard RML screen. However, it is much more satisfactory to use it on the eighty character screen. Although TXED will change the format of text from the style used when it was typed in, it does not show this change on the screen in the same way as WordStar, and in any reformatting the complete document must be processed. This can cause frustrating delays. All the standard features of a wordprocessor are available within the program, including continuous processing of files larger than the available RAM, and list processing, for which you have to pay extra with WordStar. With care, TXED will allow the continuous processing of documents with up to 70 000 characters, or almost thirty pages of A4.

Unfortunately, most users do not find TXED very 'friendly'. It takes a great deal of effort in learning to use, although it helps if the student is familiar with the 380Z. There are no simple training manuals readily available either, and it is unlikely that a school secretary will fully master TXED for office use without a great deal of personal instruction. However, it is half the price of WordStar, and many schools may have been provided with it as standard software. If the choice lies between WordStar and TXED schools will be forced to balance the expense of installing the former against the difficulties of training and use which the latter presents.

(iii) Magic Wand This is another competitor to WordStar for wordprocessing on any microcomputer with the CP/M disk operating system, but you may have difficulty in getting a version suitable for the 380Z. It is rated as 'friendlier' and considerably easier to use than WordStar. It has all the usual editing and formatting facilities, some of which are more powerful than WordStar's. It also incorporates a 'list processing' facility inclusive within the price of the program.

However, there are some disadvantages with Magic Wand. The text editor and text formatter are two separate programs, and you can't see exactly how your text will look until the formatter has printed it. Magic Wand does not file an overlong document to disk. The longest document it will hold depends on the available RAM. You are warned in advance if this is nearly full and all the text must then be filed to disk. However, since less memory is taken by the Magic Wand program, the files created in long documents may not be much shorter in length than those of WordStar. The documentation with Magic Wand is excellent, with lessons to take you through its facilities in easy steps.

CBM PET

(i) Wordpro Earlier versions of Wordpro were written for the 3000 or 4000 series PETS. I don't consider forty column machines suitable for office wordprocessing but Wordpro 4 plus is written for the 8000 series and offers most of the features of a standard office machine.

Wordpro requires a ROM to be inserted in one of the spare PET sockets. This is merely a security device to protect the program, since it comes on a disk which will only run on a machine fitted with the necessary ROM. This is a useful way to stop you giving copies of the program away, but could prove a problem if your ROM machine doesn't function when you need it and you don't have your second machine equipped.

This program has all the usual facilities and, like WordStar, is an all-in-one package. However, it has one disadvantage in screen presentation – it does not have automatic word wrap, and words are split where they end at the margin on the screen. Wordpro does not file automatically to disk either, and its memory can only hold 350 lines of text (just under nine pages of A4). When full this memory must be filed to disk. However, these short files can be linked automatically for printing and in this way over fifty A4 pages might be printed continuously. Although the final format of text is not evident on the screen when entered to memory, Wordpro has a facility to print text to the screen, instead of the printer for examination in this way.

Wordpro's editing and formatting are both straightforward with few frills. It is rated as easy to use and learn.

(ii) Superscript This is a very similar program to Wordpro, but can usually be bought much more cheaply. Like Wordpro it does not have automatic word wrap. It also uses the idea of linking short files together to compose long documents, with the facility to print the final document in its formatted form to the screen for checking. Superscript's files, however, can be somewhat longer than Wordpro's and this means that it is much easier to move around large blocks of text within a long document. In general, Superscript's methods of moving blocks of text are superior to Wordpro's. However, Wordpro is superior in its list processing techniques, which you might wish to use for pupils' testimonials or reports.

APPLE
For use as an office wordprocessor, the APPLE will need to be equipped with an eighty column display board. The addition of a Z80 card will allow the CP/M

disk operating system to run. In this case WordStar can be used on APPLE if sufficient memory is available.

(i) Format-80 Aside from WordStar this is one of the more expensive and full-feature wordprocessing programs for the APPLE. It includes a list processing facility which will allow different names held in a file to be printed in successive documents.

One limitation of Format-80 is its file size. Each file can only hold about 900 words, so long documents have to be split up into a large number of files. However, these files can be numbered sequentially for use with printing and search and replace facilities. A disk will hold up to seventeen of these files.

Format-80 is very suitable for general office use in wordprocessing. It is quite user friendly, and relatively easy to learn how to use.

TRS-80

The Tandy organization markets a wordprocessing program for its own microcomputers. This program is called SCRIPSIT, and whatever model of the TRS-80 you have, there is a version of SCRIPSIT to suit you. SCRIPSIT has all the features of wordprocessor programs which might cost twice as much or more, including automatic word wrap, search and replace, and a list processing facility. Even the problem of the fourteen lines by sixty-four character screen is overcome by using the screen as a 'window' to view lines up to 132 characters wide and pages up to ninety lines long.

SCRIPSIT is one of the easiest programs to see in operation and learn to use. Any Tandy Computer Centre will be pleased to let you see it and use it. Some even offer useful training courses for schools.

BBC microcomputer

Software has been slow arriving since this microcomputer was introduced, and wordprocessing programs have been no exception. However, quite recently two programs have been introduced. Both differ in one significant way from others described in this section in that they are provided on a ROM chip which can be inserted into one of the spare sockets on the printed circuit board of the BBC Model B microcomputer, either by the user or a dealer.

(i) Wordwise Wordwise operates in two modes – the 'menu' mode and the 'edit' mode. The edit mode is used for typing text into memory. Word wrap is automatic and the nine red function keys on the microcomputer are assigned special tasks in connection with text editing. The menu mode deals, for the most part, with saving or loading text from disk or cassette, but a search and replace facility is also included here. It is possible to view the formatted text on the screen before printing, in either forty or eighty column mode, depending on the amount of RAM left available.

The two major limitations with Wordwise are that it cannot carry out either 'list processing' or 'continuous processing'. The longest document it can handle is about 4000 words – roughly seven pages of A4 text. Of course, it is possible to produce longer documents by instalments.

Wordwise is one of the few wordprocessors to make use of colour with a colour monitor, in such a way as to enhance still further the ease with which most users find they can operate this package.

(ii) View Acorn, the makers of the BBC microcomputer, have introduced View as their own offering in the wordprocessing field.

View has all the facilities one would expect to find in a wordprocessing package, including automatic word wrap, search and replace, block text movement and on-screen formatting. Here again, the red keys are made to fulfil specific functions, but by devious means no fewer than twenty-nine different tasks can be carried out. Like Wordwise, View also operates in two modes – the 'command' mode and the 'text' mode. There is no menu, and most operations take place in the text mode where editing and formatting are viewed as they happen on the screen.

The size of document which can be held in memory depends on the amount of RAM available. Because of the way in which the BBC microcomputer controls its screen display, View can work with several variations between forty characters by twenty-five lines and eighty characters by thirty-two lines. In the forty by twenty-five mode, 25K will be available, enough for, say, a dozen pages of A4. In the eighty by thirty-two mode only 5K RAM will be left – a distinct limitation unless disks are used. With disks this is no problem since 'continuous processing' is allowed, with text being transferred to a single file on disk. This file is limited to half the available disk space – 50K on the cheaper disk drives – a massive 100K, or roughly 175 pages of A4, on the high density system. This should be quite adequate for most school documents.

The View program has many useful facilities, including a type of 'list processing', and its only minor disadvantage would appear to be that it needs an extra program, supplied at extra cost on cassette or disk, to make use of any special printer facilities such as underlining or bold typing.

The consensus of opinion among users familiar with both Wordwise and View seems to be that the former is the easier to use, and thus is the best package of the two for teaching wordprocessing in the commerce department. However, View has the greater number of features likely to be required for office work and is more suitable for use in school administration. Where the BBC microcomputer is chosen for both administration and teaching purposes, it would seem to be bad practice to have different wordprocessors in action. For the sake of compatibility and hardware back-up a choice might have to be made between the two programs.

4.14 Accounts

Accounts packages seem to be divided between those devised to help teachers control the 'capitation' or 'school fund' type of accounts, and very much more sophisticated packages designed for the world of business and commerce. The cost and complexity of the latter will probably confine their use to the bursar's office of the non-maintained sector for the time being. Very few of the former type of programs are publicly available, and currently I can only draw attention to two for RML 380Z.

(i) ACCOUNTS (Eric Vincent)
This suite requires a 380Z equipped with at least 47K memory and twin mini-floppy disk drives. The suite handles either a single account – say the school capitation as a whole – or a number of accounts, such as those sums of money allocated to individual departments.

Commands within the suite allow data files (or accounts) to be created, opened and amended as necessary. Transactions are then entered and each account is kept up to date automatically. Accounts can be displayed on the screen or printed as required. These can be by department or show an overall statement of balances, for all departments and for the accounts as a whole.

The suite is written in Microsoft compiled BASIC, which makes it extremely fast in operation. However, the appropriate 'systems' software (a Microsoft 'run-time compiler') will be necessary before it can be run on the 380Z.

(ii) The Lakes accounts suite (Alex Redhead)
This suite is also written for the RML 380Z, with twin mini-floppy disks and at least 47K memory. It is written in BASIC Version 5.

The suite operates using a file of orders placed, with estimated cost included, if required. A series of transaction files are created when an invoice is received for payment. The accounts are made up by departments, and there is provision, too, for utilities such as fuel, telephone, PTA, and so on, to be included.

The system provides for:

1   Entry of estimates
2   A printout of the estimate file
3   The entry of transactions
4   A printout of transactions
5   Correction of estimates and payments
6   A printout of account statements
7   The carrying forward of balances to a new file of accounts
8   An analysis of spending (e.g. on books, equipment, etc.)

It is estimated that between one and two hours per week will be necessary for data entry to keep the accounts up to date. After that the routines will look after the remaining account keeping business on their own.

4.15   Library applications

The first public demonstration of SIR (schools information retrieval) was given during early 1983. SIR is a general purpose database management system developed by the British Library Research and Development Department with use in school libraries particularly in mind. It is reported, on the basis of trials in six schools, to be a powerful system with facilities for the construction of various databases which can be searched by random access techniques. One of the problems with general database management systems is that they can be quite difficult to use effectively without considerable training. However, SIR has been designed for 'hands-on' use by pupils in the school library, not only to retrieve information about books but also to learn the skills of information technology generally. SIR will be available during the course of 1983 for both RML 380Z and the BBC micro with twin-disk systems at a reported cost of about £60. At this price SIR could find some uses in general administration as well as in the school library.

4.16 Stock control

Some schools have adapted general database management systems for the purpose of stock and resources control, but the maintenance of the database in a rapidly changing situation, as is found with central stationery control, can be rather time consuming and tedious, and possibly less efficient than a manual system. A specifically dedicated program might improve the situation but, unhappily, I have nothing to report. It would seem that those with working programs are insufficiently confident to release them just yet. As with everything else in the world of microcomputers, no doubt the situation will change very shortly.

5 A practical guide for individual schools

or 'How will we get there?' (Part 3)

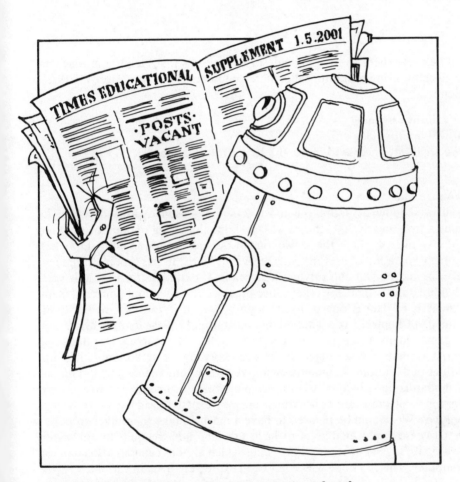

'Required for September – microcomputer to undertake
curriculum development and timetabling. Scale 4
allowance available. Apply via data post to . . . '

A practical guide for individual schools

Before ever starting to introduce MCBA you must have a clear idea of precisely why you want to do it. If you fail to do this you will never have any yardstick against which to judge progress or, indeed, be able to evaluate whether you have made any gains at all. I suppose this is true of any changes we want to make in schools. Nevertheless, we are often neglectful about setting out our precise objectives. With the introduction of MCBA it is actually very much easier than with almost any other innovation you may wish to make. So don't lose this opportunity to apply management by objectives.

5.1 Reasons for beginning MCBA

It will be useful here to look at some of the reasons that Heads and teachers have given for using computers and microcomputers in this way. Here are three of them:

1 It will save us time
2 It will improve our efficiency
3 We shall have access to more and better information

1 To save time

Beyond a shadow of doubt the most common reason expressed to me in responses from nearly 300 schools was the hope that using the microcomputer would save time. Perhaps this is why one of the most common initial tasks has been the preparation of lists and rolls of various kinds. In this task pupils names have to be rearranged and retyped many times. A computer can do this very much more quickly than any other office process. The collation, rearrangement and analysis of data is one of its strengths. In fact, if you look at the tasks examined in Chapter 2, you will find that most would appear to offer significant time gains. Many teachers and secretaries felt that the computer had the potential to remove the drudgery from their everyday tasks. Accumulating vast quantities of data from documents such as registers, totalling long lists of marks and standardizing individual scores, retyping long documents just to add one paragraph – all these are tasks which are not exactly designed to enliven a school day. We should be pleased to have a machine take these over from us. Such a release might enable us to have the time and freedom to apply our professional judgement to those problems which are not capable of resolution by computer. This is a hope which has been expressed to me in various ways by many Heads and teachers. Certainly those who identified themselves as 'classroom teachers' hoped that it would release 'administrators' more often for classroom duties. If saving time is to be your prime objective, then state it clearly. But be prepared to measure the time carefully, for you may be surprised to find that you do not save a significant amount of time at all. At the very least a considerable investment of time might be necessary before any can be saved.

2 Improving efficiency

The second most important objective stated by those using MCBA is to 'improve efficiency'. At first sight this is the same as 'saving time', but further consideration often reveals it to be subtly different. In the school office it could mean the ability to undertake more tasks for teachers as opposed to administrators. The former would then be able to undertake their teaching and pastoral roles more effectively. In one school, for example, it is reckoned that the school office can do more typing and duplication work for teachers as a result of the computer undertaking some routine tasks. In another, it has meant that teachers are relieved of the task of sorting out timetable problems for pupils, as a result of the way timetable data is printed by the microcomputer. In yet another, parents are able to understand their children's reports much more easily because of the uniformity of presentation of the data on the report slip. All these are examples of improved efficiency, yet not all can be equated with time saving. Indeed, in some cases the improved efficiency is only bought by spending extra time. The judgement as to whether the improvement is worthwhile is difficult to make objectively. But time is valuable, and the judgement must be made. Here is a case where the opinions of all those involved will be useful in an assessment. These opinions will probably have to be sought by a senior member of staff who has an overall view of the exercise, yet can judge dispassionately. It may be that no-one less than the Head Teacher can do this.

3 Improving the quality of information

The third objective is not nearly so often given as the preceding two. This is to gain access to more accurate and effective information. It seems to me that this is an objective which has much greater priority in the industrial and commercial use of computers. Figures on production, sales and cash flow are vital information for managers who have to make critical decisions. To these people, the techniques of database management and interrogation, and mathematical modelling used to explore potential outcomes of plans and policies, are much more important than the purely clerical function of the computer. This is an area which we have barely begun to appreciate in school management, and one which emphasizes the difference between our 'managerial' and 'administrative' functions which I discussed in Chapter 1. The problem is that few mathematical models have been developed at school level to use as vehicles for the technique. In Section 2.4 this problem is discussed in relation to models proposed both by T. I. Davies (1969) and by B. Wilcox and P. Eustace (1980). In Section 4.9 I have shown one way in which such models might be exploited.

The use of better and more accurate information does not just apply to the curriculum designer or senior manager. In one school which I know, the change was made recently from a manual system of examination administration to one based on a microcomputer. In the old system, because of the methods used, teachers were not aware of the total examination load being carried by their candidates. In consequence it was not uncommon for some candidates to be carrying far too many 'double entries' for comfort. With the computer system a list was published at an early stage showing entries for each candidate. Form Tutors, who had not been part of the old system, quickly picked out members of their tutor group who seemed overburdened and opened a debate which soon involved parents in rationalizing decisions. Here is clear example of the reorganization and circulation of information being used to the benefit of pupils and teachers.

There must be other areas where such information would prove useful. These are a few which have been considered in some schools:

(i)   planning for, and keeping track of, capitation spending
(ii)   monitoring patterns of absence to combat truancy
(iii) monitoring test results to combat underachievement
(iv)   checking the 'quality' of successive annual pupil intakes to assess the nature of remedial or other curriculum provision which might be necessary

Having said all that, let us guard against going too far. I should hate to see that terrible '1984' when a Form Tutor is called to the Head's study to be told: 'The computer predicts an alarming rise in anti-social behaviour in your form, Miss Brown. A crash programme of social education is called for!'

4   Other reasons

A number of other minor reasons have been given for using a microcomputer for administrative tasks. Some Heads and Deputies want to learn to use the microcomputer in order to broaden their own education and become familiar with the new technology. There is no doubt in my mind that you can do this best by using the computer to solve real problems, and for a teacher, that may often mean attempting administrative chores. A very similar reason is given by some teachers who want to demonstrate to pupils that microcomputers have a real and practical use aside from playing games and a few trivial applications in the home. There are also some teachers who are microcomputer hobbyists and can happily combine this pleasure with their job. Laudable though these reasons are, it is unlikely that they will form a firm rationale for the introduction of MBCA in a school. Consequently, I conclude that the three main reasons why schools wish to use their microcomputer in this way are those given at the head of this Section.

5.2   The initiative to begin MCBA

So whose initiative begins MCBA in schools? This is a question which has particularly interested me since the very early stages of my investigations into MCBA. The observations might help guide those who are about to set out along the trail. The majority of Heads and Deputies I met knew little about microcomputers or their potential, although they did have a fairly good idea of which tasks the computer might aid. On the other hand, teachers who had a good working knowledge of the computer were often not heavily involved with the major tasks of school administration. There were incentives to them, however, to lend a hand in this field. Some saw the opportunity as a way to get extra equipment, while for others it was just a way in which they could give something extra to the school, possibly influencing promotion prospects. It must be recalled that as recently as 1979 it was unusual to have large memories or disk systems for school microcomputers. Some schools did not have printers either. Teachers anxious to acquire such refinements often volunteered the administrative use of the school machine in order to make a case to those responsible for distributing the money.

Schools divided themselves into three roughly equal groups when it came to beginning MCBA. The first group included those where the Head or a Deputy had initiated developments. In the second group those teachers in the 'middle management' bracket – Heads of Departments and Faculties – had begun to explore the possibilities. The third group comprised those teachers, many quite new to the profession, who had considerable microcomputer expertise, and great enthusiasm to make progress using it. It was very unusual to find a school where someone other than a teacher had been the prime mover in introducing MCBA. In 50 per cent of the schools, only one teacher was involved with the process and apart from the dangers of this approach it was significant that such schools had generally made less progress than in those schools where there were two, three or more teachers involved.

What came through very clearly, both in survey returns and in talking to individual teachers, was that the Head's interest and attitude was of absolutely paramount importance in making progress. Perhaps this is true of any innovation which a school makes – drive from the top seems to be an essential factor. A Deputy Head's interest and backing did seem to be a reasonable substitute for this ingredient, particularly where the top management was run on a team basis. The team idea seemed particularly successful where MCBA was concerned too, involving as it sometimes did a Head or Deputy, a Head of Department, a young enthusiastic teacher, a secretary and perhaps a pupil or two. This would appear to be an ideal combination for rapid and effective progress, especially where everyone has a clearly defined role to play.

5.3 Problems in beginning MCBA

Even in schools which had the right team approach there were still numerous problems to be overcome. These problems took much time and determination to resolve for those working absolutely on their own, especially when this was in the face of considerable opposition within their schools. It will be useful to examine some of these problems, and to note their effects, before looking at suggestions for beginning MCBA in a way in which the pitfalls might be avoided.

Problems encountered can be identified as:

1 Getting software
2 Lack of support and coherence in external software
3 The transfer of workloads
4 Depending too heavily on one person
5 Conflict over hardware
6 Personal and general 'social' insecurity

1 Getting software

The first problem always concerns software. Without it you just can't begin. In the early days, say up to 1980, for those who knew a lot about microcomputers and were interested in using their skills the answer was easy – they wrote their own programs. For those without these skills the early period with microcomputers in school was almost barren for obtaining software. Little, if any software for administration was advertised and unless you happened to make a chance contact on a flimsy and unofficial network there was no advice available. In the spring of 1980, despite contacts with thirty-three schools involved in developing MCBA, I could only find one program which was being advertised for use in other schools. Contrast this with the sixty-one individual programs which were reported as in use and you realize how great was the proportion of DIY work going on. By 1982, matters had scarcely improved. After making contact with over 200 schools I identified only about thirty programs in use which had been obtained from outside the user school. Of these, however, only three were in use in more than one or two schools. There were an awful lot of 'wheels' still being reinvented.

In what I have said so far, I hope that I do not denigrate the work of those pioneers who did set out, and still are setting out, on their own. For many, this was the only way forward, and I'm sure much of value was created. I question, however, whether this is still the correct tactic today. It is very easy to write a program to produce pupil lists. It is a little more difficult to write programs which carry out statistical analyses from a database. It is even more difficult to write programs which give real help in matters such as sifting option group structures or real timetable planning. It is virtually impossible for a mere mortal to write an interactive timetabling program. Yet all these tasks are interrelated, and once you set out on the course, one thing must inevitably lead to another. Here we have an example of what Bernard Chapman (1980) has described as 'a style which grows more easily than it can change direction'.

I think that this approach has some grave disadvantages. First of all there is the whole question of the time it takes to develop programs. Really good, well documented programs, immediately usable by anyone other than the author, take many, many man-hours to develop. If the author is not to be programmer, data collection and entry person, computer operator, and distributor of output then other personnel will have to use the system. Therefore, so much time must be spent on software creation that it is often at the expense of other real duties –

such as good and efficient teaching of children! Some have realized the truth. At least ten people told me during my investigation: 'I am not willing to give that extra time.' Others said, 'It saves the secretary's time, but not mine!', and, 'I found that whilst the microcomputer could be of use in administration it was taking up too much of my time as I normally do not do administration. Suppose I put in ten hours and it saves someone else 100 hours – I shall still have to find that ten hours'.

There is a much better chance of getting ready-made software today, and the choice is improving all the time. There are caveats, however.

2   Lack of support and coherence in external software

Unfortunately, the decision to go totally 'external' for software has not always proved satisfactory either. At one school, the Head took a very bold decision at an early stage to buy a complete microcomputer system for school administration. He realized the impossibility of creating the necessary software internally and researched the available market very thoroughly. Eventually, he decided to work with an external consultant in the preparation of a total school administration suite. There was a conscious attempt to identify and analyse the needs of the school and a comprehensive software specification was drawn up. After this there were considerable delays in the preparation of the programs and twelve months later the school was still waiting to put the microcomputer into action. Eventually, and at very short notice, the consultant withdrew leaving the school with a sketchy documentation and an incomplete suite of programs. In the consultant's eyes there was, potentially, too little financial reward working in this field. The school, very rightly, felt badly let down. Almost two years' effort to introduce MCBA had been wasted. It might be thought that with the quantity of software now available for school administration on various microcomputers this situation could not arise again. Unfortunately, with the proliferation of microcomputers it is only too easy. I know of Heads who have fallen prey to high pressure salespeople anxious to sell sophisticated systems for 'management' tasks at excellent discount prices. They have promised far more than can be expected from the software available and the unfortunate purchasers have been forced ultimately to seek either training in the use of expensive software which they could not understand or alternative programs which will 'really do the job'.

Following some enquiries at an exhibition, I received a follow-up call from such a salesperson. The system I had seen would be excellent for the school office I was told; the new software which had been prepared for this machine was all-embracing. (Actually it was a fairly sophisticated database management system.) I enquired exactly what it could do for me. 'Oh – everything!', came the reply. 'What about the school timetable?' I asked. 'Oh, that would be easy for this system', cooed the delightful young lady! I made an excuse and hung up! To be fair, there are many excellent database management systems available, but sales staff are not always aware of the special problems of schools.

The other important point about external software is that it takes time to master. Good documentation and a 'crash proof' program will help here, but those involved in its use will have to allow plenty of time initially to 'play' with trial data while thumbing through the manual to experiment with commands. On first use a program might take more time than the task would have taken manually. It will mean less time than actually developing the program, however, and time gains in subsequent runs, if that is the objective, should be more reasonable on account of the familiarity gained. In Chapter 4, I discussed the 'tailoring' of externally acquired software to make it more specific to the individual school's needs. I pointed out that this was likely to be relatively easy in BASIC but much more difficult with machine code programs. In choosing external software it's worthwhile bearing this in mind, especially in relation to one specific factor – the proliferation of databases. If you buy your software from various sources for several different tasks, you may find yourself having to enter the same data many times over to different programs in a variety of ways. Supposing you want to print the 4th Year pupils' timetables after option choices are established. You may find yourself having to enter the timetable data both for the option program and for the program you use to print the school timetable. How very much more sensible if you were able to use the same timetable data for both programs. Often it will be possible to write a very simple BASIC program to link the databases. If such techniques are possible in your school, this may give you greater flexibility in choosing software. The ideal, of course, is a single system which embraces all the tasks we need to do, having a coherence which avoids the necessity for us to write linking programs at all. More of this in Chapter 6.

3 Workload transfer

The comments made by teachers at the end of sub-section 1 illustrate another facet of what is likely to happen if MCBA is introduced with insufficient planning – the phenomenon of workload transfer. During my investigations into MCBA it was school secretaries who most frequently claimed that their time was being saved. In the same school a teacher might indicate that the administrative use of the microcomputer was demanding much more time. If two secretaries save three days each in dictating and typing up the school timetable it is but little consolation to the teacher who has spent fifty hours writing the program to print the timetable and a further two days entering up the data. That each teacher on the staff has saved fifteen minutes 'heading up' report slips is but little consolation to the Deputy Head who has to spend three hours watching over the running of a computer program and picking up report slips which have been disgorged from the printer, not to mention the time already spent by a secretary entering up the data. Workload transfer is a serious MCBA problem. As I have indicated previously, the time gains are not all they might appear. Heads must learn to judge whether the overall gains are significant in terms of the school's uses of its time resources, or whether the inroads which it makes into useful time is a reasonable expenditure in terms of improved effectiveness in the various operations involved.

Workload transfer might be totally avoided if those who normally do a particular job manually can be persuaded to undertake the work as part of a team approach using the microcomputer. For example, if secretaries normally undertake Form 7 analysis, then extraction of the statistics from the microcomputer should also be by them rather than a Head of computer science 'because he knows how to run the program'. Equally, if a Head or Deputy normally undertakes analysis of the examination results then it should not be passed over to another merely because a microcomputer is being used. Of course, you cannot spread all jobs out like this. Some jobs, like report heading, are more sensibly done as a package, but the team approach will help.

4 Depending too heavily on one person

Despite the problems of time and workload transfer there are still those individuals who plough on. Eventually, and with determination, or perhaps because of their dedication and enthusiasm, they beat the software and workload problems, only to run their school into another trap – person dependence. In at least 36 per cent of the schools I surveyed, MCBA systems would have collapsed if one teacher left the school. Allowing for uncertainties, the number could have been as great as 50 per cent of the schools. In such schools a number of vital factors are missing. One of these is that documentation for programs being used is often so sketchy that even if the programs are left upon departure of the author, no-one else can use them because no-one else understands them. A factor in this situation is the lack of involvement of other staff. Sometimes this is due to lack of interest, sometimes to lack of training, and sometimes, unfortunately, due to an active policy of discouragement: 'This is my empire – kindly keep out!' I have seen some small disasters in schools where the computer man has left taking his expertise with him. Usually, the chaos is minor and the position made good by quick recourse to manual methods, but where there is heavy reliance on MCBA systems which are person-dependent, such a removal could deal a heavy blow to school organization. Once again, it is the Head's job to see to it that this situation doesn't arise. It is rarer not to have one or two timetablers trained and in reserve these days. So it should be with MCBA.

5 Conflict over hardware

Software and hardware are complementary. You can't really choose one without thoroughly examining the other. The choice of hardware in its own right was examined in Chapter 3 but it's worthwhile stressing again the influence which software will have on that choice. Most companies making microcomputers now realize that an essential ingredient for successful sales is a good software range.

Also mentioned in Chapter 3 were difficulties noted in schools which had only one microcomputer, namely the conflict between administrative and instructional use. Some teachers felt very strongly that administration was 'taking over' and being given unfair priority. Where the machine had clearly been purchased for curricular purposes one was forced to sympathize with their views. The tensions between skilled computer personnel and school administrators did not further the cause of MCBA. Now that there is usually more than one microcomputer in a school it makes sense to identify one machine for administration. In some schools the Head has 'purchased' from the computer studies department an older, yet powerful machine, and quite suitable for administration, by buying a number of smaller machines with more recent and useful features. The 'administration' machine can always be used by pupils during its less active moments.

Another 'hardware' difficulty which arises is the siting of the administrative machine. This is especially important where secretaries and senior staff are going to make frequent use of it. It is unsatisfactory to site this hardware in some remote computer room often frequented by hordes of pupils, as sometimes the work is confidential. But apart from that important fact, secretaries are not used to working in such close proximity to pupils, and for many that I met this was given as an extra reason to avoid using the machine. Several told me that they have found it rather embarrassing having to ask small boys or girls how to use the machine. It was even worse having them constantly peering over their shoulders, ready in a flash to correct the slightest error with a flow of technical jargon. Strangely, the school office itself is not always a good site either. Even in the busiest office the machine does not seem to be in use for 100 per cent of the time. It is inefficient to waste the spare capacity, and pupils, particularly senior ones, might well make use of the time to get extra wordprocessing or programming practice. In this case the school office is not the place for them to work.

I have been lucky in being able to site my machine in a small converted cloakroom near to the school office. Here there is room for two or three people to sit around the keyboard and screen. The machine can be booked by secretaries, selected pupils and staff as required. This seems to make the best use of it for all parties. An alternative would be to site the microcomputer on a trolley which could be wheeled from the school office into a nearby classroom for use by anyone who needs an alternative environment. This is a slightly more untidy arrangement and often rather hard upon the printer and all the connecting cables.

6 Personnel and general 'social' insecurity

This seems an appropriate point to examine the problems which some innovators have experienced with MCBA and the personnel who become involved. Let us begin with school secretaries.

Most, but certainly not all, of the secretaries I interviewed appeared to have been initially reluctant to work with the new technology of microcomputers. Although the work which they were being asked to do was essentially an extension of the normal typewriting task, and it was their speed on the keyboard which was being used, they did not always see it quite that way. As one of their number put it to me: 'My typewriter doesn't answer back.' It was not always fully appreciated that the keyboards they were being asked to use did not react in exactly the same way as typewriter keyboards. There were strange keys with 'RETURN', 'ENTER', or 'ESCAPE' on them. The 'shift lock' did not seem to affect all keys in exactly the same way. To those with only 'manual' keyboard experience, the computer keys were grouped much more closely and had a very different 'touch'. I have seen very competent typists reduced to two-fingered 'pecking' in such circumstances. In particular, for those not recently trained, the habitual use of the letter 'l' for number 'one' and capital 'O' for 'zero' often produced quite inexplicable results. In one school, the secretary's habit of typing a 'space' after every name caused some consternation when other operators tried to access particular pupil records from the database.

One secretary admitted to me that much training would be necessary before we should know if 'older people can adapt to these technologies'. In such circumstances it is not surprising to note that the older the secretary involved, the more reluctant she might be to approach the task with any enthusiasm. In fact experience has shown that, even with a bare minimum of training, an enthusiastic secretary can become very competent in using a microcomputer program in a comparatively short space of time. Someone will have to provide the initial training, however. One of the biggest complaints voiced by school secretaries was that their employers seemed to offer them very little, if anything, in training with any kind of new technology.

Another worry, which a few school secretaries had, was that new technology would substantially change their role, reduce staffing levels in already busy offices, or even render them redundant. These particular fears seemed significantly reduced when they had a clearer idea of what computers could and could not do. However, there was evidence that where the school office was 'unionized' resistance could be considerably harder. One particular organization was said to have a policy against the 'electronic office' and in one Local Authority this was given as the reason why that Authority had been unable to establish a consistent policy for MCBA software in its schools. In most school offices however, the staff were willing to consider the innovation, and some have become quite bitten by the computer 'bug'. It is clear that school secretaries have an important part to play in establishing MCBA in schools and should be among those consulted at an early stage of the innovation.

Ever since the first computers started to process data, there has been suspicion in the human mind about the computer's speed in doing so, its ability to communicate its information in any reorganized form to other electronic devices and its apparent infallibility. These fears have been cultivated by the media to the point where society unquestioningly accepts them as real. It should come as no surprise that the most important reservations which teachers have about the application of computers to school administration are in this connection. My observations in schools indicate that 'social' reasons form the bulk of the objections made by teachers who are not connected with the innovation itself, but who will be the collectors and users of the information.

The objections expressed can be categorized under three headings.

Firstly, comes the question of depersonalization. Since the computer deals with numbers, there is a perception that every individual within a record system becomes a number. This perception is reinforced every time that coded information is collected or dispersed. Some examples of such cases are where examination candidates become just candidate numbers, where comments on reports are drawn together by a selection of numbers, or where staff cover is organized by a machine in a seemingly random fashion.

The second heading concerns the security of data. The recent code of practice relating to the use of computers in schools, drawn up by the Assistant Masters and Mistresses Association (AMMA *Report*, April 1982), specifically tries to 'ensure that the use of computers in no way compromises the security of information which, at present, is regarded as being of a confidential nature'. I have always felt that information is going to be more confidential when held on a floppy disk than it is on paper in a filing cabinet in my room. But there is more to it than that. Teachers are just like the general public in respect of computer data. Firstly, they fear that information will be so well hidden that only those with knowledge of the computer will be able to see it. Secondly, they worry that personal data will be transmitted electronically into a large computer network. It is essential to be open and honest about what information is being kept, and how it is used.

The third heading, in a way, relates to this. All data entry to a computer needs to be very carefully checked. Once incorrect information is in the computer, it may tend to stay there. Such 'bad' data – a misspelt name, an inaccurate examination result, a poor attendance report, a wrong birthdate – could have unwelcomed consequences. On a computer system such 'bad' data is much more likely to be perpetuated and some teachers are very worried about this.

The AMMA Code of Practice is worth reproducing in full since not only does it exemplify the concerns I noted in teachers' attitudes to MCBA but also it offers some answers to overcoming objections.

1   Any personal records which are computerized should be for use with microcomputers only and not be for use with mainframe computers.
2   Each Local Authority or other body acting in the capacity of an employer should decide what categories of information in respect of pupils and of teachers it will allow to be placed on computer files. This decision should be taken in conjunction with representatives of the teachers' organizations and, in the case of pupils only, after consultation with representatives of parents' associations.
3   Parents or guardians and teachers should be informed on request what categories of information are being placed on a computer file.
4   Parents or guardians and teachers should be able to see the information that is on file and which is of their direct concern.
5   Information regarding pupils must be factual and must not be placed on computer file where a specific request has been made that this should be the case.
6   Information regarding teachers should be of a factual, routine, and non-confidential nature.

7   Nothing should be placed on a computer file if it would not otherwise have been placed on a written file at that location.

8   Personal files of pupils and teachers should be stored securely, separately from each other and in a separate place from all other non-personal computer materials.

9   Code and program information relating to personal files should be recorded separately from other similar information relating to non-confidential material.

10   The code and program information relating to personal files should be kept secure, but in a separate place from the personal files themselves.

11   Access to personal files and the associated code and program information should be limited to a small number of known individuals.

[Reproduced by courtesy of the Assistant Masters and Mistresses Association]

Apart from the social issues there are other reasons why teachers may not always welcome the introduction of MCBA. The 'time' problem for those directly involved has already been mentioned. However, this is an issue often taken up by other staff. In the eyes of many teachers the activities of 'administrative' staff, particularly Heads, Deputies and pastoral staff such as Year/House Heads appear,to an extent, non-productive. One can draw a parallel between 'office staff' and 'shop floor workers' in the industrial situation. Teachers hope that the application of computers will release some of this 'administration' time for use in the classroom. All too often they notice that the opposite becomes the case. We have already noted that time is necessary for program preparation and data entry. Where this is allocated to a teacher/programmer at the expense of teaching time, MCBA is given a poor image in colleagues' minds. Without being told, it is difficult for teachers to know that this is an investment which may pay dividends later on.

Some teachers also question the quality of the computer's output. In one school I visited, staff were critical about the quality of output from an old lineprinter which had been given to the school. It could only print upper case letters and the quality of form lists being produced certainly left a great deal to be desired. When it was suggested that this same printer be used for heading up reports that would go out to parents there was quite an outcry. As one teacher said, 'my handwriting may not be much, but it's better than that!'. The complaints were heeded. Eventually a good quality dot matrix printer was purchased. Sometimes the criticism is simply of the actual physical output as in this case. Elsewhere it is the actual quality or nature of the information which is being questioned. In any event, staff opinion on such issues must always be useful to those organizing MCBA.

In my own school, some years ago, we experimented with Peter Andrews' original TT timetable printing package. At that time the output only allowed two characters for staff, rooms, and forms, and no subjects could be printed. Unfortunately nearly all our staff codes had three characters, as did many of the rooms. All of the classes had three or four characters. In our experiment we reduced all staff to two characters. This was not too difficult except that there were three JB's, two of whom had to become XB and YB to avoid confusion. Classes reverted to a 4A, 4B, 4C two character style.

Rooms were more difficult and complex rules were made up. For example: 'To determine the real room number for those shown between 31 and 60, subtract 30 and place L before the answer'. The staff tried their best, but were very confused and said so. It was clear that pupils would never be able to cope. Several members of staff suggested that we should renumber all the rooms in the school. I rejected that suggestion. To me it was the tail wagging the dog. If the computer can't do things the way you want it to, then it should not be used. I like to think that the positive suggestions which my staff were able to make helped Peter Andrews towards designing that very useful facility in TTX – the ability to write a simple BASIC program to print the timetable the way you want it. My staff have certainly been very happy with the output.

Staff need to be consulted, then, about the use of MCBA so that they are able to feed back their opinions. Quite often, collectively, they will be able to make useful and positive contributions to developments. This procedure may help to overcome the general scepticism and disinterest noted by respondents in some schools I contacted. A senior member of staff at one school reported:

Staff have resisted attempts to introduce the computer into school by non-action on documentation issued and a poor attendance at 'hands on' training sessions.

At least this school was trying to overcome the uncertainty which some teachers expressed about the technology. It seems that this kind of familiarity is not so important as a general explanation and consultation about what the computer can be expected to undertake and how. Sometimes the resistance was vectored in the opposite direction within the hierarchy. This could be largely ascribed to a fear of loss of control of vital or sensitive aspects of the organization. For example, one junior member of a school's staff wrote:

There is a general misapprehension that the computer (or its relatively junior operator/programmer) would have the power to control timetable/options/staff cover, possibly in an unsympathetic or inappropriate direction.

It's obviously not just the workforce which fears control by computer!

A final grouse which staff had in several schools was that it was all going to cost too much for too little gain. Particularly in those schools where the capitation debate was an open one, the realization that full implementation of MCBA could cost in excess of £3000 raised many doubts. Certainly this was the case among those for whom the capitation to run quite a large department for a whole year would be considerably less, and at a time when they were often short of many vital materials. In such circumstances, it is the task of management to convince others of the correctness of the action. The gains could be cumulative, over the long term but it is certainly open to question, even then, whether financial resources would not be better deployed elsewhere when considered in terms of other potential benefits.

The influence of microcomputers on school administration systems might appear to be minimal, but both secretarial and teaching staff will experience change. A perceptive article by Tomeski and Lazarus in 1973 had something to say about this influence of the computer on organization:

It is virtually impossible to introduce a computer into an organization without producing changes in workflow, structure and organizational relationships.

In such a climate of change, teachers will certainly expect their voices to be heard.

5.4   Key factors for success

In schools where MCBA is being implemented it has been possible to identify seven factors which will contribute to the success or failure of the innovation. In summary they are:

1   The sponsorship and direction of the Head and the Management Team
2   The identification of a person to spearhead the innovation
3   Having the necessary technical skills available
4   Gaining the co-operation of teaching staff
5   Encouraging the support of clerical staff
6   Choosing good software
7   Having available, and being willing to seek, advice and support external to the school

1   Sponsorship and direction

By far the most important factor is whether the innovation has backing from the top. I have observed that not only do teaching staff rate this as the most important, but in schools where the Head or Deputy is actively involved, there appears to be substantially greater progress. In part it can be claimed that this is due to the Head's influence over finance. The introduction of MCBA is likely to be more rapid and successful when substantial amounts of money are spent on powerful software and quality hardware. However, when teachers are questioned further, it becomes clear that the leadership example of a Head's involvement can carry a lot of weight. Those involved with the introduction of computers into business would not be surprised. A report by the McKinsey organization in 1968 entitled *Unlocking the computer's profit potential* observes that:

The key to computer success was strong leadership from senior management in directing applications of the computer. Where computers were ineffective it was generally because senior management had abdicated responsibility.

Management Consultant Michael Turner in his book *The first computer handbook* says:

It is therefore only the Board of Directors that can define the business framework within which computerization is to be considered . . .. The Board needs to be involved with the computerization project; and for there to be a half chance of a successful system resulting, the Board also needs to be in control of the project.

For 'the Board' read 'Senior Management Team' in a school and this quotation will define the key position occupied by the Head and Deputies, especially at the initial stage of any project.

2 The identification of a key person

This factor would be identified as very important in the business world – that of having one particular member of staff in charge of the project called, perhaps, the Project Director or Manager. What sort of qualities does the Project Director need? Ideally he or she should have good communications skills and be sufficiently senior to relate easily with any member of the school staff. A good working knowledge of the administrative systems of the school and some familiarity with microcomputer systems is also necessary. A Deputy Head or teacher operating as Head of Year/Head of Faculty would seem to be an ideal person to undertake such a role.

3 Having the technical skills available

If the project is not to interfere with the normal day-to-day work of the Project Director, some help will be needed from other identified staff. This relates to another important factor identified by teachers – the need to have some programming skills on the staff. Eric Vincent, in a *Times Educational Supplement* article in 1982 attributed the success of certain schools in computerized administration to their staff who wrote the software. Here is the role for the teacher who is also a computer enthusiast. This 'assistant' will need good programming skills, a passion for lots of hard work and a conviction that MCBA will benefit the school. It might be useful, too, at this stage to identify a person who will eventually hold responsiblity for the routine operation of the computer. This person needs rather different qualities from the first 'assistant' – good keyboard skills and a willingness to undertake routine work with strict observance of a few rules. It seems likely that this person will be a second assistant to the Project Director, and probably a secretary. I have also seen junior teachers and senior pupils with appropriate keyboard skills used in this role.

4 Gaining the co-operation of staff

I have noted the effects that introduction of some computerization is likely to have on teaching staff. The general support and enthusiasm of teaching staff was seen as another important ingredient for the success of MCBA by teachers. Michael Turner suggests that:

The effects on your staff of computerization of procedures are not well understood. And unfortunately this means that this impact is invariably underestimated. One of the most important factors in determining your chances of success with the installation of your first computer is the accuracy with which you estimate this effect.

The key to this, as with so much innovation, would appear to be consultation. The staff must know what is going on and have the opportunity to voice their opinions about it and modify the innovation if necessary.

5   Encouraging the support of clerical staff
Strangely, similar support and enthusiasm from the school office was not rated so highly as a key factor by teachers. Nevertheless, a key factor it is, since some of the biggest changes are likely to be felt here. Skills which are found in the school office are likely to be in great demand as the tempo of MCBA increases and if its main objectives are to be met.

6   The selection of software
Enough has been said about the importance of software to establish that choice of this commodity will be another key factor in the success of MCBA. There are schools, for example, where the choice of a crude cassette based wordprocessing system has killed any interest which office secretaries might have generated. A professional disk based system might have promoted extra enthusiasm.

7   Using external advice and support
The selection of software is linked with the final key factor – the availability of external advice or support to the school in its innovation. This factor was not rated very highly by teachers, but schools are notoriously introverted. Few businesses would think of an initial computerization without seeking the advice of some external consultant. No school should think that it has all the answers in such a technical innovation. Evidence gleaned from some schools which started out alone in the early days suggests that they would have made better progress and avoided some pitfalls by building on the experience of others. This presupposes, of course, that external advice is available. In the early days of the innovation there was no network to tap. Today a great deal more information and knowledge is diffusing through the system, albeit in a somewhat haphazard way. The experience is certainly there if you seek it out.

5.5   How to begin MCBA

I find that those who have not been dissuaded from using MCBA, and have a willingness to begin, or even to extend operations, are eager to have some simple plan of action. Based on the pitfalls I have observed, and the key factors relating to success, I suggest the following as one method of proceeding:

1   The reasons for beginning MCBA should be firmly established. This should certainly involve the Head and his senior management team. External advice, perhaps from a County Adviser, could be sought. There should be some clear idea at this stage about the aims of the innovation and how progress towards these might be judged, perhaps in terms of what the school expects to gain. These aims may not be realized in the short term but will guide overall direction for the project.

2   One senior member of staff should be identified as 'Project Director'. This is the person who will spearhead the innovation and to whom other staff can look for support, advice and direction. At this stage a number of staff should be formed into a planning team under the Project Director.

163

Ideally this team will have at least four members of contrasting skills who will provide mutual support and enthusiasm. The qualitites of the Project Director and some of his team were dealt with in the previous section. I envisage that the team will include at least one good computer person, and one with professional keyboard skills.

3 The Project Team will identify short term objectives which they feel might be comfortably attained within a defined period – say a year – and which will mark a stage towards attainment of the project's aims. The suggested objectives will need to be arrived at through discussion between the Project Director and the school's Senior Management Team in order that all are agreed on what is to be attempted. It would be prudent not to be over-ambitious at this stage. One task achieved well will be much better than several done badly or left unfinished. Recently, I observed a school which had set out to place the records of two Year Groups on the microcomputer with a view to to attempting some tasks from this database. In the event, staff were so pleased with the results that records for all Year Groups were entered. This injected extra impetus to the next stage of the project.

4 The Project Team must establish their requirements for hardware and software. If the hardware is installed already at the school for other purposes, then this will limit the search to software for that particular microcomputer. However, if both hardware and software are to be installed, then this gives much greater flexibility. There will be many factors to take into account. These have been dealt with in previous chapters, but a disk system, 32K of memory and a printer will be minimum requirements. Simultaneously with these considerations, a number of other activities should take place, as in sub-sections 5, 6 and 7 below.

5 Both software and hardware choices might be influenced by making contact with other schools. Once again, the services of some external consultant could be enlisted to identify schools where good practices have been established. It might be possible to see in action some of the software under consideration. Suppliers might be able to help here. There could be merit in using similar systems to nearby schools so that emergency back-up of both software and hardware might be close at hand. The existence of local experience should certainly be fully explored and exploited. It is my view that internally created software should only be used as a very last resort.

6 The Project Team must take decisions on the final division of the workload. Someone must take responsibility for being familiar with the hardware. Someone else might be given the task of learning everything about the software being used and teaching others who might have to use it. One or two people might be responsible for data entry and producing hard copy. Another will certainly have to act as a focal point for data collection and distribution – this might be best undertaken by the Project Director.

There is merit in involving as many staff as possible in sitting at the microcomputer and using software – including the timetabler, the Director of Studies, the Bursar, or even the Head. A shared approach is always best, and the more people involved the less likely is the hazard of person dependence.

7   In the school context some kind of time allowance might have to be made to the key personnel involved. To an extent this will depend on other decisions, such as the number of tasks to be attempted and whether software creation is part of the programme. The Project Team will need to make recommendations for consideration by the Senior Management Team.

8   Final decisions on all recommendations under headings 5, 6 and 7 might be expected to be taken by the Senior Management Team, especially if they are ultimately responsible for finding the necessary resources of money and time.

9   As the systems are brought into operation, the Project Team will have to consider the various aspects of training which will be required.

Before any plans are implemented there should be a general introduction for staff. This might occupy half of an in-service training day at most or as little as a one hour after-school staff meeting. In any event, the objectives should be clearly stated and an indication given of how they are to be achieved, and what will be expected of staff generally. There must be some opportunity for staff to question the plans and identify potential problems.

Other training may be necessary for other key roles, particularly where personnel within the Project Team are likely to leave the school. Eventually most training can be provided in school and on the job, but initially some outside support may be necessary. I shall return to the theme of training in the wider sense, particularly by the Local Authority, in the final chapter.

10   The Project Director and his team must arrange for a continuous review of progress as systems become established. There must be contingency plans for any kind of systems failure especially when manual methods of operation are abandoned. At various points there must be provision for feed-back from teaching staff. There will be discrete review points for the Head and Senior Management Team who will help in assessing whether the innovation is meeting its objectives and take decisions on whether to go further.

Ultimately it is this group which will have to decide whether MCBA is fulfilling its original aims. Never hesitate to abandon something which has failed, even though it might be painful to admit it. What works in the environment of one school may not work in another. It is possible that an application may fail in part if not in whole. In that case a decision can rest on whether the good parts remaining will be worth keeping when the failures have been rooted out. However, if planning has been carefully done and decisions thoughtfully taken, it is more than likely that the innovations will be rated a great success.

With MCBA, it is only through a process such as I have described that you are likely to know the answer to the question: 'How shall we know when we are there?'

6 Prospects for the future

or 'Into the Kingdom of Sand'

Good schools and enterprising Local Authorities will never stand still. They will be continually thrusting forward looking for new ways to improve and fresh challenges to meet. Where MCBA is concerned they will have asked the question: 'How shall we know when we are there?'. Matters will not rest there, however, and their next questions will be: 'Where are we now? Where do we go from here?' – and so the cycle begins again. A school reaching this stage will be satisfied with its achievements so far and will be seeking further refinements or new tasks to conquer. A Local Authority surveying its schools, however, may see a different perspective.

6.1   The Local Authority's role

Everything written so far in this book concerns the individual school developing MCBA. In particular, in the last chapter I examined the main difficulties which the individual school is likely to meet and suggested some ways to overcome the problems. However, some difficulties may be beyond the resources of a single school to resolve. Let us consider just two of these.

The first concerns the multiplicity of software for various tasks. Where a school buys in its software (as I believe most schools now should), it is quite likely to end up with a variety of packages for tasks so diverse as options analysis, examinations administration and timetable production. Each package needs the creation of its own database, a task which is probably not cost-effective in terms of time when the associated data entry, validation and maintenance is considered. It is true that some schools may have sufficiently experienced programmers to reconcile the various database requirements, especially for BASIC programs. It is unlikely, however, that many will be able to do the job for the more sophisticated machine code programs, such as timetabling packages, which are likely to become available. In those schools having the skills and time to produce their own individual program suites, the chances are better. But for some major tasks they are unlikely to match the sophistication of programs which trained computer professionals will produce. Forced to purchase these externally they will face the same problem. The fully integrated and coherent school MCBA system is a rare phenomenon, and is likely to remain so for a little while.

The second problem which the individual school will find difficult to solve, is meeting the training needs of its staff. I suggested in the last chapter that a continual policy of training was a vital ingredient for success with MCBA. Those familiar with the needs of in-service training will know how impossible it is to provide for these completely within the school. For one thing the necessary expertise may not be available, and even if it is, time is always at a premium to do the job properly. With MCBA the situation is no different. A school in-service day may be sufficient to give a general introduction to staff, but the more specialized needs of programmers, and users such as Heads, Deputies, timetablers, Bursars and secretaries must certainly be satisfied elsewhere.

These are both areas where Local Education Authorities might be expected to help. But if they are to be brought in to assist only at a time when all their schools have been developing techniques of their own for a year or two, it is unlikely to be either a simple task or a very productive one. If the Local Authority asks for the first time at this stage – 'Where are we now?'- in terms of all its secondary schools, the answer is likely to be that things are in a fair degree of chaos! At the beginning of the microcomputer revolution, most Local Authorities took the wise decision to define one particular microcomputer as the standard for their schools. One reason for such a decision was to facilitate the sharing of software among schools. Programs written in one school could easily be used in another, and advice and training concerning both hardware and software could be offered on an area wide basis. Strangely, a standardization on software was rarely made. Perhaps it was never seen as necessary. But consider just one task in MCBA – wordprocessing. For most microcomputers several wordprocessing software packages are available. If schools are able to choose almost at random from these, the prospects for offering a common training session within an area will be slim. In addition both schools and LEA will have lost the opportunity to exchange documents on magnetic media.

The situation with pupil record database systems is even worse. It is possible that every school within an Authority's area will be using a different database structure. Once this situation is reached and schools have committed a great deal of data to magnetic media, they will be somewhat reluctant to change. From the LEA's point of view it is then faced with a quite impossible situation in which to provide in-service training. It will also have no reward for such effort, being unable to use electronic information gathering techniques for want of a common standard of database.

Local Authorities which ignore the development of MCBA in schools are likely, in time, to be faced with a veritable 'can of worms'. Some schools will be using a variety of packages for individual applications, while others will have attempted a more integrated approach. Some will have purchased software and others may have developed their own. In a few schools there may even be 'non-standard' microcomputers beavering away in school offices with their own unique custom-designed software. Much time and a great deal of money may well have been wasted through lack of direction and advice. Above all a great opportunity will have been lost.

It is difficult to understand how this can be allowed to happen. Although the design of curriculum and timetable is left to the individual school, when it came to constructing the timetable using a mainframe computer, LEAs usually dictated which software was to be used. And although the general style of a school's administration is left to individual Heads, the way information is transmitted is usually fairly carefully prescribed. In general, if Local Authorities feel that there is a benefit to be derived from a common policy, then that policy will be introduced. It seems that the benefits of such a common policy for MCBA have only been foreseen in a small number of wise Authorities.

Here are some benefits which should accrue:

1 The Authority will benefit as a corporate organization by virtue of its size in comparison with an individual school. It will already have a number of computer professionals on its staff, some of whom may already be familiar with the schools. Their professional expertise could provide the analysis for a software system design which could be undertaken either by the organization's computing service or by consultants identified by that service.

2 The design of professional programs for the whole organization will probably be better than those produced by individual teachers.

3 The provision of programs by the LEA will release teachers for their most important task – teaching children. This might be true both for those teachers who are presently writing and maintaining systems and for those who carry out mundane clerical tasks.

4 A Local Authority can purchase, examine and recommend a much greater range of 'off-the-shelf' software than could ever be achieved by an individual school. Standardization could be achieved in this way and services for database linkage could be provided centrally.

5 By whichever method software is obtained, the database will be standard for all schools in the area. This allows the LEA to:
Save clerical effort in manipulation of data
Transfer data electronically
Update records more regularly
Analyse data more easily

6 The training of staff in schools in the use of MCBA techniques is made easier on account of the common software and common procedures.

7 The LEA has greater control over electronic dataprocessing in its schools.

It is interesting to note how one Authority which has recognized the corporate benefits of MCBA has set about investigating the potential for a common system. Firstly, this County took a decision about the development of MCBA. Schools would not be forbidden to begin development of systems, but they would be encouraged to think very carefully about dangers and difficulties of individual initiatives. Heads were told that the County would be investigating a common system which included both hardware and software. A steering committee of Heads, Deputy Heads, Bursars, County Officers and Computer Staff was formed. This set up a pilot scheme in one school which was subsequently extended to two others, with plans being laid to bring in another ten schools at a later stage. For the first three schools the microcomputer chosen was the Superbrain. This has an 8-bit microprocessor and is not commonly found in schools but is well known in business and higher education. To form the pupil record system a standard commercial database management package called dBASE-II was used. In the first school, the pilot scheme was planned so that only the records of two year groups needed entering for various data manipulation studies. So successful was this that the Deputy Head asked to continue with the records of the remaining year groups and this was

170

accomplished. It was planned to investigate assessment, reporting and progress procedures with pupil data, in addition to making County returns. The County Officers had suggested processing resources, accommodation inventory and staff records. The schools were most interested in some kind of timetabling package. Such developments were very much at the preliminary stage in the initial pilot scheme, but results were sufficiently encouraging to press on to the next stage. It was also very pleasing to note that there had been total co-operation from both clerical and teaching staff. Some lessons had been learned. It seemed that Superbrain was not big enough for the tasks proposed and consideration was being given to trials with a 16-bit system which had the potential to be linked with a mainframe computer.

This scheme is still in its infancy, but the method employed has a great deal to commend itself, using as it does the whole range of a County's expertise and resources. Similar schemes are being tried in various places up and down the country, although so far very few are willing to openly share the knowledge gained. Some feel they are developing systems which are of commercial value. Others fear that publicity may lead to a flood of interested visitors which will make too many demands on the time of key personnel. Whatever the reason, communications about MCBA between LEAs seems to be poor. This is a great pity, since LEAs which have taken initiatives are likely to be much better placed to make full use of the microcomputer as an aid to Countywide administration, and such knowledge should be shared.

6.2   The modular concept

If LEAs are to act as integrating and standardizing agencies for MCBA, and in particular if they are to gain in terms of their own information flow and dataprocessing needs whilst still allowing schools to conduct administration using microcomputers in the way which best suits them, then a number of problems need to be resolved. One of these concerns the size and structure of the database held in each individual school. As far as the LEA is concerned, the 1974 LAMSAC report discusses the total information requirements which might have to be met. Data is identified as being required for five basic elements – pupils and students, teachers and other staff, buildings and supplies, curricula and finance. It is suggested that a totally integrated database containing such information would be an impossible task to initiate without considering installation in discrete steps or modules. Of course, an eye towards achievement of an integrated whole at every stage is absolutely vital both for LEA and for schools, otherwise the situation is unlikely to be any more coherent than that which results from individual development of a number of different MCBA applications. The report goes on to specify in some detail how this system of interrelated modules would work.

This concept is particularly useful where data collection is to be delegated to individual school microcomputers. A totally integrated database holding all the information which might be required by the LEA would almost certainly be too big for most microcomputers in all except the smallest schools. Containing the information within modules, however, yet retaining the potential for easy integration, would keep the data in a form which could be held by a microcomputer, accessed by the Local Authority and used by the individual school.

In order to make the modules usable by schools, they would have to be arranged only slightly differently from those proposed by the 1974 LAMSAC report. Data on buildings, for example, would be insufficiently variable to justify keeping in a school's own database. Such a module need only be kept centrally. An equipment module in individual schools might be justified for both inventory and resource location purposes. Modules on pupil, staff, curricular and financial data would be essential in any school, and to these I would add two more – timetable data and examination results. It can be argued that timetable data is really part of the curriculum database. However, the timetable in its raw

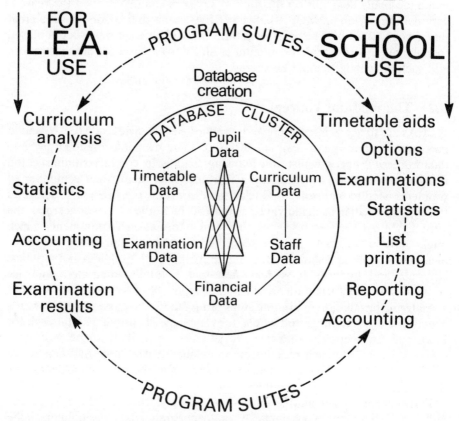

Figure 6.1 Modular concept for integrated MCBA systems.

form does not always easily reflect the nature of the curriculum from which it was planned. In any case, the timetable data will be considerable, so I conclude that these two should be in separate databases. Likewise, examination results could form part of the pupil record, although I have found that Local Authorities usually prefer results disassociated from particular pupils' names. Also, many schools handle the examination database as a separate entity on account of the amount of RAM which the essential data occupies. I conclude that it makes sense to separate these two – pupils and examination entries – in a modular system.

Figure 6.1 shows the database cluster which might be needed in each individual school working on a modular system. The cluster is accessed, both by LEA and school using a number of associated program suites. It may be that for LEA purposes the access programs would not be used on the school microcomputer – the contents of the database cluster could be transmitted in raw form to a much larger machine. There are two ways to achieve this. Either the microcomputer can be used as a terminal to transmit the data via a telephone line to a mainframe, or disks can be sent by post to the appropriate computer centre, there to be read into the mainframe using the appropriate apparatus. I support the latter method, since it is considerbly cheaper and marginally more reliable. Collection of such data does not seem to warrant the urgency or expense of on-line methods.

It is quite likely, then, that the LEA's program suites will only be required for a mainframe computer. The same cannot be said either for the database creation program, which ensures standardization of the cluster, for those programs which will be used by the school. Since these programs must run on the host microcomputer, the question immediately arises as to which language should be used. If the programs are to be produced professionally by a central agency it is doubtful that BASIC will find favour. As I indicated in Chapter 4, this language is not greatly admired by purists and has the disadvantage for real application purposes, of being uncommonly slow. Many professional program-mers might prefer COBOL because it has become the standard and most popular language for business software running on mainframes. It is the natural language for data management and has many 'built-in' facilities, such as sorting. At the moment COBOL is not available for all the 'standard' school microcomputers, and where it is, the compilers are rather expensive, usually of the order of £400.

The most viable alternative is probably to use machine code. This has no compiler cost and is extremely fast and efficient in operation and in use of memory. The code is tedious to write and 'debug' and may not be cost-effective to produce. However, some teachers have successfully produced useful and error free programs in this medium (Peter Andrews's TTX for RML 380Z is an excellent example). Many of the most impressive professionally produced general purpose microcomputer programs are written in machine code.

Whichever language is used to produce the programs for school use, there will be one significant disadvantage if BASIC is not used. Schools are unique and, as I have suggested before, it is unusual to find standard programs which can be adapted without amendment in any school. It is quite common to find that schools make minor amendments to purchased MCBA programs which modify them for more effective use in their particular situation. This opportunity is lost if programs are written in other languages, since few schools have staff who can easily amend programs apart from those in BASIC. In order to discourage schools from attempting to 'tailor' the database creation program, thereby corrupting the database structure, it will be best that this program is not in BASIC. Assuming this, only a small number of alternatives present themselves as a solution to the problem of writing the remaining programs for school use:

1 Write the school access programs in the same language as the database creation programs but allow individual schools to suggest modifications to the central programming agency. This could be time-consuming for the central agency.
2 Write the school suites in BASIC, despite the disadvantages of the language. This is the compromise middle route, effective both from producer's and school's points of view. However, BASIC might be inefficient in terms of practical use for the most complex tasks.
3 Create the databases in such a way that they can be accessed by BASIC programs which are created in the various schools. Although inefficient in terms of use of the teacher/programmer's time this allows maximum flexibility for each school. (Once again TTX is a prime example on account of its facility for formatting timetable output.)

All this assumes that a Local Authority will set up a central agency to co-ordinate MCBA in its schools. Such an agency might be based at the Authority's computer centre, where its mainframe data is processed; at an educational computing centre; at a resources centre; or as an off-shoot of an Authority's teacher or in-service training centre.

6.3 The requirements of in-service training

In addition to its co-ordinating, standardizing and resource producing roles for MCBA, the LEA has one other function – the duty of providing training for its staff who are, or will be, involved. At various points in preceding chapters the need for in-service training for the school personnel involved has been identified as a matter of prime importance. There are four general areas which I see as needing particular attention. This will be the case whether the Authority assumes a co-ordinating role or is content to allow piecemeal development. If the latter is the case, however, then the task will certainly be that much more difficult. The four areas are:

1 A general introduction to MCBA for all teaching and clerical staff in a school prior to its introduction. This need take no more than half of one

school based in-service training day. It should provide staff with the opportunity to know which tasks are to be undertaken; to understand how these will be done and what their involvement will be; to discuss the implications; to decide what benefits will accrue to themselves, to the pupils and to the school; and to provide feedback and suggestions for a smooth introduction. Such a session is absolutely necessary to minimize the suspicion and mistrust which often accompanies the introduction of computerization into an organization.

2 A detailed introduction to the software for those teachers with program-ming skills who might need to amend or write programs for individual schools. The nature of this course and the length of time necessary for it will depend very much on the circumstances. Such a course will be very much easier to organize where the LEA has agreed to standardize on software. It will involve a small number of teachers from each school (perhaps some members of the Planning Team discussed in the previous chapter) who have been identified as being responsible for maintaining the programs and associated databases. Such staff will need to be extremely familiar with both hardware and software in order that they can speedily resolve any minor problems, and write small programs to undertake such minor tasks as might arise. Such a role often falls upon a hard-pressed computer studies teacher but there is every reason to involve others. These staff would need to know the structure of the database and the associated school-based programs. Such a course might fill three or four days full-time, assuming that the teachers were familiar with the computer language used.

Where the LEA is not exercising a co-ordinating influence, such a course presents problems of organization on account of the variety of software likely to be in use. However, if several pieces of software are identified as being in common use within a County, the course might be profitable where persons sufficiently familiar with them could usefully pass on their knowledge to others.

3 A specific introduction to the use of MCBA is essential for senior school administrative staff, particularly Heads and Deputy Heads and those who aspire to such posts. The use of microcomputers in school administration is potentially so important that there is a good case for all management focused in-service training courses to include an element of it. The nature of the material need not be as technical as that required in the previous section. Certainly a critical appraisal of the strengths and weaknesses of the MCBA approach should be included. The potential tasks for MCBA will need to be examined, together with a consideration of how systems should be set up and maintained. Some familiarity with the hardware and software will be necessary although it must be assumed that detailed technical advice will be on hand at the school. More importantly, consideration needs to be given to the interpretation of management reports produced by microcomputer as software for such tasks becomes available.

4   A basic introduction to the microcomputer as an office tool for school secretaries and Bursars/Administrative Officers. These are the personnel who are often forgotten in training programs, yet it is equally essential to train them in the application of new technology if it is to be successfully applied to school administration. It is school secretaries who will have to deal with most of the school's wordprocessing. A wordprocessor is a complex device requiring several new skills not necessary in operating a typewriter. An introductory course for school secretaries in operating such a system could well fill three or four full days. Likewise, if Bursars are to move over to computerized account keeping, this too will demand new skills together with confidence in both hardware and software. It may be that suppliers of some sophisticated accounting systems could provide training as part of the purchase arrangements. This will be particularly important in the independent sector, where such packages are quite likely to be used without the back-up of a Local Authority. LEAs requiring an integrated system, however, may well be better advised to provide their own courses.

6.4   Policies for the future

Given the piecemeal development of MCBA during the past five years, it is not surprising to find that the current status is somewhat untidy on anything but an individual school basis. The time has come now for firm co-ordination to take place and the LEA is the most effective unit within which this can happen. It is my hope that this will be the main line of development over the next five years.

In this respect we have a great deal to learn from the United States, where computers have been applied to school administration on an organized basis in school districts for a number of years. A detailed treatise on such work is K. M. Hussain's book *The development of information systems for education* published in 1973. However, it is a statement by W. M. Tondow writing on the same topic some years earlier which I feel is of great importance:

In developing the use of computers within a school district innovation is actually no more expensive that waiting for someone else. One of the characteristics of innovation is if you wait for someone else to develop a system, several things will occur. While you have waited, your program has remained static. Secondly, when you attempt to use the system developed by someone else you must either change your own system, distort your operation to conform, or make extensive modification. This means that the costs to you are about the same as to the innovator. Also, being the innovator provides a great deal of room for creativity.

In addition to encouraging LEAs to assume their co-ordinating role for MCBA, this advice should also encourage individual schools not to await LEA initiative. Beginning MCBA in a small way will give confidence in the hardware and provide experience of working with computers, thus ensuring a good foundation for the next step forward. In this respect, purchase of software to run on existing hardware and costing only a few hundred pounds could provide a sound investment in experience for the future. Those involved with the introduction of microcomputer hardware to schools over the past five years have had a maxim: 'Now is never the right time to buy.' As this implies, there is always something better just around the corner. The same is now true about software. Some software written in the late 1970s already looks dated. Those schools which have been happily using it for four of five years might soon have to buy more polished versions or entirely new packages. The life of software is limited, possibly more so than hardware. Schools beginning now will have some advantage over those who began earlier, but they in turn will be leapfrogged by those coming up from behind. Whenever you start the time will come when circumstances force you to change your systems, because hardware, software, or the LEA dictates it. So simply waiting for the LEA initiative might not be the best policy, especially if there is no sign of it developing. The process of continual development will go on. As R. W. Ewart wrote in 1977:

The one message that is essential to put over is that to go back to the beginning is unnecessary; start by using the experience of others – build on their development of computer systems and on the appreciation and knowledge of their administrators.

6.5 Hardware for the future

Just as today's software will be replaced by more sophisticated programs so, too, will hardware be regularly superseded as innovation in microprocessor and memory chip design reaches the commercial market. Already schools are beginning to consider the microcomputer dedicated to school administration and based in the school office. If the compatibility of the hardware with that used for teaching is not important then a considerable array of powerful equipment offers itself for consideration. A short appraisal of the possibilites in this field may prove useful.

A natural step to take in buying dedicated equipment for the school office is to move 'up-market'. In this particular case it might be wise to remember that software development might have to begin all over again. With some packages the translation might be a fairly simple exercise, but with the more sophisticated tasks, such as timetabling, it might be an impossibility. However, you might wish to innovate!

The latest business microcomputers employ a 16-bit microprocessor. One of the earliest machines to be introduced using this technology was the ACT Sirius I. Designed as 'a third generation microcomputer for the business environment' by the man who produced the original Commodore PET, the Sirius is becoming increasingly popular in small businesses, perhaps on account of the publicity associated with its launch and the strong advertising of the associated ACT Pulsar software. It is produced in three units, rather like the RML 380Z, but smartly constructed to produce an important-looking 'executive' image. The main cabinet houses the electronics and twin floppy disk units. These are of the 5.25″ variety and even in single-sided single-density form will store 1.2Mb of data. The disk operating system is CP/M-86 which will appear very familiar to 380Z users. The memory is an ample 128K RAM, expandable internally to 0.5Mb and externally to 1Mb.

The 12″ green screen is mounted on a turntable and can also tilt to be positioned for the operator's comfort. It has a twenty-five line by eighty column display. The slimline keyboard has been specially designed and incorporates special clusters of keys as well as the standard typewriter arrangement. It is connected to the main box by a neatly coiled cable. It is said that this microcomputer insists on repeating 'I am the Sirius One, the number one choice in personal computers', every time it is switched on. Certainly it does have a speaker for sounds, but I would imagine that this feature gets very wearing.

Perhaps because of the disk operating system, the Sirius behaves rather like the 380Z, and BASIC must be loaded from disk before BASIC programs are run. Although the BASIC is not identical to RML BASIC it is somewhat similar and this may aid software translation of MCBA. WordStar is available for wordprocessing. It is said that the Intel 8088 16-bit chip used was 'designed so it can interface to the 8-bit microcomputer world'. This seems to suggest that software prepared for the 8-bit Z80 family might run on the Sirius. One should not place too much reliance on this suggestion without good technical advice being readily available.

Other microcomputers using 16-bit chips are becoming available. Principal rivals to the Sirius 1 at the moment are the IBM Personal Computer and the Tandy Model-16. Both are more expensive than the Sirius and, as far as MCBA is concerned, suffer from the same lack of software. There is no doubt that these or similar sophisticated microcomputers will, before long, find a place in the school office, but at the present time it would be a highly innovative school which undertook development of suitable software systems for these machines purely for internal use.

There are two more technological innovations which are likely to affect MCBA soon – the 'network' of microcomputers and the hard disk system. A 'network' means that a whole group of microcomputers can be linked together by wires in order to communicate with each other, with a 'master' station, and to share peripheral devices such as a disk system or printer. The technology of such systems need not concern us here, but suffice it to say that with some networks anything from one to over 100 'slave' systems can be connected to one master system. Some networks use glass fibre optic cables rather than conventional wire along which laser beams carry data and other communications for distances as great as 9 km at the speed of light. So fast can parcels of data be carried that 'slave' stations can appear to load programs simultaneously from the same disk system. What is in fact happening is that each 'slave' is getting its turn to collect information under control of the microprocessor in the master station. There are two ways in which networks could be used. Ultimately, they might be used to form a linking administrative system for all secondary schools in an LEA. Immediately, however, it is more likely that networks will be installed only in individual schools.

Recently I was discussing the possibility of a school using a network of BBC microcomputers as a dedicated MCBA system. This system would have 'slave' stations in the school office, the Head's office and in the offices of the two Deputies. A fifth BBC microcomputer would be necessary as the 'master' station. In such a system it was assumed that the 800K dual floppy disk unit would be adequate, plus a suitable printer. Even including suitable monitor screens at each station and connecting cable the cost would still be under £5000. Such a system holds exciting possibilities for Heads and other senior school staff. For those who can type documents as quickly as they can be drafted by hand, these can be prepared electronically on the desk-top slave unit and transmitted directly to disk storage in the school office. Here it will be the secretary's task to oversee the printing and to edit minor errors before the final version is produced. Thus the skills of both Head and secretary can be linked in the interests of a more efficient school office. The time may not be too far away when dictation into a microphone at the 'slave' unit is all that is necessary to produce electronic text. Although traditional typing skills will not be necessary with such a process, the need for careful editing by secretary, Head, or both will still be vital.

'Hard' or 'Winchester' disk technology has improved the prospects for networks by allowing the storage of much greater quantities of information which can be continuously 'on-line'. First introduced to the microcomputer world in 1980, the early systems stored up to 5Mb of data – as much as twenty disk surfaces of the best mini-floppy disks of the day. For a microcomputer including such a drive the user could expect to pay in the region of £5000. Looking through magazines only three years old, the units pictured look quite old fashioned. By mid-1982 the frontier for hard disk storage had risen to 35Mb, and by 1983 the 80Mb drive has become a practical possibility. All the time the cost of these systems has been decreasing. The cheapest hard disk system is now under £1000 while even a 20Mb system is under £2000. Would any school administration system need the equivalent of 100 mini-floppy disk surfaces on-line at the same time?

Already schools have begun to experiment with network systems for teaching purposes. These systems might have twenty or more microcomputers connected in the computer laboratory alone. However, the system can be extended further afield with slave stations in science laboratories, technology workshops, 6th Form centre, and administrative offices. With the large capacity of hard disk systems, storage is not a problem. Security of data is, however! One can imagine some agitation amongst teachers if pupil records could be accessed from terminals in the computer room. There would be quite a row if staff records could be called up in the 6th Form centre! Certainly, within such network systems security codes can be given which effectively lock out files to users who do not know the code, but I should always be worried that the odd 'computer junkie' among the pupils would spend months attempting nothing else on the network but breaking the code system. There is a good probability that someone, sometime would succeed. For this reason alone I believe that school administration systems should be totally separate from the school's teaching network system.

Beyond the school network lies the system which links several schools. In a small LEA it might soon be technically possible to link all its schools on a microcomputer network. In Scotland at the moment, under the guidance of the Scottish Microelectronics Development Project, one of the most advanced experiments in the use of microcomputers in school administration is taking place. The Schools Computer Administration and Management Project (SCAMP) is presently involved in a three year initial pilot scheme spanning seven Scottish Regions. Twelve schools will be involved over the course of that time. The hardware installed in these lucky pilot schools leaves one almost breathless:

1 master station with 256K memory
1 slave station with 128K memory
(These systems are built by Future Technology Systems of Beith, Ayrshire and are 16-bit systems using the 8086 chip)
Peripherals include:
1 80Mb Winchester hard disk
1 16Mb cartridge disk store for back-up
1 Florida Data printer with Tractor, cutsheet feeder and stand (This printer will operate multimode between 600 c.p.s. and 100 c.p.s. letter quality printing)
One most important inclusion will be a communication device, probably an accoustic coupler, which will transmit data from school to school, or from school to a central site via a telephone line

The budget, including maintenance on the hardware, systems software and wordprocessing software is £20 000 for each school!

Just as exciting, is the user software which is being prepared for the project. This will probably be professionally written in COBOL to a specification designed by the team's systems analyst in consultation with educationalists, particularly teachers on secondment. It will be aimed directly at the systematization of secondary school record keeping and administration, and in so doing provide for the internal information needs of the school while at the same time taking account of the need to service Regional and other requirements.

While schools will not be able to modify the code of the programs, flexibility will be maintained by allowing the school to map its own 'personality' on the system. So initialization of procedures at the school will allow definition of the basic administrative parameters at that institution such as registration classes, house systems, setting systems, courses offered and so on. It is this exercise which forms the basis of the whole SCAMP system.

Phase 1 of the project will also include: software to tackle class formation in the S1 year; course allocations in years S2/S3; marks processing to produce reports for teachers and parents; and essential information in a pupil record system.

Phase 2 will take in data for processing on: staffing; the school roll; the school timetable; and the organization of subject departments.

Returns of data can be made both to the Scottish Education Department and the National Examination Board, who will return data in machine readable form to schools. It is also intended to include units on school attendance, to extend the course allocation unit, and to assist examination timetabling. This forward-looking programme could well show us the way ahead for MCBA for a decade or more.

In the concluding section of my research report to the Department of Education and Science written towards the end of 1981 I said:

Those closely associated with microcomputer development know only too well that one has but to blink and the scene has changed. For this reason the material assembled in this project will be out-dated almost before the ink is dry upon the paper.

Even then I should have found it difficult to imagine how far things would have progressed in little less than two years, and the enormous explosion of interest which has been generated in the wake of this progress. The genesis of microcomputing lies in a tiny slice of silicon, yet to quote David Everett's immortal lines fittingly written for a School Declamation:

Large streams from little fountains flow
Tall oaks from little acorns grow

We stand on the edge of on age where gigabytes of information can be stored on disks read by lasers, and sophisticated microprocessor chips drive microcomputers which will make the present generation of 16-bit machines appear as pedestrian as an eight digit calculator. Perhaps the day when the school timetable is automatically generated in fractions of a second can still be with us. In these respects a memorable quotation with which Professor W. Gosling, formerly of the University of Bath School of Electronics, ends his paper 'Microcircuits, society and education' says it all:

In the Kingdom of Sand all things become possible, and only imagination rules

Appendix 1

Software sources for microcomputers in school administration

Every effort has been made to ensure accuracy of the details contained in this list. Most of the programs are known to have had substantial use in schools. Nevertheless, it will be prudent to seek full details from suppliers before placing orders. In any case queries should always be directed to suppliers, not to the author of this book.

Software is listed according to make of machine. Where programs are available for more than one type of machine cross references are given for details.

On account of fluctuations which are likely to take place, prices are only shown in general categories as follows:

Price code A: under £25
Price code B: £25 – £50
Price code C: £50 – £75
Price code D: £75 – £100
Price code E: over £100

Programs for RML 380Z

1R   The TTX extended timetable program (Peter Andrews)
A machine code program for the 380Z which assists in the construction of a school timetable. In addition to the standard printout routines provided, facilities are included to enable the user to format the output to his own needs by writing simple BASIC programs. Full details are given in the twenty-eight page manual.
Requires COS 3.0 or later with a minimum of 32K (depending on the size of school). Available on cassette or disk.

Price code B. Send SAE for full details and official order form to: P. J. Andrews, 43 Rickmansworth Road, Watford WD1 7HS.

2R   Manpower/curriculum analysis (Patrick Bird)
Useful in the planning stages while moving from curriculum design to timetable construction, and for a final analysis of the completed timetable.
The program offers the following facilities:

1   Accepts school and department or faculty data by year groups. This can be permanently displayed using the low resolution graphics facility

2 Stores data on disk file for subsequent amendment or re-use in further calculations
3 Evaluates contact ratios
4 Summarizes the demands of the curriculum against supply from manpower
5 Evaluates 'bonus' distribution, etc., using two methods – T. I. Davies/ COSMOS and *Displaying the curriculum* (Jagger) Sufficiently flexible for any type of school. Full documentation available. Minimum 32K memory required, and mini-floppy disk drive.

Price code A. Contact: Hutchinson Education, FREEPOST 5, London W1E 4QZ.

Also available for BBC Model B and APPLE – see appropriate sections.

3R   Programs from Timetabling – OPT1-6 and TT1-6 (Keith Johnson)
A suite of twelve programs connecting option choices (OPT1-6) and timetable production, and for basic timetable planning (TT1-6), as published in the book *Timetabling* by Keith Johnson.

Price code A (for each suite). Full details of these, and the extensions to the programs (see section on CBM PET) from: Hutchinson Education, address as in 3R above.

Also available for PET, APPLE, TRS-80 and BBC – see appropriate sections.

4R   A school administration suite (Ian O'Neill and David Jewell)
A suite of twelve programs which can be used for the following functions:

1 Lists of whole school, years, tutor groups, option groups
2 Sorting of data files into alphabetical order by name
3 DES Form 7 dates of birth statistics
4 Tutor group and option group sizes (boys, girls, total)
Requires 5.25″ disk system, minimum 32K, with printer, also a text editor for data file creation/maintenance. Comprehensive documentation explains how to use and adapt the suite.

Price code B inclusive of disks, documentation and delivery. Contact: I. M. O'Neill, 4 Charles Road, West Ealing, London W13 0ND.

5   R The Lakes school registration package (Alex Redhead)
This suite stores pupils' records in files from which can be produced:

1 Alphabetical lists, with addresses if required
2 Lists of pupils' ages
3 Address labels
4 Clash table and subject choices
5 Lists of subjects taken by a pupil
6 Lists of pupils taking a subject
7 Form 7 and other statistical data

Also included: The Lakes school finance package – capitation control and accounting suite.

Requires 32K+HRG or 56K, + drives ABCD.

Price code B. Contact: A. Redhead, The Lakes School, Windermere, Cumbria.

6R Pupil list administration (Christopher Glover)
This suite:

1 Creates an alphabetical year file
2 Accepts amendments to year file
3 Creates form files and prints form lists with totals
4 Creates subject set files and prints set lists with totals
5 Accepts amendments to set lists
6 Analyses number of pupils in each form of a given age and prints a matrix of results with totals
7 Prints names of pupils who are out of normal year
8 Is compatible with examination administration programs 7R

Price code B. Contact: C. M. Glover, 10 Sundays Hill, Lower Almondsbury, Bristol BS12 4DR.

7R Examination administration (Garry Norman and Christopher Glover)
This suite has the following functions:

1 Reads pupils' names from an alphabetical file of the year group
2 Accepts entries for each pupil from a data sheet
3 Bills parents where charges are necessary
4 Accepts results and prints individual results lists
5 Analyses results by subjects
6 Summarizes the school's results

Price code B. Contact: C. M. Glover, address as in 6R.

8R Kingsdown external examination entry system (Gareth Cole)
This suite has the following functions:

1 Sets up a pupil database
2 Allows amendments to data
3 Lists pupils for entry checking
4 Lists pupils for form filling
5 Prints entry forms for Boards
6 Enters pupils' final results
7 Lists final results
8 Analyses final results
Plus other utility progams.

Price code B. Contact: G. Cole, Kingsdown School, Stratton St. Margaret, Swindon, Wilts. SN2 6JS.

9R T/TABLE – Aids timetable construction (Timetable Systems)

Requires 32K memory and HRGB or 48K memory. Available in versions to suit all sorts and sizes of schools – up to 100 teachers, any number of periods per day or days per cycle. User remains in control and decides on priorities, building up the timetable in any order, and at any stage supplies status information. Has ability to suggest rearrangements of the timetable in order to accommodate lessons which are difficult to fit in. Rooms are allocated automatically, according to rules of priority user determines. Any sort of timetable can be printed – staff, year, room, individual teachers and classes and lists of empty rooms. Enhanced version planned for curriculum analysis, departmental funding and staff substitution.

Price code B/C (inc. instruction manual). Contact: Timetable Systems, 39 Somerset Road, Frome, Somerset BA11 1HD.

BBC version planned.

10R OPTION – arranging option choices (Timetable Systems)

Provides a database which holds for each pupil a name (of any length), sex, tutor group, separate teaching set if appropriate, and a selection of up to eight subjects with a predictive grade for each subject. Offers pupils a choice of subjects from a predetermined set of option blocks, or else allows an open choice of subjects and builds an option system which maximizes pupil 'satisfaction'. Either way, allocates pupils to classes, with control of class size; this is done automatically, or under 'manual control', one pupil at a time. The database can be updated and amended in any respect, at any time, and alphabetic lists can be printed in any category (year group, tutor group, subject etc.). A general student record system is planned to link with this program.

Price code B (inc. instruction manual). Contact: Timetable Systems – address in 9R above.

BBC version planned.

11R School administration – a general suite (M. Wilding)

A package containing some twenty-two programs interlinked via an index. The programs will:

1 Create/correct/update pupil files
2 Completely update the files on a yearly basis
3 Output pastoral/tutor groups
4 Output any year in numerical or alphabetical order
5 Output student timetables, pupil lists per subject, clash tables
6 Input and output external examination results
7 Input external examination results O level, CSE, and A level
8 Input/output of observed and expected examination results
9 Calculate the Chi squared value between the observed and expected results
10 Output past and present files

Hardware used for development: twin(dual) mini-disks with HRG board, eighty character screen and Microline-80 printer. (Most programs are also available with forty character screen.)

Price on application to: M. A. Wilding, 62 Keble Street, Ince, Wigan, Greater Manchester WN2 2AY.

12R   TEXT GRADER (John Maloney and Peter Meiklejohn)
Will automatically provide you with the reading age of any text you type in. It gives the reading age on nine different measures: FJP Index, Flesch Grade, Flesch Reading Ease Score, FOG Index, FORCAST, FRY X and Y Coordinates, Mugford Word Length Score and Smog Grade.

Price code B. Contact: Hutchinson Education, FREEPOST 5, LONDON W1E 4QZ.

Also available for BBC Micro and 480Z.

13R   Disk directory (Peter Andrews)
DSKDIR is a program to produce an alphabetical list of all the files on a number of RML 380Z disks. The user can give each disk an identifying name thus enabling a file to be quickly found. DSKDIR can handle up to 100 different disks and about 1000 filenames – many more on a system which exceeds 32K. Very useful for those with a great many administrative programs and files to keep track of.

Price code A. Contact: P. J. Andrews, address as given in R1.

14R   Fourth year options (Michael Lovett)
Provides the school timetabler with a powerful aid for solving some of the difficult administrative problems associated with options schemes. Designed to eliminate much of the repetitive work normally involved, while allowing the timetabler to have considerable control over the outcome. Tasks covered are:

1   Creation and updating of a list of pupils
2   Analysing pupils' subject preferences
3   Fitting the preferences to an options scheme
4   Amending the pupils' choices at any time
5   Printing options lists in several useful formats
6   Printing pupils' personal timetables
7   Creating and updating a staff names list

Comprehensive documentation included. Requires COS 3.4 or later, with minimum 32K memory and two mini-drives.

Price code D. Contact: Longman Micro Software, 33-35 Tanner Row, York.

15R   GCE/CSE external examination package (Robin Ingledew)
The ten programs in this package cover creation of files of examination subjects and pupil entry details; listing of entries by subjects for Departmental checking, and double entries; insertion of grades once results are published; and analysis of results with lists of various statistics. Price code B.

Exam timetables package
Five programs, which allow creation of a file of exam details; sorting into chronological order; production of individual pupil exam timetables, and school exam timetables for the CSE/GCE period; and a list of exam clashes for pupils. Price code A.

Entry schedule packages
At present available for the JMB, Univ. of London, and North Regional Exam Boards. Produces the completed entry schedule. Price code A.

Random access files
Creation of database files for each year group which can be displayed/amended using random access BASIC (Software Systems Associates). Produces other files without further need to type in pupil names. A second program produces exam entry file from 5th Year database. Price code A.

Contact: R. A. Ingledew, 1 Jesmond Ave, Linthorpe, Middlesbrough, Cleveland.

16R ROLL and OPTIONS (Clare Computing)
ROLL
Allows creation, maintenance and searching of a pupil database. Enquiry program produces individual details or lists. Price code B.

OPTIONS
Suite of eight programs for use with ROLL or independently. Up to 300 pupils taking up to five options. Start with free choice, finish with printed subject and form lists. Requires 2 disk drives + HRGB. Price code B.

Contact: Clare Computing, 35 Wilton Grove, London SW19 3QU.

17R RECORDER and ACCOUNTS (Eric Vincent)
RECORDER
An information storage and retrieval system to handle a file size of up to 900 records, with a maximum record size of 252 characters and twenty-four fields. Prints output in columns or sequence of fields or on labels, with selection on one or more fields. Suitable for a pupil record system, with facilities for batch printing class lists and for making global form changes. Price code B.

ACCOUNTS
A simple accounting system to serve the needs of schools and colleges. Deals with sub-accounts for nineteen Departments, or more if necessary. Price code A.
Both suites require at least 47K and dual disk drives.

Contact: E. Vincent, 23 Greenhill Rd, Moseley, Birmingham.

18R   OPTIONS (System)
A machine code options system to give extremely fast response on all edits, analyses etc. Allows up to fifty pupils per form, up to thirty-four forms per year group, up to forty different subjects with three sub-sets per subject and up to sixteen options per pupil. Will provide form lists, option lists, analyses of various subject combinations and totals per subject within form and year. Price code A.

OPTIONS II also provides clash matrices and block fit. Price to be fixed. Needs only one disk drive and will operate with a variety of printers (e.g. Epson, Anadex, Microline, various Daisywheels).

Contact: SYSTEM, Weston House, West Bar Green, Sheffield S1 2DA.

Also available for 480Z (free standing only – not network), BBC B, APPLE II.

19R   Library record and retrieval system (Cheshire Education Committee)
Requires 48K memory.

Price code A. Contact: Mrs C. Gerrard, Supplies Section, Cheshire Education Committee, Education Dept., County Hall, Chester CH1 1SQ.

20R   School option block structuring and pupil allocation system (Cleveland County Council)
Accepts free choices by pupils and structures the option blocks so as to satisfy as many as possible of the these choices. Subsequent amendments allowed to suggested blocks if required. All the usual lists produced from final choices. Requires 48K twin mini disk system and XDB BASIC.

Price code C including disk and user's manual. Contact: Cleveland County Council Research and Intelligence Unit, PO Box 17, Rede House, Middlesbrough, Cleveland.

21R   QADMIN (David Blow, Malcolm Fraser and John Porter)
Allows a school to create a general database of its own pupil records which is in the format required by MicroQUERY or QUEST, thus allowing the powerful editing and interrogation facilities of these database management systems to be used. QADMIN itself will produce various lists, including form lists, option lists and examination entries.

Price code C. Machine configuration to be fixed. Contact: Hutchinson Education, FREEPOST 5, London W1E 4QZ.

QUEST or MicroQUERY are obtainable from AUCBE, Endymion Road, Hatfield, Herts. AL10 8AU. Price code A/B.

Also available for BBC Model B and RML 480Z

22R   Pupil reports and testimonials (Phil Neal)
A package which uses Wordstar and Mailmerge to produce pupil reports and testimonials. The package contains a pamphlet explaining the

system, and disks containing a 'testimonial kit' and a complete set of report comments for one subject.

Will require 380Z with 56K + Varitext board and WordStar plus MailMerge.

Price code to be fixed. Contact: P. Neal, 34 Derwent Rise, Flitwick, Bedford MK4S 1QS.

WordStar is available from Research Machines Limited, PO Box 75, Mill Street, Oxford OX2 0BW. Price code E.

MailMerge is available from Hutchinson Education, address as in 21R. Price code D.

23R   Examination entry programs (Peter Rhodes)

Makes the job of collection, collation and transcription of examination entries very much easier for all concerned. Produces lists to collect entries from teachers, collates the data, produces individual notes for pupils and parents informing of subjects entered.

Price code A. Contact: Hutchinson Education, address as in 21R.

24R   Exam Entries (D. J. Hancock)

The programs produce: form lists, subject lists, exam entry letters, clearance forms for school leavers, examination result statistical analysis. Requires 56K + disk system.

Price code A. Contact: D. J. Hancock, 63 Victoria Crescent, Hansforth, Leeds, Yorkshire.

Other programs

Details of some administration programs for 380Z were given in *Educational Computing*, vol. 4, no. 2, March 1983. Aside from those already listed here there were programs for Options(2), Form 101a and marks standardization.

Programs for CBM PET

P1   Timetabling, options analysis, and exam results analysis (Keith Johnson)

A suite of programs connecting option choices and timetable production, and for basictime table planning, as published in the book *Timetabling* by Keith Johnson. *OPT1-6* deal with options listing and analysis. Price code A.

TT1-6 deal with timetable planning and listing and are well documented in the book. Price code A.

Some extra programs are now available:

OPT7 finds pupils with particular subject combinations.
TT7 is a machine code program to do the actual scheduling of the timetable, with the order of entries determined by the timetabler.

TT8 and *TT9* will do the actual scheduling by scanning all the school data and running either interactively or automatically.

EXAM 1 and *EXAM 2* analyse the school's external examination results (mean of ten methods) and use the pupils' results to cross-moderate departments so that the success of departments may be compared.

Details from: Hutchinson Education, FREEPOST 5, London W1E 4QZ.

Some of these also available for 380Z, TRS-80, APPLE and BBC.

2P   Examinations, options and set listings (Graham Cluer)
1   A program to rank, standardize and print examination lists
2   'Option Zero'. This program enables you to keep track of 4th and 5th Year pupils' options programme, and to search for pupils doing certain combinations of options, etc.
3   'Set sorter'. A useful program for printing set lists
4   'Name writer'. To prepare data tapes of names for the above three programs
All for 16K (minimum) cassette machines.

Price code A, with documentation. Contact: G. Cluer, Sylvan High School, Maberley Rd, Upper Norwood, London SE19 2JH.

3P   Administration listing and examination entries (Studysoft)
1   Class and school lists
2   Form 7 Numbers
3   Feeder school lists
4   Examination entries
For 32K 5.25″ disk machines.

Price code E with documentation. Contact: Studysoft Educational Software, 30 Lee Dale Close, Denton, Manchester M34 1BG.

4P   School administration (Ian O'Neill)
A suite of sixteen programs to: create and maintain data files; sort data files by name/tutor group; print pupil records; print address labels to parents/pupils; list the whole school, or any subset thereof, especially years, forms, tutor groups, option groups, and print any information for each pupil in the list; print DES Form 7 dates of birth statistics; tutor group sizes and option group sizes; update disk files for next school year. Hardware required: PET series 4000 (i.e. version 4.0 BASIC), with dual mini-disk drives and a printer, 32K memory and 'new' ROMs.

Price code D including disk, full documentation and delivery. Contact: Hutchinson Education, FREEPOST 5, London W1E 4QZ.

5P   Staff absence cover, and Parent-teacher meetings (Alan Dean)
Staff absence cover
Works out and prints individual slips and noticeboard copies. Deals with 'supply'

teachers, normal absence cover, exams, etc. Calculates the best substitute based on six different factors, keeps detailed records and prints summary sheets. The relative importance of the various factors considered may be changed by the users.

Parent-teacher meeting appointments program
Calculates and prints appointment times for parents and teachers. Ensures parents do not have long waiting times. Accepts time restrictions for both parents and teachers.
Hardware required: PET 3032 or 4032 with disk drive and CBM printer.

Price code A includes both programs supplied on CBM 4040 format disk. Contact: A. Dean, 6 Birkland Drive, Edwinstow, Notts NG21 9LU.

6 P Choice (DMA Software)
A suite of eleven programs to assist option choices systems. Increases the efficiency of the option system, produces all the lists required and individual timetables for each child. Has the following features:

1 Pupil lists can be produced by subject and by sets within a subject – in alphabetical or any other predetermined order.
2 Individual timetables, including the common core subjects, can be produced in standard timetable format with the option of adding the homework timetable.
3 Maximum numbers may be preset for each subject in an option block.
4 Additional pupils may be added at any time in the most appropriate place.

Separate versions for 3000 and 4000 series. Disks required.

Price code A. Fully documented. Contact: DMA Software, 21 Homefield Rd, Seaford, East Sussex BN25 3DP.

7P The MACPACK. An aid to timetabling and list printing (Don McNiven)
Deals with option choices and various lists therefrom. Prints individual timetables for pupils, rooms, staff etc. Requires PET disk system.

Price code B. Contact : Don McNiven, Spurn Haven, Crossroads, Tetney, Grimsby DN36 5NG.

8P A general database for PET (John Cocks)
Up to 1000 records with fifty fields. Full editing facilities. Searching and sorting with any combination of fields output to screen or printer. The package has a number of programs for use in schools and colleges including class lists and a number of programs to assist with option and timetable production. The latter culminates in individual pupil/student timetables. Requires 4032 or 8032, a dual disk unit and printer.

Estimated price code A/B. Contact: MEP Southern Region, Furnace Drive, Furnace Green, Crawley RH10 6JB.

Also available for BBC Model B.

Other programs
Software for the PET was listed in *Educational Computing*, vol. 3, no. 7, September 1982. Aside from administration programs already listed here there was one on sorting and listing year groups.

Programs for APPLE

1A OPT1-6, TT1-6 (Keith Johnson)
For details see CBM PET no. 1P.

Price code A. Available for APPLE from: J. Gray, 10 Hawthorne Grove, Paulton-le-Fylde, Lancs. FY6 7PN.

2A Parents' evening scheduling (Tony Thornley)
Calculates appointments required both by parents and teachers and prints the necessary timetables and lists. Tried and tested in many schools. Documentation: twenty pages. Requires 32K + 5.25" disk system.

Price code B. Contact: A. N. Thornley, Highfields School, Lumsdale Rd, Matlock, Derbyshire.

3A Curriculum analysis (Peter Broome)
This is a program derived from R2 in the 380Z list. An invaluable planning tool, this disk-based program analyses the curriculum in four ways–Pupil/period, Teacher/period, T. I. Davies/COSMOS Standard, and Department/Year per cent analysis–to show the balance of resources across the year groups. Alternative strategies can be speedily reviewed, the results being printed out if required for further consideration. Simply put the disk into the drive, turn on the APPLE, and the program runs itself. The user is prompted at each stage, various main functions being selected from a 'menu'. An APPLE II (48K) with single disk drive and optional printer is required. There are two versions:

1 With year group, periods/day and days/week specified
2 In which these parameters are variable

Price code A. Contact: P. R. Broome, 48 Pagets Rd, Bishops Cleeve, Cheltenham GL52 4AG.

4A ROSTAR III – an interactive options and timetabling package (Paralax)
ROSTAR is a powerful interactive timetabling system. After data entry it will produce 4/5th Year options for individual students. Then the timetabler uses the program to timetable the whole school making his own decisions. At any stage 'state of play' information is available. Prints out full timetable and

by individual teacher, class, room etc.

Price code E. Contact: Hutchinson Education, FREEPOST 5, London W1E 4QZ.

5A   Timetable storage/retrieval system (J. Goodier)
Extremely rapid and efficient. Send SAE for full details to: Mr J. Goodier, Southlands High School, Clover Rd, Chorley, Lancs.

6A   Normalizing of marks (Jel Computer Services)
Standardizes examination marks. Requires 48K and one disk drive. DOS 3.3.

Price code A. Contact: Jel Computer Services, 3 Kings Rd, Cleethorpes, Lancs. DN35 0AJ.

7A   Options on the APPLE II
For full details see 18R. Contact: SYSTEM of Sheffield.

Programs for TRS-80

1T   OPT1-6 and TT1-6 (Keith Johnson)
For full details see CBM PET no. 1P.

Available for TRS-80 from P. Rhodes, 16 Mountfield Rd, Bramhall, Stockport, Cheshire SK7 1LZ.

2T   Programs from TEAM

Staff cover	Requires 32K, disk + printer
Nominal roll	Requires 32K, disk + PROFILE disk package
Labels	Requires 32K, disk + printer
Exams I	Requires 32K, 1 disk drive, printer + PROFILE
Exams II	Results entry, summaries and statistics to EXAMS I. Requires 32K LII + disk drives
Class records	Requires 16K LII
Timetable I	Based on K. Johnson's programs.(See item P1.) Requires 32K LII, disk drives + printer
Timetable II	Stores timetable and prints out using SCRIPSIT. Requires 48K LII, disk drives and SCRIPSIT

Price code A (all programs). Contact: TEAM Software Library, EDC, 36 Wolverhampton Rd, Walsall, West Midlands WS2 8PN.

3T   Examination entry programs (Peter Rhodes)
For full details see RML 380Z no. 23R. Disks required.

Price code A. Contact: Hutchinson Education, FREEPOST 5, London W1E 4QZ.

Other programs
The Tandy list of educational software was published in *Educational Computing* in February 1983. There were two administration programs, both connected with timetabling.

Programs for the BBC microcomputer

1B   OPT1-6 and TT1-6 (Keith Johnson)
For details see CBM PET no. 1P.

Price code A. Contact: Hutchinson Education, FREEPOST 5, London W1E 4QZ.

2B   TEXT GRADER (John Maloney and Peter Meiklejohn)
For details see RML 380Z no. 12R.

Price code A. Contact: Hutchinson Education, address in 1B above.

3B   General database package (Richard Green)
Five programs menu driven to form a random access database. The database can be amended or interrogated as required. Information from interrogation appears on screen or printer as required. Suitable for pupil record systems and associated tasks. Disks required. Size of records limited only by disk capacity.

Price code A. Contact: MUSE, FREEPOST, Bromsgrove, Worcs. B61 7BR.

4B   Options (System)
For full details see 18R.

Price code A. Contact: System of Sheffield.

5B   General database (John Cocks)
For details see PET section 8P.

Estimated price code A/B. Contact: MEP Southern Region

6B   Manpower/Curriculum Analysis (Patrick Bird)
For full details see 2R. For Model B with at least one mini-floppy disk drive.

Price code A. Contact: Hutchinson Education, FREEPOST 5, London W1E 4QZ.

7B   T/TABLE and OPTION (Timetable Systems)
For full details see 9R and 10R.

Price code B/C. Contact: Timetable Systems, 39 Somerset Rd, Frome, Somerset BA11 1HD.

8B Examination entry programs (Peter Rhodes)
For full details see RML 380Z no. 23R. Disks required.

Price code A. Contact: Hutchinson Education, FREEPOST 5, London W1E 4QZ.

9B QADMIN (David Blow, Malcolm Fraser and John Porter)
Allows a school to create a general database of its own pupil records which is in the format required by MicroQUERY or QUEST. Full details under 21R.

Price code C. Machine configuration to be fixed. Contact: Hutchinson Education, FREEPOST 5, London W1E 4QZ.

QUEST or MicroQUERY are obtainable from AUCBE, Endymion Road, Hatfield, Herts. AL10 8AU. Price code A/B.

10B DATABASE/CLASS LISTS/OPTIONS/TIMETABLING (EAS)
Operates on the whole school. Printout includes:

1 Class lists (one to four per page)
2 Class lists with pupil choices
3 Option/set group lists (one to fifteen per page)
4 Alphabetic lists (year or whole school)
5 Register lists (name, address, DOB, parents' name, telephone)
6 Teachers' names, addresses, responsibilities

Will print out all lists for the whole school at one press of a button. Free choice option scheme (max. six pools and four reserve choices with core subjects added later). Timetabling and Form 7 available soon, compatible with suite. Full screen editing on database. Requires disk system.

Price code D. Contact: J. Callaghan, Educational Administration Software, Somerville House, Brunswick Road, Withington, Manchester M20 9GA.

Other programs
BBC microcomputer software was listed in *Educational Computing* in November and December 1982. Administration programs listed were wordprocessing (Wordwise) and a general database system.

Programs for SWTP 6800

1S General school administration programs (T. Boyd)
Offering:

1 Calculation and reporting of marks
2 Cross-referencing of pupils' statistics, e.g. age, form, etc.
3 Tallying performances with '+' and '-' (machine code)
4 Tabulation of performance in individual sports (swimming, athletics)

5   Tabulations of scores by teams, forms, etc., in an on-going competition

Price code A/B.

Also available:
6 Text Editor. Price code A.
7 Wordprocessor. Price code A.
All with documentation. Require 5.25″ disk system. Newsletter of products/software for SS-50/6800.

Contact: T. K. Boyd, Seaford College, Petworth, West Sussex GU28 0NB.

Programs for Sinclair SPECTRUM

1Z   Database package (M. Wilding)

Six programs for the 48K Spectrum (three with printer, three without). The database can store 200 records. Each record holds a name file of thirty characters with facility to add seven files, each file storing up to ten characters. Alphabetical/numerical sorting is available on both name and data files. Calculations will give mean, standard deviation.

Price code A including tape, postage and packing. Contact: M.A. Wilding, 62 Keble St., Ince, Wigan, Gtr. Manchester WN2 2AY.

2Z   Supervision (M. Wilding)

A program to help with the supervision of the school day. Output includes: absent member of staff's timetable with supervising staff included and/or individual notification slips.

Price code A including tape, postage and packing. Contact: M. A. Wilding, 62 Keble St., Ince, Wigan, Gtr. Manchester WN2 2AY

Appendix 2

Useful addresses

The following companies are national suppliers of all kinds of computer peripheral supplies such as disks, cassettes, ribbons, continuous stationery, etc. They offer a comprehensive catalogue and price list and a quick phone-in and delivery service for urgent orders.

Action Computer Supplies
6 Abercorn Trading Estate, Manor Farm Road, Alperton, Wembley, Middlesex HA0 1BR. Tel: 01-903 3921

Data Efficiency Limited
Maxted Road, Maylands Avenue, Hemel Hempstead, Hertfordshire HP2 7LE. Tel: 0442-60155

Inmac (UK) Limited
Davy Road, Astmoor, Runcorn, Cheshire WA7 1BR. Tel: 09285-67551

Particularly useful for cables, connectors and other similar hardware.

Willis Computer Supplies Limited
PO Box 10, South Mill Road, Bishop's Stortford, Hertfordshire CM23 3DN. Tel: 0279-506491

The following companies are specialists in continuous stationery, especially stationery specifically designed to the customer's needs.

Datamatic Limited
Trecenydd Industrial Estate, Caerphilly, Mid-Glamorgan CF8 2RZ.Tel: 0222-866444

Very competitive prices.

Moore Paragon Business Forms
Paragon Works, London E16 1NW. Tel: 01-476 3232

Specialists in wordprocessing products.

The following companies will be able to provide, or direct you towards technical advice on their microcomputers.

Commodore Business Machines (UK) Limited
Customer Liaison Department, 675 Ajax Avenue, Trading Estate, Slough, Berkshire SL1 4BG. Tel: 0753-74111

Research Machines Limited
PO Box 75, Oxford OX2 0BW. Tel: 0865-249866

Tandy Corporation
Tameway Tower, Bridge Street, Walsall, West Midlands WS1 1CA. Tel: 0922-648181

To produce printing acetates direct from WordStar or TXED files

A. J. Eden, 118A St John's Road, Woking, Surrey GU21 1PS.

Other addresses

Bytech Limited
Sutton's Industrial Park, London Road, Earley, Reading RG6 1AZ. Tel: 0734-61031
Suppliers of various microcomputer and printer components.

Datalink Microcomputer Systems Limited
10 Waring House, Redcliffe Hill, Bristol BS1 6TB. Tel: 0272-213427
APPLE dealers. Advice on, and sales of APPLE software. Disks at competitive prices.

Micro Workshop
Mill House, Freshford, Bath BA3 6BX. Tel: 022122-2469
Courses on WordStar. One day intensive courses, disk-based training package, consultancy service.

Bibliography

AMMA, 'A code of practice relating to the use of computers in schools', *Report* – Journal of the Assistant Masters and Mistresses Association, vol. 5, no. 7 (April 1982), p. 17

Appleby, J. S., Blake, D. V., and Newman, E. A., 'Techniques for producing school timetables on a computer and their application to other scheduling problems', *The Computer Journal*, vol. 3 (1960), pp. 237-45

Armitage, P. H., 'The development and use of mathematical models in educational planning' in L. Dobson, T. Gear and A. Westoby (eds.), *Management in Education – some Techniques and Systems*, Ward Lock, 1975

Barker, P. and Williams, R., *Computers in School Administration*, Occasional Paper no. 8, Scottish Centre for Studies in School Administration, 1977

Barraclough, E. D., 'The application of a digital computer to the construction of timetables', *The Computer Journal*, vol. 8 (1965), pp. 136-46

Barry, C. H. and Tye, F., *Running a School*, Temple Smith, 1972

Bird, P. J., *The Use of Low Cost Microprocessor Based Computer Systems in School Administration and Management*, a report to the DES, 1982

Bird, P. J., 'The use of low cost microprocessor based computer systems in school administration and management', unpublished MEd dissertation, University of Bristol, 1982

Bloch, A., *Murphy's Law and other reasons why things go wrong*, Price/Stern/Sloan Inc., Los Angeles, 1982

Boch, R. E., 'The management case for separation of administrative and instructional computing', *Journal of Educational Data Processing*, vol. 15, no. 4, (1978), pp. 6-13

British Computer Society Schools Committee, 'The use of the computer as a management aid in schools: a report', *Computer Education*, no. 23 (1976), pp. 13-17

Brook, H., 'Comprehensive time-saver', *The Teacher*, vol. 29 no. 6, (6 Aug. 1976), p. 3

Brookes, J. E., *Timetable Planning*, Heinemann, 1979

Brookes, J. E., Dixon, C., and Zarraga, M. N., *STAG – Two Years On*, School Timetabling Applications Group, Basingstoke, 1973

Bush, T., Glatter, R., Goodey, J., and Riches, C. (eds.), *Approaches to School Management*, Harper and Row, 1980

Bushnell, D. D., *The Automation of School Information Systems*, Department of Audiovisual Instruction of the NEA, 1964

Chapman, B. L. M., 'Microcomputers and the school', mimeograph,

University of Bristol School of Education, 1980

Council for Educational Technology, *A Guide to the Selection of Microcomputers*, USPEC 32, CET, 1980

Coventry, W. F., *Management Made Easy*, W. H. Allen, 1970

Cowie, F. P., 'Some experiences in the use of a computer in school administration', *Computer Education*, no. 22 (1976), pp. 11-15

Csima, J., and Gotlieb, C. C., 'Tests on a computer method for constructing school timetables', *CACM*, vol. 7 (1964), pp. 160-3

David, C., 'The use of the computer in certain aspects of school administration', *Education for Development*, vol. 4, no. 3 (1977), pp. 33-9

Davies, T. I., *School Organization*, Pergamon, 1969

Davies, T. I., 'School timetabling by computer', *Trends in Education*, no. 35 (1974), pp. 33-8

Dempster, M. A. H., Lethbridge, D. G., and Ulph, A. M., 'School timetabling by computer – a technical history', *Educational Research*, vol. 18, no. 1 (1975), pp. 24-31

Drucker, P. F., *The Effective Executive*, Heinemann, 1967

Drury, B., 'Databases for pupil records', *Computers in Schools*, vol. 3, no. 2 (1980), pp. 20-21

Dunsire, A., *Administration – the Word and the Science*, Martin Robertson, 1973

Egner, W. E., 'School timetabling and the electronic computer', *Brit. J. Ed. Tech.*, vol. 6, no. 3 (1975), pp. 4-14

Ettlin, W. A., *WordStar Made Easy*, Osborne/McGraw-Hill, Berkeley, California, 1981

Eustace, P. J., and Wilcox, B., *Tooling up for Curriculum Review*, NFER, 1980

Everett, D., 'Lines written for a school declamation', in J. M. Cohen and M. J. Cohen (eds.), *The Penguin Dictionary of Quotations*, Penguin, 1960

Ewart, R. W., *Computers in Educational Administration Today and Tomorrow*, CET, 1977

Gallagher, T., 'The taming of Form 7', *Educational Computing*, vol. 3, no. 9 (Nov. 1982), p. 21

Gosling, W., '*Microcircuits, Society and Education*', Occasional Paper no. 8, CET, 1978

Gotlieb, C. C., 'The construction of class-teacher timetables', in C. M. Popplewell (ed.), 'Information processing', *Proceedings of the IFIP Congress 1962*, pp. 73-7, North-Holland, 1963

Green, R., 'Administration on a school microprocessor?', *Computer Education*, no. 33 (1979), p. 12

Hammond, V. J., 'School administration by computer', unpublished dissertation for the Diploma in Computer Education, Westhill College, Birmingham, 1980

Harnack, R. S., 'Use of the computer in curriculum planning', *International Review of Education*, no. 14 (1968), pp. 154-67

Havelock, R. G., *Planning for Innovation through Dissemination and Utilization of Knowledge*, Centre for Research on Utilization of Scientific Knowledge, Institute for Social Research, Ann Arbor, Michigan, 1969

Horner, G., and Teskey, F. J., 'Microcomputers and the school library', *School Librarian*, vol. 27, no. 4 (1979), pp. 339-40

Howard, A. W., 'Management information systems', *Computer Education*, no. 32 (1979), p. 27

Hussain, K. M., *Development of Information Systems for Education*, Prentice-Hall, New Jersey, 1973

Jagger, T. F. B., *Displaying the Curriculum*, ILEA Learning Materials Service, 1979

Johnson, K., *Timetabling*, Hutchinson, 1980

Joyner, W. D., 'Pupil records by computer', *Computer Education*, no. 30 (1978), p. 29

Kendall, M. G., 'Models for thinking with', in L. Dobson, T. Gear and A. Westoby (eds.), *Management in Education – Some Techniques and Systems*, Ward Lock, 1975

LAMSAC, *Towards a Computer Based Education Management Information System*, Local Authority Management Services and Computer Committee, 1974

LAMSAC, *Computer Assisted School Timetabling*, Local Authority Management Services and Computer Committee, 1978

Lancaster, D., (ed.), 'Microcomputers in School Administration', Sheffield Papers in Education Management No. 34, Sheffield City Polytechnic, Department of Education Management, 1983

Lawrie, N., and Veitch, H., *Timetabling and Organization in Secondary Schools*, NFER, 1975

Lewis, C. F., *The School Timetable*, OUP, 1961

Lyons, G., *Heads' Tasks – A Handbook of Secondary School Administration*, NFER, 1976

McKinsey and Co., *Unlocking the Computer's Profit Potential: a Research Report into Management*, McKinsey and Company, New York, 1968

Miles, R., 'Computer timetabling: a bibliography', *Brit. J. Ed. Tech.*, vol. 6, no. 3 (Oct. 1975), pp. 15-20

Millard, D., 'A bursar's view – computerised accounting', *Conference*, vol. 10, no. 1 (1973), pp. 24-6

Milner, S. D., and Wildberger, A. M., 'Determining appropriate uses of computers in education', *Computers and Education*, vol. 1, no. 2 (1977), pp. 117-23

Moseley, C., and Greenwell, A., 'The computer and the school library', *Conference*, vol. 17, no. 1 (1980), p. 11

MUSE, 'Database standards', published with *Computers in Schools*, vol. 2, no. 9 (1980)

Neal, P., 'Computer references', *Times Educational Supplement*, no. 3475 (Feb. 1983), p. 20

Oettinger, A. G., *Run Computer, Run! The Mythology of Educational Innovation*, Harvard University Press, Cambridge, Mass., 1969

Piddock, P., 'Computers in school administration. DES Form 7', *Computer Education*, no. 21 (1975), pp. 19-21

Pratt, S., 'Computer assistance for curriculum planning in secondary schools', *Educational Administration*, vol. 8, no. 1 (1979), pp. 180-200

Ransom, N. L., 'Timetabling in the secondary school – a simulation', unpublished course material, Educational Courses, Rearsby, Leicester, 1974

Schmidt, G., and Strohlein, T., 'Timetable construction – an annotated bibliography', *The Computer Journal*, vol. 23, no. 4 (1979), pp. 307-16

Sweeten, C., 'Timetabling for schools', *Personal Computer World*, vol. 1, no. 6 (Oct. 1978), pp. 62-6

Times Educational Supplement, 'An experiment in computer administration', a report in *Times Educational Supplement*, no. 2773 (July 1968), p. 97

Tomeski, E. A., and Lazarus, H., 'A humanized approach to computers', *Computers and Automation*, (June 1973), pp. 21-5.

Tondow, W. M., 'Computer utilization by schools: an example', *International Review of Education*, no. 14 (1968), pp. 182-209

Turner, M. J. L., *The First Computer Handbook*, Computer Handbooks, Whitney on Wye, Hereford, 1980

Vincent, E., 'Management objectives: the administrative applications of microcomputers', *Times Educational Supplement*, no. 3440 (June 1982), p. 39

Wilson, P. A., 'School timetabling by computer in ILEA schools in 1978', mimeograph, Operational Research Unit, Greater London Council, 1979(a)

Wilson, P. A., 'Computer assisted timetabling – use of the Oxford system in 1979', mimeograph, Operational Research Unit, Greater London Council, 1979(b)

Zarraga, M. N., and Bates, S., 'Computer timetabling and curriculum planning', *Educational Research*, vol. 22, no. 2 (Feb. 1980), pp. 107-20

Glossary

Most technical and jargon terms are defined in the text and are indexed. This glossary confines itself to those few which are not so defined and, for convenience, the main acronyms which are used.

ALU	arithmetic and logic unit
BCSSC	British Computer Society Schools Committee
bit	an abbreviation for binary digit
bug	an error in program code
byte	in the case of many microprocessors, an 8-bit binary number
CET	Council for Educational Technology
COS	cassette operating system
COSMOS	courses on staffing and management of schools – commonly organized by Her Majesty's Inspectorate
CP/M	control program for microcomputers – a disk operating system for Z80 based microcomputers
c.p.s.	characters per second – a unit used to measure the speed of printers
CPU	central processing unit
CRAC	Careers Research Advisory Council
CSE	Certificate of Secondary Education
cursor	a point on a VDU screen marking where the next input will be displayed
database	an organized and integrated collection of data which may be arranged in a number of datafiles
datafile	an ordered collection of data held by a microcomputer in one package
DBMS	database management system
debug	eradicate errors in program code
DES	Department of Education and Science
DFS	disk filing system – a disk file control or operating system
DOI	Department of Industry
DOS	disk operating system
GCE	General Certificate of Education

graphics	pictures produced by the microcomputer on its VDU screen
high resolution graphics	fine detail in graphics made possible by plotting a large number of very small points accurately on the microcomputer's screen
ILEA	Inner London Education Authority
K	kilobyte (1024 bytes)
KSR	keyboard send and receive – a keyboard which can be used on the printer directly and also to send messages to the computer
LAMSAC	Local Authorities Management Services and Computer Committee
LEA	Local Education Authority
LGORU	Local Government Operational Research Unit
Mb	megabyte (1024 kilobytes)
MCBA	microcomputer based administration
MEP	Microelectronics in Education Project
MUSE	Microcomputer Users in Education
QWERTY	the order of letters on the top row on the standard typewriter keyboard
RAM	random access memory
ROM	read only memory
SAM	school administration by microcomputer
SCAMP	Schools Computer Administration and Management Project
SMDP	Scottish Microelectronics Development Project
STAG	Schools Timetabling Applications Group
UCCA	Universities' Central Council for Admissions
VDU	visual display unit

Index

absent staff cover, 135
accounting, 33, 65, 144
administration, 16
advice and support, 163
aims and objectives, 148, 164
arithmetic and logic unit (ALU), 71
applications software, 101
APPLE microcomputer, 88, 93,
    software for, 113, 124, 126, 130,
    136, 142, 192
attendance, 30

back-up
    disks, 97
    stores, 84
BASIC, 101, 103, 173, 174
batch processing, 15, 16, 26
BBC microcomputer, 96, 101, 178
    software for, 113, 122, 124, 126,
    143, 146, 194
BCSSC, 27, 32, 33, 34, 36, 87
beginning MCBA, 148-66
benefits of computerization, 34-6
bi-directional printers, 78
binary numbers, 71, 100
bits (binary digits), 72
block moves of text, 139
bytes, 73

cables, 76, 83
capitation distribution, 65, 66, 150
carbon film ribbons, 83, 97
careers, 33, 67
    CRAC, 68
cassette operating system (COS), 100
cassettes, 84
cathode ray tube, 77

central processing unit (CPU), 71
change, 39, 157, 160-1
chips, 14, 71-2, 73
clash
    matrix, 25, 49, 115, 117
    table, 58, 114
clerical staff, 156-7, 163
clerical tasks, 17
COBOL, 101, 173, 180
code of practice, 158-9
combing chart, 57, 128
Commodore PET microcomputer,
    77, 88, 90, 92, 177
    software for, 109, 113, 122, 126,
    129, 135, 142, 189-92
compatibility of hardware, 87
compilers (languages), 101
conflict matrix, 58, 128, 130
consultation, 60, 160, 162-3
contact ratio, 125, 126, 128
continuous processing, 140
co-operation of staff, 162
core store, 73
corporate policy, benefits of, 170
cost of implementation, 160
cover for absent staff, 135
crash proof, 104, 106, 154
curriculum
    analysis, 124-8
    design, 56-8
cut sheet feed, 83

daisywheel printer, 79, 89, 95, 97
data, 28
    fields, 43
    incorrect, 157-8
    saving, 107

security, 36-7, 159, 179
  sensitivity, 36
  protection Act, 37, 43
  protection Bill, 37
  validation, 29, 43
database management systems, 112
databases, 28, 31, 42-7
  contents of, 42, 45
  for microcomputers, 42-7
  modular concept for, 171-4
  proliferation of, 154, 168
depersonalization, 158
Deputy Head's role, 150-1, 161-3
disk
  drives, 85-7, 89, 97
  filing system (DFS), 96
  operating system (DOS), 100
disks
  back-up copies, 97
  density format, 86
  double-sided, 86
  hard, 86-7, 179
  mini-floppy, 85
  single-sided, 86
  storage capacity, 44-7, 86
documentation, 104
dot matrix printers, 78-84

editing, 26
efficiency, improvement in, 148
electronic pegboard, 59
examinations
  administration, 18, 31-2, 44, 51-5,
    117-24
  invigilation, 52, 55, 134
  papers, 63
  results analysis, 31, 52, 54, 122-4
eyestrain, 77

fabric ribbons, 83, 97
fan-fold stationery, 82, 97
fast tape systems, 85
fields of a record, 43
file names, 85
firmware, 97

floppy disks, 85
Form 7, 31, 44, 48, 109, 110, 111
form lists, 42-4, 108-13
friction feed, 82

general database management
  systems, 112

hard copy, 78
hard disks, 86-7, 179
hardware, 70, 177
  choosing, 87-97, 164
  conflict over, 87, 155
  siting of, 156
Head's role, 149, 150-1, 155, 161-2,
  165
high level language, 100

information, improving, 149-50
initiative, 150-1
ink jet printers, 79
innovation in software, 102, 176
instruction set, 100
in-service training, 39, 165, 174-6
integrated circuits, 14
interface, 83
interpretive languages, 101
introduction of MCBA, 163-6
invasion of privacy, 36

key factors, 161-3
key personnel, 162, 163-4
keyboards, 75-6, 82, 156
  send and receive type (KSR), 82
kilobytes, 74

LAMSAC reports, 24, 26, 27, 28, 29,
  30, 34, 35, 36, 37, 38, 39, 43, 44,
  45, 62, 86, 171
languages, 100
large scale integrated circuits, 14
LGORU, 22
library, 32, 67, 145
list
  making, 27, 42, 44, 47, 108-13

processing, 139
listing paper, 97
Local Education Authorities, 168-71
lower case descenders, 78

machine code, 100-1, 103, 133, 173
mainframe, 14
management, computers in, 16-18
marks, 29, 47
  processing, 28
mathematical models, 17
MCBA, 18
megabytc (Mb), 74
megahertz (MHz), 71
memory, 73-4
  back-up, 84-7
  random access (RAM), 74-5
  read only (ROM), 74-5
menu driven, 106
MicroLEEP, 112
microprocessors, 14, 71, 100
MicroQUERY, 112
mini-floppy disks, 85
monitors, 77

networks, 178
Nor-Data system, 22-3

on-line processing, 15, 86
options
  choices, 24-6, 48-50, 113-17, 130
  clash table or matrix, 25, 49, 115,
    117
operating system, 100
  disk, 100
  cassette, 100
Oxford Systems Associates (OSA),
  21

parents' evening timetables, 136-8
peripherals, 87
person dependence, 23, 103-4, 151,
  155
personnel, 156-61
PET/CBM microcomputer *see*

Commodore PET
pin feed, 82
pixels, 77
Prestel, 67
printers, 78-83, 95
  quality of, 78-81, 159
programs, 72, 88, 100-8
project team, 164
pupil record systems, 26-9, 42-7,
  108-13, 170, 180

quality of information, 149-50, 158
quality of print, 159
QWERTY, 76

random access memory (RAM), 74-5
random file handling, 116
read only memory (ROM), 74-5
record systems, *see* pupil record
  systems
red/green/blue (RGB), 77
reliability, 14
reports, 29-30, 50-1, 141
resolution screen, 77
resource lists, 66
ribbons, 83, 97
right justification, 139
RML 380Z, 88, 90-2
  software for, 108, 110, 112-28,
    132-5, 140-2, 144-6, 182-9
roll feed, 82
rooming a timetable, 59, 133, 134

SAM, 18
schematic diagram, 57
school fund accounting, 65, 145
screens, 76-8
search and replace, 139
secretaries, 76, 85, 109, 111, 114, 136,
  141, 156-7, 162, 163, 176
security of data, 36-7, 159, 179
senior management team, 161-2,
  163-6
sensitivity of data, 36
sequential file handling, 116

silicon chip, 14, 71
single-sided disks, 86
Sirius 1, 177
siting of hardware, 156
social implications of
 computerization, 29, 36-9 156-61
software, 88, 100ff.
 developing, 101-4
 external, 152-4, 176-7
 innovation, 102, 103
 multiplicity of, 168-9
 selection of, 104-8, 153-4, 163
 simultaneous development of, 26,
  102, 152
SPL (NZ) scheme, 24-5
sponsorship and direction, 161-2
staff co-operation, 162-3
staffing, 57, 124-8
STAG, 22, 57
standard video signal, 77
stationery, 82, 97
statistics, 27, 30-2, 44, 48
stock control, 66
supplies, 97

Tandy TRS-80, 94-5
 software for, 113, 126, 143, 194-5
tapes
 cassette, 84
 fast, 85
technical skills, 162
television screens, 76-8
terminals, 15
testimonials, 51, 64, 141
text editors, 64, 141
thermal printers, 78
thimble printers, 81

time saving, 16, 38, 42, 148, 154, 159
timetable, 55-63, 124-35
 amendments, 62, 135
 apparatus, 58-9
 changes, 62, 135
 checking, 60
 construction, 19-24, 58-60, 128-33
 history of computer aided, 19-24
 inconsistencies, 57
 interactive, 21
 planning, 56-8, 124-8
 printing, 60-2, 128-35
 scheduling, 19-24, 58-60, 128-33
 storing, 60-2, 128-35
tractor feed, 82, 89
training, 39, 165, 174-6
turnkey systems, 101, 105
typesetting, 64

UCCA, 67
user friendliness, 104-7

validation of data, 29, 43
Varitext board, 91
VDU eyestrain, 77
visual display unit (VDU), 77
visual planner, 57
volatile memory, 74

Winchester disk drives, 86, 179
wordprocessing, 63-5, 89, 138-44, 169
word wrap, 139
workloads, 152-3, 154-5
workload transfer, 154-5

Zarraga's rule, 58, 128